Microsoft® Office Specialist 2010 Series

Microsoft®
Word 2010
Core Certification

Courseware 3240-1

Exam 77-881

August 2010
© CCI Learning Solutions Inc.

Microsoft® Word 2010 Core Certification

Courseware Developer: Sue Wong

Microsite Developer: Lorin Ledger

Editors: Marguerite Caunt, Jonathan Jacobsen

CCI Publishing Team: Kelly Hegedus, Kevin Yulo

This courseware is one in a series prepared by CCI Learning Solutions Inc. for use by students and instructors in courses on computer software applications. CCI designed these materials to assist students and instructors in making the learning process both effective and enjoyable.

CCI Learning Solutions Inc. would like to acknowledge the financial support of the Government of Canada through the Book Publishing Industry Development Program for our publishing activities.

© 2010 CCI Learning Solutions Inc.   All rights reserved.   ISBN: 978-1-55332-293-1   Printed in Canada

Working With the Data Files

The exercises in this courseware require you to use the data files provided for the book. Follow the instructions shown to download the data files for this courseware.

1   Launch your browser and navigate to the CCI Web site location http://www.ccilearning.com/data.

2   Enter: *3240* in the **Courseware #** box and click [Find Data].

3   Click **Run** in the File Download – Security Warning window. (Alternatively, you can choose to **Save** the file to a location on your computer.)

4   In the Internet Explorer – Security Warning window click **Run** again.

5   In the **WinZip Self-Extractor** dialog box, use the **Browse** button to specify the Windows Desktop as the location to unzip the file and then click **Unzip**.

5   The **3240 Student Files** folder containing the required student work files has now been downloaded to your desktop. It is recommended that you rename the folder using your own name before starting the exercises in this courseware. You can reinstall and use the work files as many times as you like.

What is the Microsoft ® Office Specialist Program?

The Microsoft Office Specialist Program enables candidates to show that they have something exceptional to offer – proven expertise in certain Microsoft programs. Recognized by businesses and schools around the world, over 4 million certifications have been obtained in over 100 different countries. The Microsoft Office Specialist Program is the only Microsoft-approved certification program of its kind.

What is the Microsoft Office Specialist Certification?

The Microsoft Office Specialist certification validates through the use of exams that you have obtained specific skill sets within the applicable Microsoft Office programs and other Microsoft programs included in the Microsoft Office Specialist Program. The candidate can choose which exam(s) they want to take according to which skills they want to validate.

The available Microsoft Office Specialist Program exams include*:

- Using Windows Vista®
- Using Microsoft® Office Word 2007
- Using Microsoft® Office Word 2007 - Expert
- Using Microsoft® Office Excel® 2007
- Using Microsoft® Office Excel® 2007 - Expert
- Using Microsoft® Office PowerPoint® 2007
- Using Microsoft® Office Access® 2007
- Using Microsoft® Office Outlook® 2007
- Using Microsoft SharePoint® 2007

The Microsoft Office Specialist Program 2010 exams will include*:

- Microsoft Word 2010
- Microsoft Word 2010 Expert
- Microsoft Excel® 2010
- Microsoft Excel® 2010 Expert
- Microsoft PowerPoint® 2010
- Microsoft Access® 2010
- Microsoft Outlook® 2010
- Microsoft SharePoint® 2010
- Microsoft Project 2010

What does the Microsoft Office Specialist Approved Courseware logo represent?

The logo indicates that this courseware has been approved by Microsoft to cover the course objectives that will be included in the relevant exam. It also means that after utilizing this courseware, you may be better prepared to pass the exams required to become a certified Microsoft Office Specialist.

For more information:

To learn more about Microsoft Office Specialist exams, visit www.microsoft.com/learning/en/us/certification/mos.aspx

To learn about other Microsoft approved courseware from CCI Learning Solutions, visit mos.ccilearning.com

* The availability of Microsoft Office Specialist certification exams varies by Microsoft program, program version and language. Visit www.microsoft.com/learning for exam availability.

Microsoft, Access, Excel, the Office Logo, Outlook, PowerPoint, SharePoint, and Windows Vista are either registered trademarks or trademarks of Microsoft Corporation in the United States and/or other countries. The Microsoft Office Specialist logo and the Microsoft Office Specialist Approved Courseware logo are used under license from Microsoft Corporation.

Table of Contents

About This Courseware

Lesson 1: Getting Started

Lesson 2: Manipulating Text

                                  3240-1 v1.00 © CCI Learning Solutions Inc.

Lesson 3: Formatting Content

Lesson 4: Working with Tabs

Lesson 5: Formatting Documents

Lesson 6: Getting Ready to Print

Lesson 7: Using Tables

Lesson 8: Working with Illustrations

                                                        3240-1 v1.00 © CCI Learning Solutions Inc.

Lesson 9: Creating Mass Mailing Documents

Lesson 10: Sharing Documents

Appendices

Course Description

Microsoft® Word 2010 Core teaches the information worker how to work with different types of documents using a variety of core and intermediate features to create and format business documents such as letters, forms, and newsletters. Some topics may appear to be basic skill sets but are discussed in more detail, exploring at a higher level different options that can be chosen or applied for that skill set.

Students who complete this course will have reviewed all of the exam objectives and be on their way to preparing for Microsoft Word 2010 Core Exam #77-881.

Course Series

This *Microsoft Word 2010 Core Certification* courseware is one of nine courses in CCI's Microsoft Office Specialist 2010 series. Other courses available in the series include:

- Excel 2010 Core
- Access 2010
- PowerPoint 2010
- Outlook 2010
- Project 2010
- SharePoint 2010
- Word 2010 Expert
- Excel 2010 Expert

The Microsoft Office Specialist 2010 Series contains exercises that students can use to learn each of the features discussed. Additional resources to practice and apply the skill sets are available from the CCI Office 2010 Microsite. Students are encouraged to register at http://2010.ccilearning.com in order access these additional activities both during and after completing the course.

Instructor Resources are available and are produced specifically to help and assist an instructor in preparing to deliver the course using the CCI materials. Contact your coordinator or administrator, or call your CCI Account Manager for information on how to access these resources.

Course Prerequisites

This course is designed for students who are familiar with personal computers, using a keyboard and using a mouse. The course assumes that students have completed the *Microsoft Windows* course or have equivalent Microsoft Windows knowledge and experience.

- ☐ start and run Windows
- ☐ use Minimize, Restore Down/Maximize, or Close
- ☐ use the taskbar
- ☐ use the left and right mouse buttons appropriately
- ☐ use the Start button
- ☐ understand file management techniques
- ☐ use the Help feature
- ☐ navigate between files, folders, or drives

System Requirements

According to the Microsoft Office System User's Guide, you must have the following in place prior to using the program:

- personal computer with a 500 megahertz (MHz) processor or higher
- 1 gigabyte (GB) hard disk drive to save the files used in this courseware
- 256 megabytes (MB) RAM or higher
- 1024x 768 or higher resolution monitor
- Windows XP with Service Pack (SP) 3 (32-bit), Windows Vista with SP1 (32-bit or 64-bit), Windows Server 2003 R2 (32-bit or 64-bit) with MSXML 6.0 installed, Windows Server 2008 with SP2 (32-bit or 64-bit), Windows 7 (32-bit or 64-bit)
- mouse or other pointing device compatible with Windows

In the materials contained in this courseware, we assume that you have met these criteria, and that you have successfully installed both Windows and Word on your computer.

Classroom Setup

The features and exercises shown in this courseware were developed using the standard installation of Microsoft Office 2010 on a system with Windows 7.0. If your computers have Windows Vista installed, you will need to adjust accordingly to accommodate for the differences in dialog boxes when saving or opening files.

It is likely your instructor set up the classroom computers based on the system requirements to run the software for this course. Most software configurations on your computer are identical to those on your instructor's computer. However, your instructor may use additional software to demonstrate network interaction or related technologies.

MMM
More Materials
on the
Microsite!

The Microsoft Office Specialist Series contains exercises that students can use to learn each of the features discussed. More materials to practice and apply the skill sets are available from the CCI Office 2010 Microsite. Students are encouraged to register at http://2010.ccilearning.com in order access these additional activities both during and after completing the course.

Course Design

This course book was developed for instructor-led training and will assist you during class. Together with comprehensive instructional text and objectives checklists, this course book provides easy-to-follow hands-on lab exercises and a glossary of course-specific terms.

This course book is organized in the following manner:

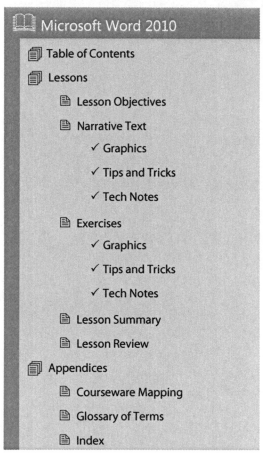

When you return to your home or office, you will find this course book to be a valuable resource for reviewing exercises and applying the skills you have learned. Each lesson concludes with questions that review the material. Lesson review questions are provided as a study resource only and in no way guarantee a passing score on a certification exam. Appendices in the back of this course book provide additional information.

Course Objectives

This course book teaches the skills you will need to successfully complete the Word 2010 Core exam. These skill sets are introduced using a fictional company named Tolano Adventures, a travel service that is a department within Tolano Environmental Consulting. Tolano Adventures offers tours to the public that are friendly to the environment.

You will use Word to create a variety of business documents, including letters, memos, and proposals. As you begin to build your skills, you will then create a variety of flyers and other promotional materials as well as explore different ways to share the information with internal and external customers.

After completing this course, you will be able to:

- Use the Word interface to access commands and features to complete specific tasks
- Use Backstage to save, open, close or switch between documents
- Manipulate the document by selecting text to perform editing tasks such as copy and paste, or find and replace
- Apply simple formatting to characters and paragraphs
- Set tabs to align text in columns
- Apply bullets or numbers to simple lists
- Apply multi-level bullets or numbers for longer lists
- Create and manipulate outlines to draft topic flow
- Apply page formatting such as changing the margins, paper size, or orientation for a document
- Use specific types of breaks to apply different page formats in a document
- Apply headers or footers to a document
- Apply backgrounds or themes for online documents
- Proof your documents for spelling or grammar errors, as well as recognize contextual errors
- Use AutoCorrect to store common spelling errors you make, or to store items Word will complete for you
- Use comments as reminders or to share information in a document with others
- Use Backstage to preview or print a document
- Create or draw a table, then manipulate the appearance of the table using formatting or table options
- Insert, format, or arrange pictures, shapes, text boxes, WordArt, or SmartArt illustrations
- Use documents to merge information for mass mailings
- Use QuickParts to assist with frequent-use items such as salutations or inserting and formatting footers
- Navigate in a document using hyperlinks, bookmarks or a table of contents
- Use footnotes or endnotes to reference items in a document
- Manage versions of a shared document
- Protect your document through passwords or restricting access to change parts of the document

Conventions and Graphics

The following conventions are used in CCI learning materials.

File Names or Database Field Names	File names or database field names are indicated in *italic* font style.
Exercise Text	Content to be entered by the student during an exercise appears in `Consolas` font.
Procedures	Procedures and commands you are instructed to activate are indicated in **bold** font style.
Features or Command Options	Menu options and features are listed in the left hand column and corresponding descriptions are in the right hand column.

The following graphics are used in CCI learning materials.

 Specific Keyboard Graphics to easily identify the key to press on the keyboard.

 This icon indicates the numbered objective from the Microsoft Office Specialist exam being covered in this topic. Refer to the Appendix for a complete listing of exam objectives.

Notes, tips or tricks or alternative ways to accomplish a task are shown as memo notes.

Technical Notes point out exceptions or special circumstances that you may find when working with a particular procedure, or may indicate there is another method to complete the task.

MMM
See:
Understanding
Basic
Terminology

Whenever you see this icon, navigate to http://2010.ccilearning.com for **M**ore **M**aterials on the **M**icrosite. These additional activities include online exercises, creative application exercises, fun activities and additional review. They're designed to give you more practice using Word 2010. Use the microsite in class or at home to practice some of the skills you are having trouble mastering, or to try your skills using different materials.

Learn the Skill

Learn the Skill graphics signal the start of step-by-step hands-on exercises or other activities.

Microsoft®
Word 2010
Core Certification

Lesson 1: Getting Started

Lesson Objectives

This lesson teaches you to create simple documents and introduces you to some file management tools available in Word. Upon completion of this lesson, you should be able to:

☐ identify elements on the screen

☐ use the Quick Access Toolbar

☐ use the Ribbon

☐ work with text

☐ identify screen symbols

☐ move around the document

☐ use Backstage to save, open, or create new documents

☐ switch between documents

☐ save in different file formats

☐ close a document

☐ add document properties

Looking at the Screen

When Word starts, a new document opens and the screen displays as follows:

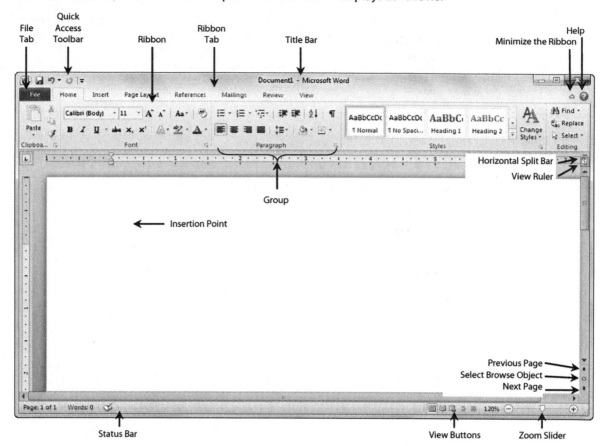

File Tab	When clicked, this displays the Backstage view from which you can select commands for a file (e.g. New, Open, Save). A panel at the left displays commands that may include tabs with a set of sub-commands to manage the file.
Quick Access Toolbar	Located above the Ribbon, this provides quick access to frequently used commands. You can customize the toolbar to contain commands you use regularly.
Title Bar	Located at the top of the screen, the title bar displays the contents of the window (e.g. *Document 2 – Microsoft Word, Letter to J. Woods - Microsoft Word.*) If more than one window is open on the screen, the one with a title bar that is a different color or intensity is the active window.
Microsoft Office Word Help	Displays the Help window to obtain the latest help on a feature; Microsoft's Help option links to the Microsoft Web site for the latest information. You can also use the help topics installed with Office.
Minimize the Ribbon	Minimizing the Ribbon displays the Ribbon Tabs only, enabling you to see more lines of text in the document on screen.
Ribbon	A collection of tabs (e.g. File, Home, Insert, Page Layout) providing quick access to commands.
Ribbon Tab	Each tab represents a group of commands for specific purposes such as editing, inserting graphics, viewing options, or page layout.

Ribbon Group	Each tab contains groups of related commands to edit, format, or enhance items in your documents. Some groups have a Dialog box launcher button at the bottom right that displays a dialog box or window with more commands and options.
Horizontal Split Bar	Click and drag this button down to split the document into two parts to view different areas of the same document.
View Ruler	Rulers display when you click this button above the top arrow of the vertical scroll bar. Use the ruler to set or modify tabs, indents, and margins.
Insertion Point	This symbol displays the cursor position in a document. In a new blank document, it displays at the top of the page.
Scroll Bars	Use the vertical scroll bar to move up and down within the document. The horizontal scroll bar only appears if the document is wider than the screen display; use this scroll bar to move sideways within the document.
Previous Page/ Next Page	Use these buttons to move from the top of one page to the top of the next or previous page.
Select Browse Object	Use this button to choose what you would like Word to find, e.g. page, table, headings, comments, sections, bookmarks.
Status Bar	Displays document information such as current page, total number of words, proofing errors, language, as well as the View buttons and the Zoom slider at the far right.
View Buttons	Quickly alternate between document views. Each view offers advantages based on document type, e.g. use Print Layout to see the overall layout of the document; Full Screen Reading to view the entire document in book layout; Web Layout to view documents saved as web pages; Outline view to organize headings, and Draft view to focus on entering or editing text.
Zoom Slider	Click the buttons at either side of the slider to increase or decrease the zoom percentage by 10%, or drag the slider button to choose a particular zoom percentage. Word displays the current zoom percentage in the Zoom level button, at the right of the View buttons. You can also click this button to set a custom or specific zoom percentage.

The previous screen displays commonly used areas of the Word screen. As you can customize the screen's appearance, not all parts always appear. For instance, you can choose to turn the ruler on i.e., for precise alignment of financial reports. You can also set up defaults, such as the font or the margins, for each new document.

ScreenTips help identify buttons or elements on the tabs of the Ribbon and the screen. To view a ScreenTip, position the mouse cursor on the item. A tip then displays the name of the button along with a description of its purpose. For some items, a keyboard shortcut may also display as an alternative for activating this feature.

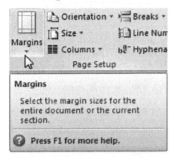
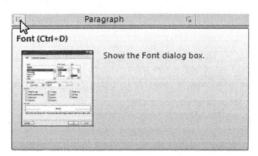

You can choose to show or hide a number of the elements shown in this section. In most cases, set items by clicking the **File** tab, clicking **Options** and then clicking the **Popular** or **Display** categories.

Using the Quick Access Toolbar

The Quick Access Toolbar, at the left of the title bar above the Ribbon, contains buttons for frequently used commands. By default, this toolbar contains the Word control icon, Save, Undo, Redo and Customize Quick Access Toolbar buttons. Use the last button to customize or display those commands you use frequently, such as a new blank document, print, or spell check.

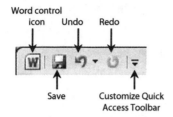

To customize the Quick Access Toolbar, use one of the following methods:

- Click **Customize Quick Access Toolbar** and click a button from the displayed list or click **More Commands**; or
- click **File**, click **Options**, and then click **Quick Access Toolbar**; or
- right-click anywhere on the Ribbon, click **Customize Quick Access Toolbar** and click a button from the list or click **More Commands**.

To move the Quick Access Toolbar to below the Ribbon:

- Click **Customize Quick Access Toolbar** and then click **Show Below the Ribbon**; or
- right-click the Ribbon, click **Customize Quick Access Toolbar** and then click **Show Quick Access Toolbar Below the Ribbon**.

Using the Ribbon

The Ribbon can help you quickly find the commands you require. Commands are grouped on tabs with each tab relating to a type of activity, e.g. inserting items into a document, changing the view of your document, or formatting text in the document. You can customize the Ribbon to display those commands you use frequently in a particular order, or to add or remove commands for a Ribbon tab (covered in the Expert course).

To reduce screen clutter, contextual tabs appear only when they are applicable, e.g. Picture Tools, Header and Footer Tools, Table Tools.

A button that appears in a different color or has an outline is active; many of these de-activate when you click the same button or click another choice. For instance, the **Bold** command can be applied to selected text by clicking that button; to turn off the boldface, click the same button again. If you want the text to be larger, click the down arrow for the **Size** button and choose the required size. When you need to change the font size again, click the down arrow for **Size** and then select the new size.

When the Ribbon displays different choices, as with the Styles list shown in the previous screen, one item will have a border around it to indicate it is active. To see how the text would appear with another style, point the mouse on one of the other items and Word displays the effect.

Each tab on the Ribbon contains groups with similar commands, e.g. the **Home** tab has a group called **Font** that contains buttons for formatting text characters; the **Insert** tab contains a group with different types of graphics or illustrations that can be inserted into a document.

If a group shows a feature with a scroll bar, it also has a button below the bottom scroll button that you can click to display the full list or gallery for that option.

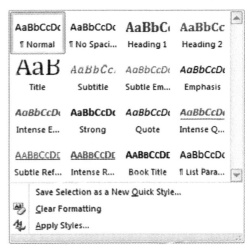

This is the **More** button which, when clicked, displays a gallery with more options as seen at the right. As you point the mouse cursor at an option, Word displays a Live Preview showing how the selected item will appear if you apply this feature. You can turn off this feature in the Word Options.

Click the ⬛ button at the lower right of a group to show a corresponding dialog box, window, or task pane with more options for this feature. Task panes appear at the left or right side of the screen. This button displays the name of the item that appears when you click the button.

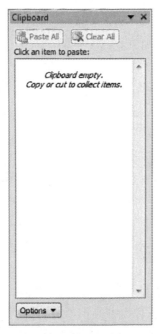

Dialog Box   Window/Task Pane

With the dialog box, you can select items from the lists, use the arrow for a list box to display more choices for that list, or click a command to turn the feature on or off. It may display a preview of the changes.

A task pane usually contains options specific to the feature as seen in the preceding graphic that focuses on the styles currently available. Another task pane is the Office Clipboard that displays any item when the Cut or Copy command is used.

The Ribbon can be minimized if you want to show more of your document or you do not want to display the Ribbon. To minimize the Ribbon:

- Click the ⌃ button at the far right of the top of the Ribbon, or
- double-click any of the ribbon tabs, or
- right-click anywhere on the Ribbon and then click Minimize the Ribbon, or
- press (Ctrl)+(F1).

You can also access the Ribbon using the keyboard; some users consider the keyboard a faster method for accessing commands. There is also consistency between Windows programs as some keyboard shortcuts are the same, such as pressing (Ctrl)+(C) to copy, (Ctrl)+(S) to save, or (Ctrl)+(P) to print.

To access the Ribbon using the keyboard, press (Alt) or (F10) to display the keyboard buttons for the commands in the Ribbon.

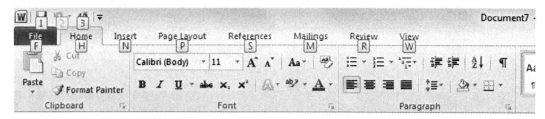

When you press the key for the appropriate feature, Word displays the next set of keys you can use to select a command or feature. For example, pressing (H) displays the **Home** tab.

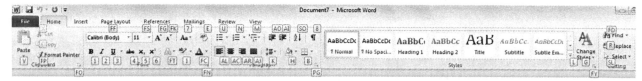

If you then press (K) you access the **Line Spacing** command which, in this case, displays a menu with more options.

You can also use the keyboard to:

- Access another tab, with the Ribbon active, press (←) or (→) to move to the appropriate tab.
- Change the highlight or focus from the active tab, the status bar, or your document, press (F6). For example, to switch view modes, press (F6) to move the focus from the document to the status bar. Then press (Tab) to move to the Full Screen Reading button, and when it is highlighted, press (Enter).
- Display a shortcut menu for the selected command, press (Shift)+(F10).
- Move from the tab to the command in the first group by pressing (Tab). Continue pressing (Tab) to move to the next command, or (Shift)+(Tab) to move to the previous command. This only occurs once you press (Alt) or (F10) to display the keyboard shortcuts on the Ribbon.

To activate the selected command, press (Enter).

- To exit or cancel a selection at any time, press (Esc). You may need to press (Esc) more than once to return to your document.

Learn the Skill

In this exercise, you will start Word and access some of the tools to see how they work.

1 Start Word.

2 Click the **File** tab and review the contents of this screen.

3 Click the **File** tab again to exit this screen.

4 Use the mouse cursor to point to the **View** tab.

Notice how the **View** tab highlights, even though you have not clicked it.

5 Click the **View** tab to activate it.

6 Point to **Two Pages** in the Zoom group and notice how the color changes.

7 Click **Two Pages** to see how the view changes.

8 Move the cursor to the bottom right of the screen to the Zoom slider. Click and drag the slider to the right until you see the zoom percentage change to approximately **200%**.

9 At the top right of the Ribbon, click the **Minimize the Ribbon** button.

Notice how you now can see a bit more of the blank document on the screen.

10 Click and drag the slider the other way so the percentage changes to approximately **100%**.

11 Click **Minimize the Ribbon** again to re-display the Ribbon.

12 Now move the mouse pointer to the top of the screen and click some of the tabs to see how the commands are categorized and grouped on the tabs.

13 Press Alt to display the keyboard shortcuts on the tab.

14 Press P to display the **Page Layout** tab.

15 Then press M to display the **Margins** options.

16 Press Esc to cancel this option.

Notice how Word still displays the keys on the tab, so you can continue to use the keyboard shortcuts to choose another command.

17 Press Esc again until the shortcut keys no longer appear.

Working with Text

Typing (keyboarding) involves using the keyboard to input text into the document displayed on the screen. Editing involves performing such tasks as inserting and deleting single characters, words or multiple lines of text, as well as inserting and deleting blank lines between paragraphs. The following are the basic concepts of typing and editing text in Word:

Insertion Point	The vertical blinking bar on the screen shows where you currently are in the document; it moves to the right as you type new text. This bar is also called the I-beam or cursor.
Deleting Text	To delete a character to the right of the insertion point, press Delete. To delete a character to the left of the insertion point, press Backspace.

<table>
<tr><td>

MMM
Word Wrap
Online
Exercise

</td><td>

Word Wrap

</td><td>

When you have typed enough words to fill a line, the next word automatically wraps to the next line. Press (Enter) at the end of each paragraph of text.

</td><td>

The paragraph mark (¶) will only appear when ¶ (Show/Hide ¶) is selected, as described in the following section.

</td></tr>
<tr><td></td><td>

Blank Lines

</td><td>

A blank line is a paragraph with no text. To insert a blank line, press (Enter) to place a paragraph mark (¶) between paragraphs. To remove a blank line, move to the paragraph mark and delete it as if it was a text character.

</td><td></td></tr>
</table>

Identifying Screen Symbols

Occasionally you may see different symbols as you enter or edit text, after performing a task, or activating a command. These symbols are visual clues provided within Word to help identify a particular status or recognize other options that may be available for this command. Some of these symbols include:

Texr	A red wavy line beneath words indicates that this text does not exist in the dictionary set up for your system or in the custom dictionary for the language selected for the document.
move the	A green wavy line indicates that Word has identified a grammatical error in this sentence.
what to where	A blue wavy line indicates a contextual error or text with the same pronunciation, but having different spellings and meanings. In this case, the text should be "wear", not "where" or "ware".
⌖ , ⌖ or ⌖	One of these symbols appears in the status bar if Word finds proofing errors in the document. The last symbol appears while Word is checking the document.
ⓒ or ℬ ▾	Word identifies this as an item that exists in the AutoCorrect list and will provide more options for this item. When you place your cursor over this symbol, it appears with a down arrow you click to display options for this item.
⧉ (Ctrl) ▾	Word recognizes that you pasted an item in the current location and now provides more options for this action. When you place your cursor over this symbol, it appears with a down arrow you click to display options for this item.
⊞ or ⊟	These symbols only appear when you can see the white space at the bottom of one page and the top of the next page. They represent the bottom and top margins respectively. Use this option to hide or show the white space so you can focus on the text in your document.
¶ (Show/Hide ¶)	On the **Home** tab, in the **Paragraph** group, click this to display non-printing formatting characters in the document. Use this tool to assist with editing documents. These characters display on the screen only; they do not print.
¶ or ↵	These non-printing characters represent each time you press (Enter) or (Shift)+(Enter). When you press (Enter), you are asking Word to end the paragraph or create a blank line in this location. Press (Shift)+(Enter) to have Word insert a manual line break or text wrapping break. Line breaks are useful to treat multiple lines as a single paragraph, as with a client's name and address.
→	This non-printing character represents each time (Tab) was pressed in the document.
·by·the·	The non-printing character between the words represents each time the Spacebar was pressed in the document.

	When you type enough text to fill a page, Word automatically begins a new page. If you have the **Show/Hide ¶** button active, you will see this soft page break code; it only appears in the Draft view.
···············Page Break···············	To start a new page, insert a manual page break. This code appears if you have the **Show/Hide ¶** button active.

A tip to help you find the end of the document is to press ⌷Enter⌷ after typing the last piece of text for the document. This will end the paragraph, and return the cursor to the left margin on a new line.

Learn the Skill

This exercise provides practice with entering text and how words wrap. You should already have a blank document on the screen. If not, open Word so you can start the exercise.

1   In the blank document on your screen, type: New Tour Proposal and then press ⌷Enter⌷.

Notice how Word allows you to enter text directly onto the screen and, when you pressed ⌷Enter⌷, the cursor moved to the beginning of the next line.

2   Type the following text as shown, pressing ⌷Enter⌷ only when you see the ¶ symbol (your text will wrap at a different location than the following as the text is formatted to fit the layout used in this book):

> One of the latest interests is in the area of paranormal activity. While this is not a new travel concept, there seems to be renewed interest in tours to places where paranormal activity has allegedly occurred. I have done some research into existing tours that have been popular and include sights such as cemeteries, haunted sites, and actual paranormal occurrences.¶
> There is a wide variety of these types of tours around the world so we should be able to offer these on a global scale.¶

As you typed the information into your document, you will have noticed that the text wrapped from the right side back to the left side when you ran out of space. This is what word wrap is and enables you to concentrate on entering your text. Word, by default, uses line spacing of 1.15 and results in the "extra" space between the lines of text. You will learn how to change the line spacing along with other formatting options later in this courseware; at this point, we will focus on entering and editing the text and managing documents.

3   Leave the document on the screen for the next exercise.

Moving Around in the Document

The insertion point indicates the location where Word will insert new text or pasted items. You can use either the mouse or the keyboard to navigate around a document.

To use the mouse to move the insertion point to a new location in the document, point to the desired new location and click.

Listed below are some keyboard methods to move quickly in a document.

Desired Movement	Press	Desired Movement	Press
Next character	→	Next line	↓
Previous character	←	Previous line	↑
Next word	Ctrl+→	Next paragraph	Ctrl+↓
Previous word	Ctrl+←	Previous paragraph	Ctrl+↑
Beginning of line	Home	Next screen	PgDn
End of line	End	Previous screen	PgUp
Beginning of document	Ctrl+Home	Next page	Ctrl+PgDn
End of document	Ctrl+End	Previous page	Ctrl+PgUp
		Go to page	Ctrl+G or F5

- When you have a multiple page document, use the vertical scroll bar to move or scroll the view of the screen through the document from top to bottom and vice-versa.
- When the document is wider than the screen displays, use the horizontal scroll bar to move or scroll the view from side-to-side, across the document.
- When you drag the scroll box along the vertical scroll bar, a ScreenTip displays your position in the document, e.g. Page: 2 . This may be a page number or a heading text, depending on how your document is set up.
- You can also use the wheel on the mouse to move up or down in the document.

Learn the Skill

This exercise provides practice moving around the document using the keyboard.

1 With the document from the previous screen active on your screen, press Ctrl+Home to move the cursor quickly to the beginning of the document.

2 Click the mouse anywhere near the end of the document.

This is an example of how easy it can be to move to the end of a short document. For longer documents, you may want to press Ctrl+End to go to that location quickly.

3 Click the mouse at the beginning of the document.

4 Press the End key to move quickly to the end of that line.

In this case, the cursor should have moved to the end of the first line of text.

5 Click any line of the next paragraph and then press End again.

Notice the cursor moved to the end of the text line, which is also the right side or margin.

6 Press Ctrl+↓.

The cursor should have moved to the beginning of the next paragraph.

7 Press Ctrl+→.

The cursor is now at the beginning of the second word.

8 Press Ctrl+→ three times.

You have now moved to the right by three words. You can use these navigation tools to move left or right by one or more words. This is true of any of the keyboard options when moving around a document.

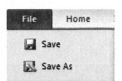

Working with Documents

As you begin working with documents, you need to consider how to organize your files for easy access. File organization includes how you name the file, where you save it, specific file type, or whether you want to add or change the properties of the file to help find it later. The Save commands are located in Backstage via the File tab.

Saving Documents

1.5

It is important to save your documents as you work on them to be able to use them again. When choosing a name for the document, consider the following:

- The file name can be a maximum of 255 characters (including the drive and folder path), and may not include these characters: / \ : * ? " < > |

- Name the file so you can identify the contents quickly.

- Word automatically assigns a .docx extension or file type at the end of the file name. You only have to type in the name for the document.

- When the file name appears in a shaded box, begin typing the new file name to insert the new file name for this document. You can use the arrow direction keys to move anywhere in the existing file name to add or delete text to the file name.

- The first time you save a new document, you will see the Save As dialog box. The next time you want to save changes to the existing document, you can use one of the Save methods.

- To save an existing document with a new name, click **File** and then click **Save As**.

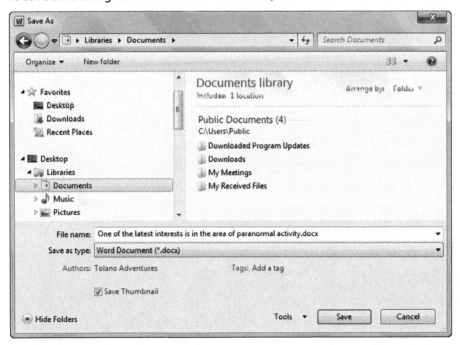

- To save a document as a different file type, such as an earlier version of Word, use **Save as type** in the Save As dialog box to find the appropriate file format.

- By default, Windows sets up the Documents library to store files and Word draws on this. You are not restricted to this folder and can:

    Libraries are available only with Windows 7.

    - Create your own folders to help organize files by clicking **New folder** on the command bar in the Save As dialog box.

    - Save in any location that you can access, e.g. hard drive, thumb drive, flash disk, network drive.

If you are unsure whether you have saved a file previously, check the title bar or use **Save As** to give the file a different name, thereby ensuring you have a copy of the current document on screen.

If the file already exists in one location, you can save the same file to another location. Be careful with files which have the same name in different locations as you will need to use other tools to help you and others determine which one is the most current or valid version.

To view the file type or extension, turn on this option using Windows Explorer. Click **Organize**, **Folder and search options**, and then on the **View** tab, deselect the **Hide extensions for known file types**. Showing file types is helpful when determining which file you want to use i.e., where two files have the same name and one shows the Word 2010 format (.docx) while the other shows the Word 2003 format (.doc).

To save changes made to the current document using the same file name, use one of the following methods:

- Click **File** and then **Save**, or
- on the Quick Access Toolbar, click **Save**, or
- press (Ctrl)+(S).

You can use **Views** in the Save As dialog box to help display the folders and files to personal preferences.

Learn the Skill

In this exercise, you will save your newly created document.

This exercise requires that you have downloaded the student data files for this courseware and extracted to a folder on the desktop. Check with your instructor if they are in a different location. Alternatively, please refer to the Preface section of this book for instructions on how to download these files.

1   With the document from the previous exercise still visible on the screen, in the Quick Access Toolbar, click **Save**.

2   Click the **Save in** arrow and navigate to where the student data files are located for this courseware. Check with your instructor if you are unsure of the location.

Whenever text is highlighted (New Tour Proposal) in a box, you can begin typing to replace existing text rather than deleting the characters first and then typing in the new name.

Notice how Word has suggested a file name for this document. You can use this name, or replace it with a name of your own.

3   In the **File name** field, press (End) to ensure you are at the end of the file name and then type: - Student where Student is your name.

> *You can also press ENTER after entering the file name to save the file.*

4   Click **Save**.

Notice the title bar now contains the new file name as visual confirmation that the file is now saved.

Creating a New Document

1.6

When Word initially starts, a blank, ready-to-type document appears on the screen. To create another document, you must use a series of commands for creating a new document.

To create a new blank document:

- click **File,** click **New**, click **Blank document**, and then click **Create**, or
- press Ctrl+N, or
- to choose from a variety of pre-designed documents, called templates, click **File**, click **New**, click a template and then click **Create**.

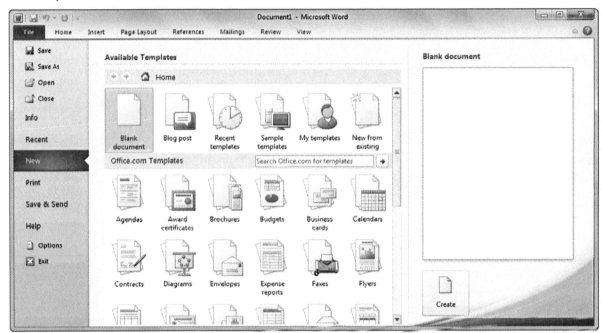

Using pre-designed templates is useful if you are unsure how to lay out a particular type of document, such as an invitation, meeting agenda, or a business memo. When you click a selection in the Office.com list, the template appears as a preview in the right pane. The new document is not created until you click **Create**, so you can move between the templates to choose the one you want.

An automatic number appears with each new document to identify it as a new document. For example, if you have three Word documents open and you create another new document, the title bar displays it as Document4 thereby ensuring it does not share the same name as the other three documents. The document numbering restarts at 1 when you start a new session of Word.

Learn the Skill

In this exercise, you will create a new document using different methods.

1   Press Ctrl+N.

You should now have a new blank document on the screen.

2   Click the **File** tab and ensure the Blank document template is selected in the Available Templates area. Then click **Create**.

You should now have a second blank document.

3   Click **File** once more and then in the Office.com templates area, click **Calendars**.

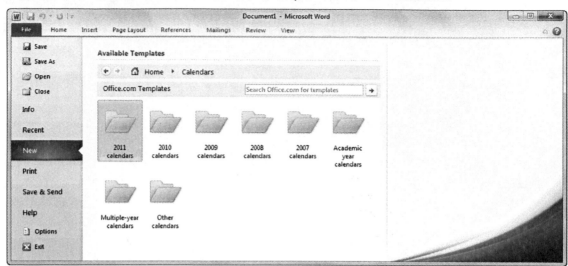

4   Click the ⬅ button to return to the previous screen for another template selection.

5   In the Office.com Templates area, click **Greeting Cards**.

6   Click **Occasions and events**.

7   Scroll in the list and then click **Welcome card**. When the preview appears in the right pane, click **Download**.

Your new document should appear similar to the following:

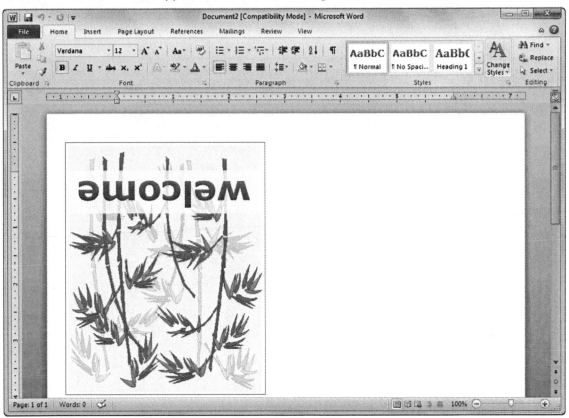

Although your document appears upside down, it is correctly set up as this is a greeting card that has been designed to be folded into four parts. This example shows how templates can save you time and effort when creating a document. Many of the elements you see in this document are covered later in this courseware.

Switching Between Documents

When you have multiple documents open on the screen, you can switch between documents quickly and easily by using one of the following methods:

- On the **View** tab, in the **Window** group, click **Switch Windows**, or

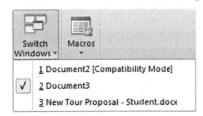

- click the **Word** button on the taskbar to display a preview of each open document, or

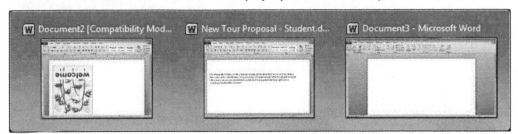

- if Word is in Restore Down view, the open documents may display in a cascading layout; click the title bar for the appropriate document to switch to that document.

Learn the Skill

You should have at least two documents open with only the most recently opened document visible. Try switching between the documents on your screen.

1   Click the **View** tab.

2   In the Windows group at the right, click **Switch Windows**.

3   Click *New Tour Proposal – Student*.

     You should now be viewing this document.

4   Click the **Word** button on the taskbar at the bottom of the screen.

5   Click one of the blank documents in the window showing all open Word documents.

6   Click the **Word** button on the taskbar and then click the greeting card document.

7   Click **File** and then **Save**.

     Notice how the Save As dialog box appears, indicating this is the first time you are saving this document.

8   Navigate to where the student data files are located.

9   In the **File name** field, with the text still highlighted, type: `Welcome card - Student` and press `Enter`.

> You can also point at the taskbar button to display any open windows for that application; clicking the button keeps the window displayed regardless of where you may move the mouse.

This file now saves; you should also notice that [Compatibility Mode] appears next to the file name. This is a reminder that the file is saved for Word 2010 and also is compatible for others if they use an earlier version of Word. The compatibility option is discussed in more detail later in this Lesson.

Saving as Another File Format

Word provides a variety of formats to save a file if you need to share the file i.e., with someone who may be using another version of Word or does not have Word installed; your Web site requires the document to be in PDF format; or to send as an attachment to an e-mail.

To save a document in another file format, click **File**, click **Save As** and then click the arrow for **Save as type** to choose the appropriate file format.

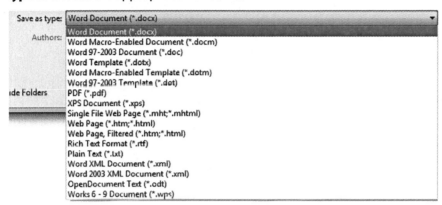

Use the **Word template** format to create your own templates or document designs. You can use one of the pre-designed templates provided by Word or create your own document, and then save the file with a new name using this file format. That file can then be selected from the Available Templates area.

Working with the Compatibility Mode

1.4

Occasionally when working with documents saved in a different format than Word 2010, you may find there are difficulties working with the file i.e., different formatting options or tab alignments changing. Word provides tools to check the document to ensure it is compatible with other Word versions, or convert the document automatically to Word 2010. These tools are available in Backstage via the **File** tab and the **Info** category.

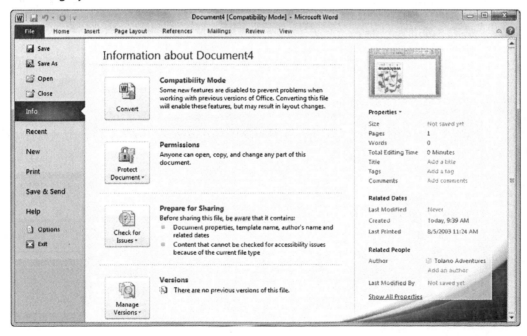

To check whether there are problems with converting your document to a different file format than Word 2010, click **File**, click **Info**, click **Check for Issues**, and then **Check Compatibility**.

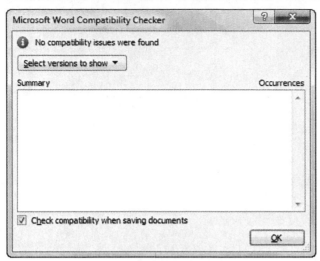

Potential problems between the versions appear in the list and you need to decide whether to continue saving the file in this file format or return to the document to make appropriate changes. For instance, the SmartArt illustration is a feature that does not exist in versions prior to Word 2007. If you continue with the conversion, this diagram changes to a drawing object and cannot be modified or ungrouped.

Converting a Document

To convert a document saved in another file format to the Word .docx format, click **File**, click **Info**, and then click **Convert**.

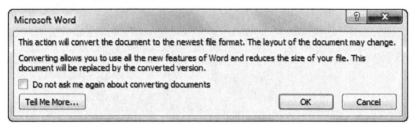

Any changes between the versions that can convert in Word 2010 appear in the list. They will not change the original document, but save this document with the Word 2010 features and format. Note that not all elements in a document created in another format can convert or are compatible with Word 2010.

Closing a Document

Once you have finished editing or revising a document, you should close the document to clear the screen and memory, enabling you to start or open another document without leaving old documents on your screen. Closing your document is much like closing a book and putting it back on the shelf before opening another book.

Although you can have multiple documents open at one time, it is best to close those you do not currently need. This saves on memory and processing time.

As Word displays each document in its own window, you can use one of the following methods to close a document and the Word application:

- Click **Close** for the Word application, or
- click **File** and then **Close**, or
- press Ctrl + W or Ctrl + F4, or

- point at the Word button in the taskbar, and then in the window with the documents, click the ⊠ button for that file.

  Using the last two methods to close all documents keeps the Word application open after you close the last document on screen. The first method displays the Windows desktop once all documents and the application are closed; this option can be changed using **Show all windows in the Taskbar** in the **Options** command of the **File** tab.

If you add or change something in a new or existing document that has not been saved yet, Word always prompts with the option of saving the document.

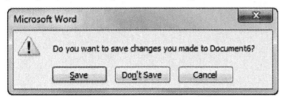

When you close all documents in Word, the screen appears similar to:

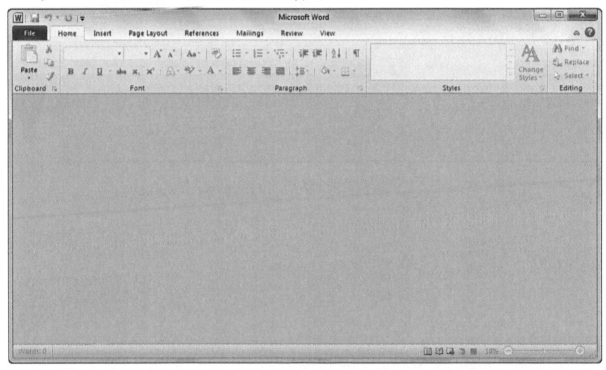

Notice no options are available to you other than the **File** tab as a reminder that there are no documents active in Word, and you must now create a new document or open an existing one before the features become available.

Learn the Skill

In this exercise, you will use several different formats to save and then close multiple documents.

1   With the *Welcome card – Student* document visible on the screen, click **File** and then **Save As**.

2   On the Command Bar in the Save As dialog box, click **New folder**.

3   With the new folder name highlighted, type: Non-Word 2010 Files and press ⬚Enter⬚.

4   Click to navigate into that folder.

5   Click the arrow for the **Save as type** list and then click **Word 97-2003 Document**.

6   Click **Save** to save the document in this location.

You now have two documents with the same name in the two different locations. The example shown here for these steps is representative of how you can organize your files by saving a copy of the original document in a different location and a different file format.

7   With the Welcome card visible, press (Ctrl)+(W) to close this file.

8   If a blank document appears, press (Ctrl)+(W) to close this file.

9   Point at the Word button in the taskbar and then click ▄▄ x ▄▄ for the other blank document.

You should now only have the New Tour proposal document active on the screen.

10 Click **File** and then click **Close**.

Opening a Document

You can open a document from any location and open it to the screen for further processing. You can open as many documents as needed; the only limitation is the amount of memory available on your system to handle multiple documents.

Use one of the following methods to open a document:

- Click **File**, click **Recent**, and then click the file from the list of recent documents; or

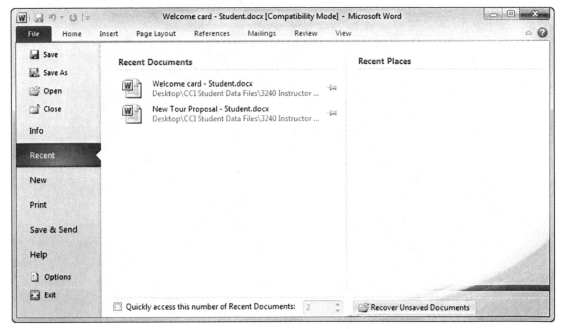

As you open documents, Word displays the files in the same order as you opened them, with the most recent at the top of the list. As you reach the maximum number of files that show in this list, the oldest drops from the list. You can click the pin icon at the right of the file name to make this file always available in the list until it is unpinned. By default, you can see a list of up to 20 recent documents at a time; this number can be customized.

- click **File** and then click **Open**; or
- press (Ctrl)+(O) or (Ctrl)+(F12).

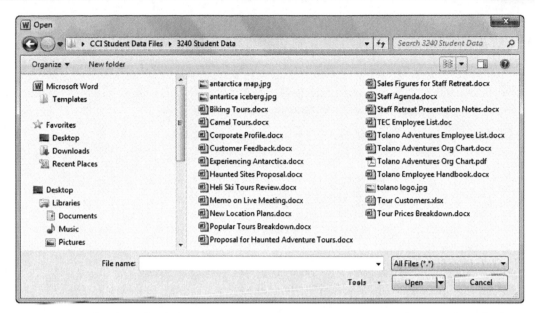

Once the Open dialog box displays, you can navigate using the mouse or keyboard to display the files or folders and then use one of the following methods to open a document:

- Double-click the file name; or

- point on the file name to select it, and then click **Open** or press ⌷Enter⌷; or

- if the file is stored in a different location, navigate to the location and then use one of the above methods to open a file.

Learn the Skill

In this exercise, you will open a document that needs to be checked for compatibility as well as open another file to convert to Word 2010 format.

1 Click **File** and then click **Open**.

2 Navigate to the location of the student data files, and then double-click *Tolano Adventures Org Chart*.

This document contains an example of a SmartArt diagram created in Word 2010 that needs to be checked for compatibility with other users.

3 Click **File** and on the left panel, ensure Info is selected.

4 Click **Check for Issues** and select **Check Compatibility**.

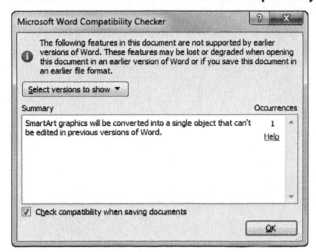

5 Click **OK**.

By accepting this issue, you have set the file so that others cannot edit the organization chart unless they have Word 2007 or 2010.

If you receive a request from Nicole Lockwood in the New York office to have the document in a format that restricts any edits, choose PDF or Portable Document Format.

6 Click **File** and then click **Save As**. In **File name**, press End to move the cursor quickly to the end of the existing file name and type: - Student.

7 Click the arrow for the **Save as Type** list and then click **PDF**.

8 Leave the defaults as displayed and click **Save**.

A PDF file is created and then opens in Adobe Reader, if it is installed on your computer. Your screen now appears similar to the following:

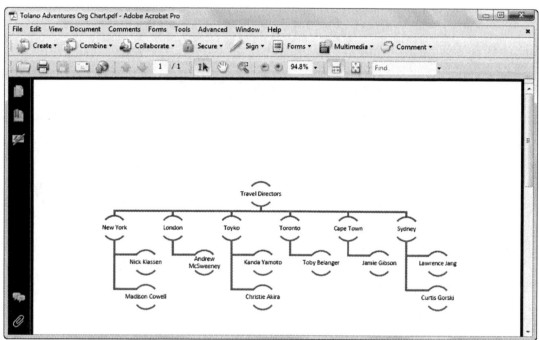

9 Close the Adobe Reader and the Word window for this document without saving.

Now try converting a file into the Word 2010 format.

10 Press Ctrl+O to display the Open dialog box.

11 Navigate to the student data files and then click *TEC Employee List*.

12 Click **File** and then **Save As**. Type: - Student at the end of this file name and then press Enter.

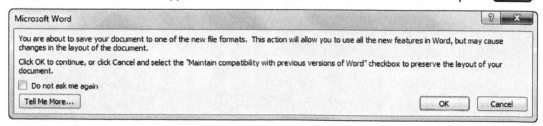

13 Click **OK** to accept that this will be saved in the Word 2010 format.

As visual confirmation that the file was converted, notice the title bar no longer displays [Compatibility Mode] next to the file name.

14 Close this document.

Using Document Properties

Document properties provide information to assist in locating this file based on specific search criteria. How much information you enter will depend on standards set up in your office, or which information you want to use to find documents later.

To view the properties for the current document, click **File**, click **Info**, and review the information in Backstage.

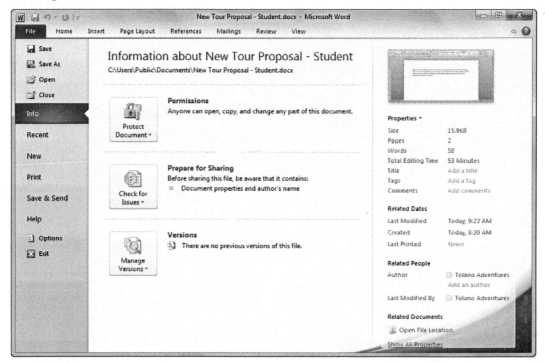

To add properties for the current document, in the right pane, click the field you want to change.

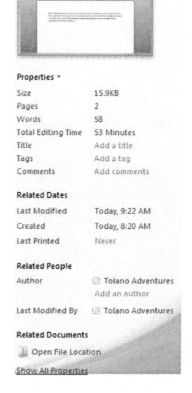

To add properties to the file using a method other than in Backstage, click **Properties** below the document preview.

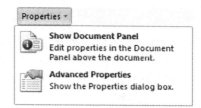

Show Document Panel   Display a panel above the document on the Word screen where you can add general information for this document. You can also click **Document Properties** to access the **Advanced Properties** option.

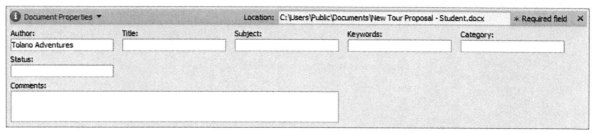

Advanced Properties   Add or customize properties for the document, i.e., who checked this document, its subject or category. Each tab in this dialog box displays different information for viewing or modifying.

Learn the Skill

In this exercise, you will add a summary to one of your documents.

1   Click **File** and then click **Open**. Double-click *New Tour Proposal – Student* to view this document on screen.

2   Click **File**, ensuring Info is highlighted at the left.

3   On the right pane, click the blank area at the right of the **Title** field.

4   Type: Proposal for Paranormal Tours and press (Enter).

5   Click **Properties** and then click **Show Document Panel**.

6   Click the blank area for **Comments** and type: Big trend currently; need to investigate how many visitors for popular sites and any eco damage results.

7   Click ☒ at the far right of the Document Panel to close the panel.

8   On the Quick Access toolbar, click **Save** and then click ☒ to close Word.

Sharing Documents

1.4

The rapid adoption of the Internet into everyday life demonstrates how communication helps people to connect in social and work settings. Today's workplace leverages the power of technology to increase worker productivity in creating, analyzing and sharing data, leading to faster and more informed decision-making. Most office workers now have at least one computer, and almost every one of them connects to the others using the corporate local area network.

Word taps into this pervasive connectivity with its built-in ability to send documents to others using e-mail, the Internet, and Microsoft SharePoint.

Using E-mail

One way of sharing documents quickly with others is to send them by e-mail. The downside of using e-mail is that every recipient gets his or her own copy of the document. These individuals often make changes or add comments to their copy of the document and send it back. The originator must then merge these copies together.

To send a document using e-mail from within Word, do the following steps:

1. Open the document.

2. On the **File** tab, click **Save & Send**.

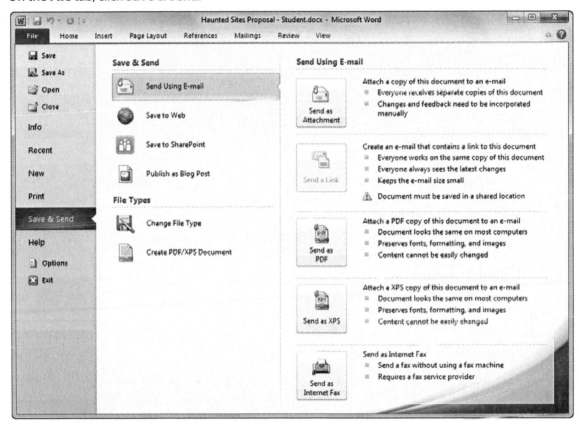

3. Ensure **Send Using E-mail** is selected and then click one of the following buttons:
    a. Send as Attachment
    b. Send a Link
    c. Send as PDF
    d. Send as XPS
    e. Send as Internet Fax

Send as Attachment	Create a new e-mail message with your document included as an attachment: 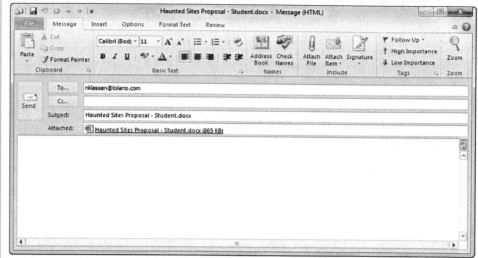 When you click the **Send** button, Outlook sends the e-mail and the attached document to the intended recipient.
Send as Link	Launch Outlook with a new e-mail message containing a hyperlink to your document. Unlike **Send as Attachment**, **Send as PDF** or **Send as XPS**, your recipients do not receive any file; instead, they open the original document by clicking on the hyperlink in the e-mail. Note that your document must be stored in a shared location (e.g., a network drive) where your recipients can access it from wherever they are located.
Send as PDF	Convert the document into a PDF (Portable Document Format) before you send it. Then Outlook creates a new e-mail message with this PDF file included as an attachment. The PDF format allows the recipient to view and print the document, but it does not permit them to make changes.
Send as XPS	Convert the document into XPS format before sending. As with **Send as PDF**, Word converts the document and then Outlook creates a new e-mail message with this XPS file included as an attachment; recipients can view and print the document but they cannot make changes to it.
Send as Internet Fax	Convert the document into an electronic fax file and send it to the internet fax software installed on your local computer.

Of these alternatives, you should select **Send as Link** as your preferred method when sharing with co-workers within the same organization. Avoid sending a document as an attachment because you will simply create more work for yourself when your co-workers make changes to their copies of the document, possibly at the same time as you are doing so. If instead you put the document into a shared location and send out a link, everyone (including you) is always updating the same document.

The **Send as PDF** or **Send as XPS** are useful alternatives if you want to prevent the recipients from making changes to the document.

Save to Web

Another way of sharing documents with others is to use a web-based storage service such as the Microsoft SkyDrive. SkyDrive is one of the components of Microsoft's Windows Live group of online services. Every registered Windows Live user has a SkyDrive with 25 GB of storage space at no cost. By default, you have two main folders: My Documents and Public. Anyone with a Windows Live ID can access any files in the Public folder at any time; any files you put into the My Documents folder are only accessible by you, except for the ones that you designate your contacts can share. You can also add other online web-based (e.g. Internet) storage services to store your documents.

To save a document to the SkyDrive from within Word, do the following:

1.   Open the document.

2.   On the **File** tab, click **Save & Send**.

3.   Under **Save & Send**, click **Save to Web**.

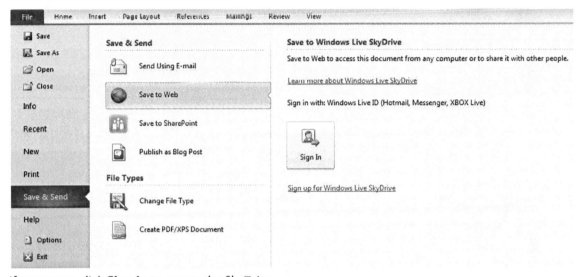

4.   If necessary, click **Sign In** to access the SkyDrive.

5.   Enter your login ID and password in Windows Live.

     Word then displays the folders in your SkyDrive.

6.   Click one of the SkyDrive folders (e.g. *Public* or *My Documents*) and then click **Save As**.

The Save As dialog box appears (there may be a short wait while the connection is completed with the SkyDrive). Although it looks like any other folder on your computer or a network drive, it is actually a remote drive provided as part of your Windows Live account. If you want to share your document with others, be sure to select the *Public* folder.

7.   If desired, change the **File name** and/or **Save as type**.

8.   Click **Save**.

9.   If necessary, make any other changes to the document and save these changes. Note that, any time you save changes, you are saving them directly to the document in the SkyDrive, not to your local computer.

10. Close the document.

The document is now accessible from the SkyDrive.

Using SharePoint

Another method of sharing documents with co-workers is by using SharePoint. Recognizing that people working together are more productive than people working alone, Microsoft designed SharePoint to facilitate document sharing within an organization and with authorized users in partner organizations. The term *web-based collaborative environment* refers to this kind of online sharing.

SharePoint brings together the many different tools that people use to share, including:

- **Shared network drives to store files and documents**—In the past, a company or IT department would designate specific computers to store these files. Access security quickly followed to ensure protection of confidential files. However, the demand for shared storage space in an organization usually exceeds the space available after a few years, representing an ongoing administrative nightmare for most IT departments.

- **Document version control**—A collaborative environment brings a new set of challenges and headaches, primarily the dispersal of ownership and loss of control over changes made, which often leads to uncontrolled and haphazard changes. For example, someone may delete a document accidentally or make changes that conflict with another person's changes. Version control ensures that only one person enters their changes at any one time. If someone accidentally deletes a document or makes unwanted changes, this feature allows you to restores a previous version easily.

- **Workflow control**—You can designate documents to be funneled through workflow processes, such as approving purchase requisitions or media releases. The system then automatically routes the document to the next person in the workflow when the current approver has completed his or her work.

- **Social networking**—Facebook is an example of social networking.

- **E-mail**—Announcements, notices and other types of team communication, which are often sent by e-mail, can be quickly lost in the daily volume of other e-mail. An effective collaboration site has a section containing the most relevant communications to the team without having to wade through e-mails.

- **Other shared communications**—These include things such as corporate or team calendars, surveys and polls.

To save a document to SharePoint from within Word, do the following:

1.   Open the document.

2.   On the **File** tab, click **Share**.

3.   Under **Share**, click **Save to SharePoint**.

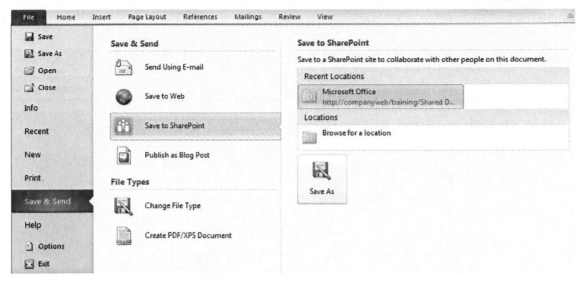

4. If necessary, click **Browse for a location**.

The Save As dialog box now appears, allowing you to navigate to the SharePoint site where the document is to be stored.

A SharePoint site can be designed in many different ways; the following illustration shows one example where documents of various types are stored.

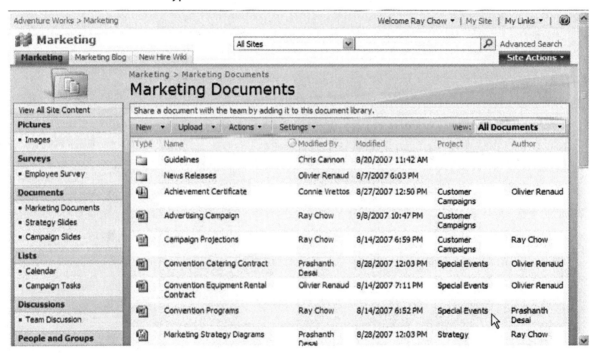

Lesson Summary

This lesson teaches you to create simple documents and introduces you to some file management tools available in Word. Upon completion of this lesson, you should be able to:

- ☑ identify elements on the screen
- ☑ use the Quick Access Toolbar
- ☑ use the Ribbon
- ☑ work with text
- ☑ identify screen symbols
- ☑ move around the document
- ☑ use Backstage to save, open, or create new documents
- ☑ switch between documents
- ☑ save in different file formats
- ☑ close a document
- ☑ add document properties

Review Questions

MMM
Go online for
Additional
Review and
Activities

1. Explain how the Ribbon is organized.

2. Provide examples of when you might use a template to create a new document.

3. Explain why you would save a file in another format other than the Word 2010 document format.

4. How can the Compatibility Mode affect a file?

5. Provide an example of how you might use the information shown for a file's properties.

Microsoft®

Word 2010

Core Certification

Lesson 2: Manipulating Text

Lesson Objectives

This lesson teaches you to create simple documents and introduces you to some file management tools available in Word. Upon completion of this lesson, you should be able to:

☐ change views

☐ select text

☐ use cut, copy and paste

☐ use the clipboard

☐ move text with drag-and-drop

☐ use Paste Options

☐ use Paste Special

☐ find text or items with Browse by

☐ replace text or items

Changing the View

1.1

You can customize the way a document displays to suit your particular requirements by choosing the appropriate options from the **View** tab.

MMM
Viewing a
Document
Online
Exercise

Print Layout	Use this view to adjust the overall layout of information on the document page, or to show how the printed document will look. As you are focusing on the layout of the printed document, you will be able to see graphical elements you cannot see with the Draft view, e.g. headers/footers, pictures and columns.
Full Screen Reading	Useful when reading a document as pages are adapted to the size of your monitor for ease of reading. The Ribbon is hidden so you can focus on reading the document at the maximum size for your monitor; a series of buttons appears across the top of the screen with options for use in this mode.
Web Layout	Useful when creating a Web page: text wraps to the screen size; backgrounds and pictures appear the same as when using a Web browser.
Outline	Enables you to create the outline of a document where you can promote or demote headings within a hierarchical layout, or collapse a document so that only the headings and subheadings appear. This makes it very easy to rearrange the topics in a document (i.e., move the headings and the appropriate text moves with it).
Draft	Appropriate for most typing, editing and formatting tasks.

You can turn this feature on or off when opening and reading documents sent as attachments to an e-mail.

An alternative to using the **View** tab is to use one of the commonly accessed view buttons located at the bottom right of the screen:

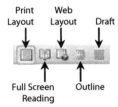

Learn the Skill

In this exercise, you will try the different views using both the View tab and View buttons.

1   Click the **File** tab and then click **Open**.

2   Navigate to the student data files location and double-click *Tolano Adventures Employee List* to open this file.

You should be viewing the document in Print Layout view which you can check on the rulers across the top and left side of the screen.

3   At the lower right of the screen, click the **Draft** view button.

Tolano Adventures

New York

300 171st Street, New York, NY 98032

(540) 555-4321 (Head Office)

Nick Klassen

Vice President

nklassen@tolano.com

Madison Cowell

Travel Director

mcowell@tolano.com

Notice the vertical ruler no longer appears and the text appears at the far left, enabling you to focus on text.

4   In the View buttons area, click the **Full Screen Reading** view button.

5   At the top of the screen, click the ▶ to go to the next page.

You should now be viewing different pages of this document. At the bottom of the screen you will see a navigation tool to help you "turn" the page:

 or

6   Click **Close** at the top right corner of the screen to exit this view.

7   Then press $Ctrl$+W to close the document.

Suppose you want to post a document on the company Web site and you want to check the document layout before sending it to the webmaster.

8   Open the *Biking Tours* document from your student data files location.

Note the position of the graphic and how the text flows around it in the Print Layout view.

9   Click the **View** tab and then, in the **Document Views** group, click **Web Layout**.

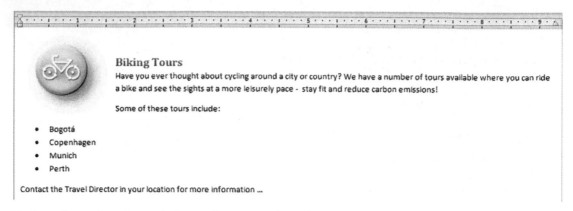

Notice where the picture is located compared to the Print Layout. This is useful when preparing documents in an environment such as the Internet where users may be viewing the document on a variety of computers. The Internet has a standard language used to enable everyone to see the same information, no matter which operating system is in use. So, documents like this will need minor modifications if the graphic is to stay at the right side.

10   Close this document.

Now take a look at when you might use the Outline view.

11   Open *Staff Agenda* in the student data files location.

This is a list that will be expanded later as the managers decide what is to be included at the retreat.

12   On the **View** tab, in the **Document Views**, click **Outline**.

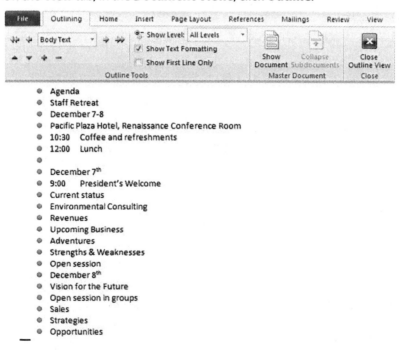

Notice how Word has changed the layout to a list format where you can set up different levels for the types of information to be discussed. For example, the Coffee and refreshments item is really a subset of the information for the hotel and conference room – currently they are at the same level. You can begin to organize the information here even though you may not have all the details. This exercise will be performed later in this courseware. This is an introduction to how you could use this view.

13   On the **View** tab, in the **Document Views**, click **Print Layout**.

14   Close the Staff Agenda document.

Adjusting the Zoom

1.1

To enlarge or reduce the text display on the screen:

- Click the **View** tab, in the **Zoom** group, click the appropriate option, or

- the **Zoom level** button on the status bar, or

- the Zoom slider or the incremental buttons on either side of the slider on the status bar.

When you use one of the first two methods, the Zoom dialog box appears with further options:

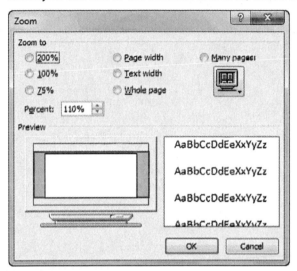

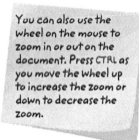

You can also use the wheel on the mouse to zoom in or out on the document. Press CTRL as you move the wheel up to increase the zoom or down to decrease the zoom.

The ability to enlarge the text display is useful when you are working with a small font size, whereas the ability to reduce the display is useful when you are working with landscape orientation.

You can set the zoom percentage between 10% to 500%, or you can have Word automatically adjust the magnification so that you can see the entire width of the page or text on the screen. When changing the view, the position of the insertion point will determine the zoom area.

100% Zoom

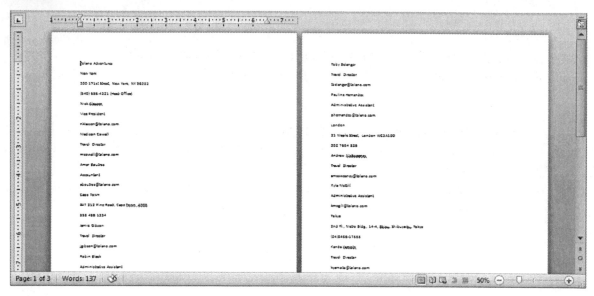

50% Zoom

Keep in mind that this feature only controls the screen display. The amount of text that displays when you change the zoom percentage is determined by the size of your monitor. For example, if you have a 19" monitor or larger, you may see more of a document at 50% than someone who has a 17", but less than someone using a 21" monitor. Changing the magnification has no effect on the document printout.

Learn the Skill

In this exercise, you will practice changing the magnification or zoom on a document.

1 Open *Tolano Adventures Employee List*.

2 On the **View** tab, in the **Zoom** group, click **One Page**.

3 Click the ⊕ button to the right of the zoom slider in the status bar three times to enlarge the view of the text.

4 Using the slider, drag the arrow to the left and right to see how the zoom changes.

5 On the **View** tab, in the **Zoom** group, click **Zoom**.

6 In the **Percent** text box, type: 82 for the percentage and then click **OK**.

   Notice how you can enter any percent value for the zoom, in addition to using the set options in the Zoom dialog box.

7 On the **View** tab, in the **Zoom** group, click **Zoom**.

8 Click the monitor button below Many pages and click at the second page on the second row, similar to the following:

2 x 2 Pages

   You should now be able to see four pages at a time, although this document only shows 3 - the total number of pages it contains.

9 On the **View** tab, in the **Zoom** group, click **100%**.

Working with Multiple Windows

1.1

Occasionally you may want to see two different parts of the same document at the same time, e.g. compare information and see which page the information is on. There are several ways to do this.

Splitting the Window

By splitting a document window you are displaying the same document in two different windows on the screen. You can only split the window horizontally into two parts. To split the window use one of the following methods:

- On the **View** tab, in the **Window** group, click **Split**. Then move the dark line to the desired height for the second window and click in that location, or

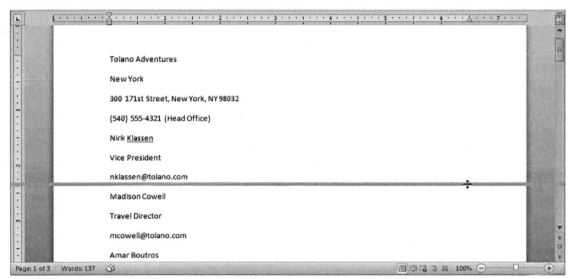

- drag **Split Horizontal** to the required height for the second window. This button is the topmost button, above **View Ruler** and the vertical scroll bar at the right of the screen.

Once the command is active, ⬍ appears as a guide to where the window will split. When you click at the location to split the window, the screen appears similar to the following:

You can change the view and scroll within each window independent of the other.

Note the following when working with split windows:

- Click in the appropriate window to access that document, or
- press (F6) or (Ctrl)+(F6) to move from one window to the other document window, or
- drag the split bar up or down to display more or less of either document window.
- To remove the split pane:
- On the **View** tab, in the **Window** group, click **Remove Split**, or
- double-click the split bar between the windows.

Learn the Skill

In this exercise, you will learn how to split a window and use the windows to view different parts of the document.

1 Ensure *Tolano Adventures Employee List* is active on the screen.

Suppose you want to see the names of the Travel Directors in New York and Sydney at the same time.

2 On the **View** tab, in the **Window** group, click **Split**.

3 Move the mouse down until you are at approximately half the screen size for the document.

4 Click in the bottom window and press (Ctrl)+(End) to move quickly to the end of the document.

5 Scroll up to show the names of the two Travel Directors in this location.

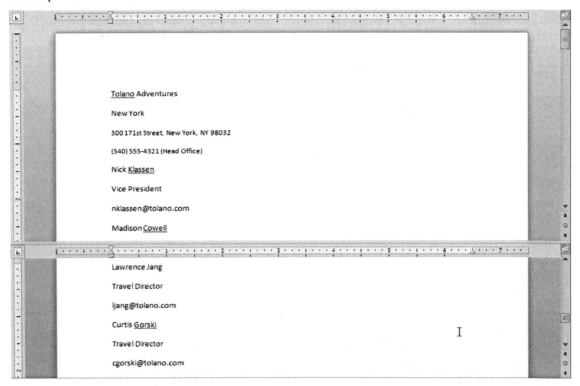

You can now view these names and then adjust the upper window to show the Travel Director there.

6 Click in the top window and scroll the document up if you cannot see who the Travel Director is in the New York office.

7 Position the cursor at the top of the bottom pane, above the ruler, and then drag to the bottom of the screen.

The split window no longer appears on the screen.

Arranging Windows

If you want to view more than one document at the same time, you can create one or more new windows to view documents side by side. You can choose to arrange the windows horizontally or vertically. As with splitting the window, you can click in each pane to work with that document, or press Ctrl + F6 to move to the next pane.

To view the documents vertically, you can use the **View Side by Side** command in the **Window** group of the **View** tab. You can only compare two documents at one time, although you can open several documents for selection.

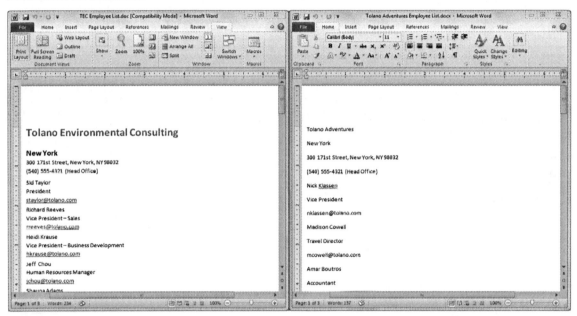

Synchronous Scrolling	Both windows scroll at the same time by the same amount (synchronous). When deactivated, you can scroll in each window separately.
Reset Window Position	Use to reset the window position if you moved or altered the window in any way.

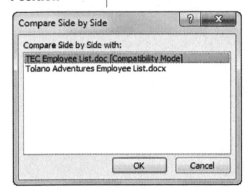

When you have more than two documents for comparison and you activate **View Side by Side**, Word automatically puts the names of the inactive documents in a window listing the file names for selection.

If you prefer to see a separate window for each document, on the **View** tab, in the **Window** group, click **Arrange All** and Word displays the documents in windows stacked one above the other, similar to:

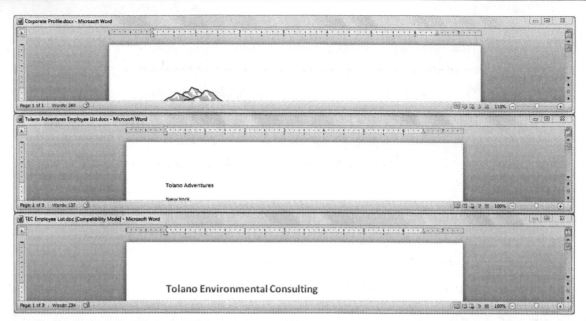

Learn the Skill

In this exercise, you will open multiple documents and then arrange the windows to view and work with each document.

1   Ensure *Tolano Adventures Employee List* is active on the screen. Then open *TEC Employees List*.

2   On the **View** tab, in the **Window** group, click **Arrange All**.

While this appears to be the same option as splitting the window, notice how two documents are open and each document appears in its own window. The active document also appears to be "elevated" and is brighter than the other document window.

Suppose you decide you would rather view the documents side by side.

3   On the **View** tab, in the **Window** group, click **View Side by Side**.

4   Click in the Tolano Adventures Employee List window.

Your cursor should now be blinking in this window so you can make any changes.

5   Scroll down the page in this window.

Notice how the TEC Employees List document scrolls at the same time by the same number of lines. This is because the files are set to scroll in a synchronous manner. This is useful if you are comparing changes from one version of a document to another, e.g. which colors and sizes did the New York office use for the text, so you can copy these for your version of that document. However, if you want to look at different areas of both documents, you will need to turn the synchronous scrolling off.

6   With the cursor still in the Tolano Adventures window, on the **View** tab, in the **Window** group, click **Synchronous Scrolling** to turn off the feature.

7   Now try scrolling up or down in this document.

You should be able to scroll in this document in any manner you want without affecting the other document.

Suppose you need to create a new window for Tolano Adventures so you can show the names of the Travel Directors along with the Environmental department.

8   On the **View** tab, in the **Window** group, click **New Window**.

A new window should appear with a copy of the Tolano Adventures Employee List.

9 On the **View** tab, in the **Window** group, click **Arrange All**.

You should now have three windows with each document in a separate window.

10 Close one of the Tolano Adventures documents and then maximize the screens.

Selecting Text

Selecting text is a fundamental step in Word prior to formatting, moving, copying, or any other manipulation of text.

Selecting a piece of text or an item such as a picture tells Word to which item you want to apply the next action. Selecting may also be called highlighting; do not confuse this with the Highlight feature in Word. Once you select text, the selection stays on the text in anticipation that you want to apply multiple actions for that selection. The only exception to this is when you delete or replace the selection with new text.

The image below shows two lines of text selected.

Proposal for Haunted Adventure Tours

Our preliminary research shows that the following tours are popular with travelers. These tours are broken down into adventure types:

Haunted Sites

The following buildings are known (with documented sightings) to be haunted:

Borley Rectory, Britain

Use the non-printing characters to help you select specific types of text, such as the line containing the title and the paragraph mark instead of just the text for the title; select the column figures and the tab character that follows. Use **Show/Hide ¶** to display the non-printing characters; this command is on the **Home** tab, in the **Paragraph** group.

If you inadvertently make the wrong selection or you wish to remove the selection, click anywhere to deselect the text or press any arrow direction key, and then begin the selection procedure again.

Selecting Consecutive Text

You can select text using the mouse or keyboard and occasionally you may want to use a combination of mouse and keyboard to select larger pieces of text.

- The basic method of selecting text is to click the mouse at the beginning of the text to be selected, and then drag to highlight the text.
- You can increase or decrease the selection as long as you continue to hold the mouse button. You can also select forwards or backwards from the starting point.
- When using the keyboard, position the insertion point, hold down (Shift), and then press the arrow keys to move the cursor to select the text. Release (Shift) when the text is selected.
- To select an entire word, double-click the word.
- To select an entire sentence, hold (Ctrl) and click anywhere within the sentence.
- To select an entire paragraph, triple-click anywhere within that paragraph.

To select the entire document, use of the following methods:

- On the **Home** tab, in the **Editing** group, click **Select** and then click **Select All**, or
- press (Ctrl)+(A).

Selecting Non-Consecutive Text

Word offers the ability to select text anywhere in the document, regardless of whether the text is consecutive or not. To select multiple pieces of text, you must select the first piece of text and then press and hold (Ctrl) as you select the next piece of text. Press and hold (Ctrl) to continue selecting more text anywhere in the document.

You can also select blocks of text using (Alt). Position the cursor at the beginning of the block of text to be selected, press and hold (Alt) as you click and drag to select the block.

Both these options can only be activated using these keys with the mouse to select text.

Using the Selection Bar

An alternative way to select larger amounts of text is with the selection bar. The selection bar is located in the white area at the left edge of the text, in the area that is the left margin. When the mouse cursor is positioned in the selection bar, it changes to a white, right pointing arrow as seen in the following:

Proposal for Haunted Adventure Tours

Our preliminary research shows that the following tours are popular with travelers. These tours are broken down into adventure types:

Haunted Sites

- The following buildings are known (with documented sightings) to be haunted:
  - Borley Rectory, Britain
  - The Whaley House, California, USA
  - Edinburgh Castle, Scotland

- To select a line of text, click at the left of the line of text in the selection bar.
- To select an entire paragraph, double-click at the left of that paragraph in the selection bar.
- To select the entire document, triple-click anywhere in the selection bar, or press and hold (Ctrl) and then click once anywhere in the selection bar.
- To select multiple lines, click and drag down to select the text.

You can also use (Ctrl) to select non-consecutive text using the selection bar by selecting a line or paragraph first, and then hold (Ctrl) as you select the next line or paragraph.

Learn the Skill

In this exercise, you will try selecting different amounts of text in the document to make changes to the document.

1   With *Tolano Adventures Employee List* active on the screen, click at the beginning of the word Adventures in the title line.

2   Click and drag across the word to select the first four characters.

Tolano Adventures

New York

3   Click anywhere away from the selection to deselect the characters.

4   Double-click the word, *Adventures*.

The entire word now highlights on the screen.

5   To select the entire New York location, click at the beginning of *New York* and drag to the end of *(Head Office)*.

6   Click anywhere away from the selection to deselect the characters.

7   Now move your cursor to the Selection bar at the left of the New York line, ensuring your arrow points to the right.

8   Click and drag down two lines, thereby selecting all three lines of the location quickly.

9   To select only the actual address information, in the Selection bar area, click at the left of the address text.

Only this line now highlights.

10 Press (Home) to move quickly to the beginning of this line, then press (Ctrl)+(→) twice.

Notice the cursor has moved two words to the right, but did not select anything. To select both words and not just move to other words, you need to use the (Shift) key.

11 Press and hold the (Shift) key, then press (Ctrl)+(→) three times.

This time all the words are selected; by using the (Shift) key, you can extend a selection in either direction.

12 Press (Shift) and then press the (↓) key twice.

Notice how Word has continued to select the text in step 11 and also to the end of Nick Klassen's name.

13 Click anywhere to deselect the text.

Editing Text

Whenever you add, delete, or change text, you are editing. Many of the commands used for editing are available on the **Home** tab for quick and easy selection. When editing it is important to select the text before you perform the next action; otherwise, the action occurs at the cursor position.

Using Undo

Use the Undo feature to reverse an action (e.g. deleting, formatting, adding text or setting tabs). To activate Undo:

*   In the Quick Access Toolbar, click **Undo**, or

*   Click the button itself to undo the last action or command performed.

*   Click the arrow for this button to undo up to the last 100 consecutive actions or commands performed. You can only undo sequential actions, e.g., undo from the first Typing at the top of the list to the second Picture. You cannot undo selective actions.

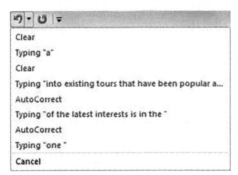

*   press (Ctrl)+(Z) to undo the last action performed. Repeat this key sequence to undo each action.

Using Repeat

To repeat the action just performed:

- In the Quick Access Toolbar, click **Repeat**, or
- press Ctrl+Y.

Using Cut, Copy and Paste

If you want to re-use text in another document or in another location in the current document, instead of retyping the information, use the **Cut, Copy** and **Paste** commands.

Cut	Cut or remove the item from the original location in the current document, and place the item in the Clipboard.
Copy	Copy the item from the original location in the current document, and place the item in the Clipboard.
Paste	Insert an item from the Clipboard into a document at the current cursor position.

Word uses the Clipboard to temporarily store any cut or copied items such as text or graphics. You can then paste these items to the required location.

To cut or move an item, after selecting it:
- On the **Home** tab, in the **Clipboard** group, click **Cut**, or
- press Ctrl+X, or
- right-click the item and then click **Cut**.

To copy an item, after selecting it:
- On the **Home** tab, in the **Clipboard** group, click **Copy**, or
- press Ctrl+C, or
- right-click the item and then click **Copy**.

To paste an item, after placing the insertion point where you want to paste the item:
- On the **Home** tab, in the **Clipboard** group, click **Paste**, or
- press Ctrl+V, or
- right-click the item and then click **Paste**, or
- click the item in the Office Clipboard, or
- click the arrow at the right of the item in the Office Clipboard, and then click **Paste**.

Once you paste an item, you will see the **Paste Options** button appear at the bottom right of the pasted item. When you point at this item, the button displays an arrow you can click to preview how the pasted item will appear in this location. The number and type of options vary based on what item was pasted, e.g. text only, formatted text, pictures.

Keep Source Formatting (K)	Keep the formatting for this item as it was set in the original document.
Merge Formatting (M)	Merge the formatting for this item from the original document with the formatting set in this document.
Use Destination Styles (S)	Use a style that exists for this document on the pasted item.
Keep Text Only (T)	Remove any formatting that existed with the original item and keep the text only.
Set Default Paste	Set how you want all pasted items of this type to appear.

Using the Office Clipboard

MMM
Using the
Clipboard
Online
Exercise

While the traditional Windows Clipboard offers the ability to store only one item at a time, the Office Clipboard offers the ability to store and retrieve up to 24 items. It will also show you a preview of the item, along with an icon representing the software program where the items are available.

To display the Clipboard task pane, on the **Home** tab, in the **Clipboard** group, click the **Office Clipboard Task Pane**.

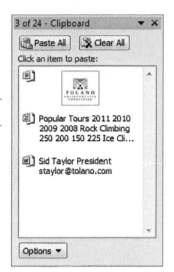

Paste All	Paste all the items currently in the Clipboard in the same order as they appear in the Clipboard.
Clear All	Clear all items from the Clipboard.
Options	Select options on how the Clipboard will work, such as when it appears, or to display an icon in the Taskbar Notification area to remind you this feature is active for collecting items.

> Show Office Clipboard Automatically
> Show Office Clipboard When Ctrl+C Pressed Twice
> Collect Without Showing Office Clipboard
> ✓ Show Office Clipboard Icon on Taskbar
> ✓ Show Status Near Taskbar When Copying
> Options ▼

The option to collect up to 24 items is useful if you are working on a report in which you would like to include text from another report, sales numbers from an Excel file, or text or pictures from the company Web site. You can collect up to 24 items from any of these programs.

Once you reach the maximum, you will need to clear individual or all items from the Clipboard to collect new items. Alternatively, you can continue to collect items and the oldest entry in the Clipboard deletes automatically.

When you move the mouse cursor over an item in the Clipboard, you will see the options available to you. A drop-down arrow appears to the right of the item and, when you click that arrow, a menu appears with other options. Use **Delete** to delete this item from the Clipboard; to paste this item into the document in the current location, use **Paste**.

Learn the Skill

In this exercise, you will practice selecting items for text replacement, undoing these changes, and then copying and pasting text blocks into the same as well as another document.

1   With *Tolano Adventures Employee List* active and the three lines of text selected, press the ⌧Delete⌧ key.

The lines of text should disappear from the screen.

2   On the Quick Access Toolbar, click **Undo**.

The deleted text now re-appears on the screen.

Suppose you want to copy the President's information from the TEC Employee List to this document.

3   Open *TEC Employee List*. Move the mouse cursor to the Selection Bar area and to the left of Sid Taylor's name.

4   Click and drag to select the three lines of information for Sid Taylor.

New York

300 171st Street, New York, NY 98032

(540) 555-4321 (Head Office)

Sid Taylor
President
staylor@tolano.com

Richard Reeves

5 On the **Home** tab, in the **Clipboard** group, click **Copy**.

While it appears that nothing has changed on the screen, you can turn on the Clipboard to check that it was placed there.

6 On the **Home** tab, in the **Clipboard** group, click the **Clipboard Task Pane** option at the lower right of group.

7 On the **View** tab, in the **Window** group, click **Switch Windows** and then click *Tolano Adventures Employee List* to switch to this document.

8 Move the cursor to the left of Nick Klassen's name. Then on the Clipboard, click the item.

(540) 555-4321 (Head Office)

Sid Taylor
President
staylor@tolano.com

Nick Klassen   (Ctrl) ▾

You have successfully copied the President's information and pasted it into this document. Notice the new icon that appears at the lower right of the pasted item. You can use the Paste Options button to affect how the pasted item appears.

9 Position the mouse cursor on **Paste Options** and then click to display the options.

10 Point at each of the four items to preview how the text would look in this document. Click **Keep Text Only (T)** so the text matches the rest of the Tolano Adventures Employee List document.

Notice how Word keeps the Paste Options available for you in case you change your mind about this option.

11 Press ⌈Enter⌋ to place Nick Klassen's name on the next line.

12 Keep this document active, but close the TEC Employee List document.

Moving Text Using Drag-and-Drop

You can also move text using the drag-and-drop method; this method is best used when you want to move text a short distance in the document. This method does not use the Clipboard and therefore leaves the contents of the Clipboard intact.

Select the text, and position the mouse cursor anywhere over the selected area, then drag the text and drop it to the new location. While dragging the text, a "ghost" cursor appears wherever you point the mouse cursor to indicate the new cursor position where the text is to be placed.

Be careful with the drag-and-drop method and be sure to release the mouse button only when at the new location for the text. If you release the mouse button too soon, use **Undo** to cancel the drag-and-drop action.

Learn the Skill

In this exercise, you practice moving text using the drag-and-drop method to move some text around in the Tolano Adventures Employee List document.

1 Scroll in the document until you see Robin Black's name in the Cape Town location.

2 Select the three lines with her information.

3 Position the mouse cursor anywhere in the selection and drag up until at the beginning of the Cape Town heading.

Cape Town

#47 212 Pine Road, Cape Town 4002

555 456 1234

Jamie Gibson

Travel Director

jgibson@tolano.com

Robin Black

Administrative Assistant

rblack@tolano.com

4 At that location, release the mouse button.

The text is now moved into this location.

Suppose another Administrative Assistant will also be moving to the New York office.

5 Scroll in the document until you see the information for Christy Akira in the Tokyo office.

6 Select the three lines for Christy's information and drag the selection to the beginning of the Cape Town heading.

Notice how the process to drag and drop this piece of text remains the same although it can be a bit tricky finding the right location as you move around in the document.

7 Close this document without saving.

Using Paste Special

You can also paste a special item such as a picture from a Web page into a document. The **Paste Special** command enables you to copy an object from another program into your document and, depending on that object, it can link to the original to update both copies, as in the scenario to update sales figures or Web pages.

On the **Home** tab, in the **Clipboard** group, click the arrow for **Paste** and then click **Paste Special**.

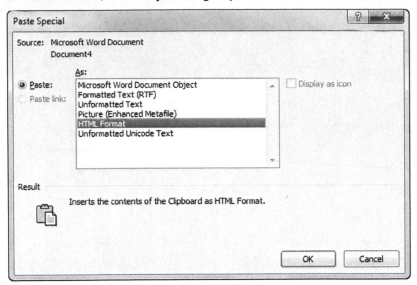

The options that appear in the subsequent window will vary based on the item being copied or cut.

Learn the Skill

This exercise demonstrates how to paste a set of annual figures in another document and set a link so you can update the figures as needed.

1   Open *Sales Figures for Staff Retreat* and then open *Popular Tours Breakdown*.

2   Copy the entire table of figures in Popular Tours Breakdown and then switch to the Sales Figure document.

3   Move to the bottom of this document and then on the **Home** tab, in the **Clipboard** group, click the arrow for **Paste**. Click **Paste Special**.

Assume we may need to update the figures for the tours breakdown as more details become available for the Staff Retreat. We also want the updated figures regardless of whether the change is made in the original file or in the Sales Figure document.

4   Click **Paste link** and then click **Microsoft Word Document Object**.

Notice how Word has pasted the table of figures into the document, but it doesn't appear any different to a regular paste command.

5   Click once in the table of figures.

	2011	2010	2009	2008
Rock Climbing	250	200	150	225
Ice Climbing	175	150	100	125
Whale Watching	350	250	100	260
Hot Air Ballooning	105	60	25	45
Heli Skiing	95	85	70	125
Cycling (Cities)	75	70	65	110

Word now displays the table with a border around it to remind you it is an object, as chosen in step 4.

6   Double-click the **175** figure in the 2011 column for Ice Climbing.

You should now be viewing the Popular Tours Breakdown document where you can make a change to that number.

7   Double-click the **175** figure in this document and type: 250.

8   Switch to the Sales Figure document.

The change for this figure is now reflected in this document as well.

9   Close the Sales Figures and the Popular Tours Breakdown documents without saving.

Finding and Replacing Items

2.2

Use the Find feature to move the insertion point to a specified location within a document. You can find a specific word, phrase, symbol or code, or any combination of these. Once found, you can choose to replace the item with something else, or continue working with your document.

To activate the Find feature:

- On the **Home** tab, in the **Editing** group, click **Find**, or
- press Ctrl+F, or

- click the **Find** tab in the Find and Replace dialog box, or
- near the bottom of the vertical scroll bar, click **Select Browse Object** and then click **Find**.

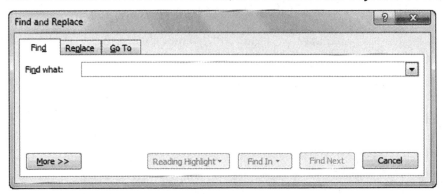

Note that the first two options shown previously display the Navigation task pane at the left of the screen, and the latter two options display the Find and Replace dialog box.

If working with the Navigation task pane, there are three tabs available for use here:

	Browse the headings in your document	Display an outline or hierarchical structure for the headings used in this document.
	Browse the results from your current search	Display each page of the document to show where the search criteria exist.
	Browse the pages in your document	Display each occurrence in the document where the search criteria were found.

When you look for items, it is probably because you want to replace those items with something else. You can instruct Word to find text that matches the characters exactly as typed, to find whole words, parts of words, or specific types of formatting. You can decide whether to replace each item individually, or replace all occurrences in the document automatically.

It is recommended that you save your document before performing a replace action. Therefore, if you decide, after replacing the text, that you really did not want the changes, you still have the original document saved.

To replace an item:

- On the **Home** tab, in the **Editing** group, click **Replace**, or
- press (Ctrl)+(H), or
- if the **Find and Replace** dialog box is open, click the **Replace** tab.

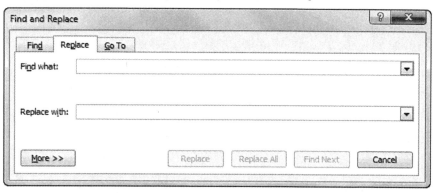

Find what	Enter the search criteria to find in the document.
More	Displays more options for the search criteria.
Reading Highlight	Highlights all items found in the main document or any headers or footers in the document.

By default, Word does not display the options for **More** when you activate the Find or Replace command. You can turn this display off in the **Find and Replace** dialog box by clicking **Less**.

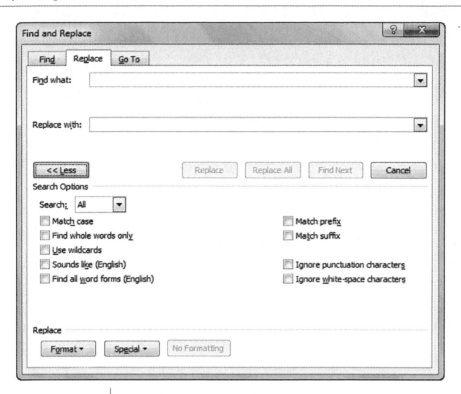

Match case	Search for any text that has the exact casing as typed into the Find what box.
Find whole words only	If you enter a small amount of text in the Find what box, we recommend you select this option if it is the complete word to be found in the document. For instance, if you type red in the Find what box without selecting this option, Word finds all occurrences of these characters including red, hundred, bred, redline, credible, etc.
Use wildcards	This feature searches for files or folders in Windows. The ? character represents a single character at a time, e.g., entering c?t finds words like cat or cot but not cart, chat, or crater. The * character represents any number of characters regardless of the word length, e.g. entering br* finds words like breath, bred, broth, or brother. To see a full list of wildcards available, use the Help option.
Sounds like	If you are unsure of the exact spelling of a word, you can use phonetic spelling to narrow the search criteria.
Find all word forms	Use this when you want Word to find all forms of the word, regardless of whether it is a noun, verb, adjective, or adverb. Word also ignores the tense form (e.g. wants, wanting, wanted) and whether it is the singular or plural form (e.g. book or books).
Match prefix	Use this when you do not know the full length or all the letters in the word to find. Insert as many characters as you know of the beginning of the word. Word then matches only those words that begin with these characters (e.g. typing psyc* finds psychology, psychic, psyche, and psychometrics.
Match suffix	Opposite of prefix; insert as many characters as you know of the end of the word. Word then matches only those words that end with these characters, e.g. *try would find symmetry, try, and poetry.
Ignore punctuation characters	Ignore any punctuation characters such as commas, colons, semi-colons, and periods.

Ignore white-space characters	White space refers to regular or non-breaking spaces or tab characters. Select this to ignore any characters, such as double spaces, that may exist in the document.
Format	Select any formatting attributes applied to the text. You could also use the corresponding buttons or shortcut keys to enter a formatting attribute to find.
Special	Search for special characters such as paragraph marks, page breaks, and tab characters.
No Formatting	Clear any options selected previously in the Find what box with the Format button.

Use a non-breaking space to keep words together such as data at the end of a line or page. Create a non-breaking space character by pressing CTRL+SHIFT +SPACEBAR instead of a regular space.

Each time you activate the Find feature, Word displays the last search criteria entered. Once you exit Word, the boxes in the **Find and Replace** dialog box will clear as will the Office Clipboard.

 ## Learn the Skill

In this exercise, you will find and replace specific items in the document.

1   Open *Memo on Live Meeting*.

You will now try some different methods to find an item in this memo.

2   On the **Home** tab, in the **Editing** group, click **Find**.

3   Click in the **Search Document** field, type: Microsoft and press Enter.

Word has found the first occurrence of this item in the document and highlighted it on the screen. If you refer to the Navigation pane, you should notice that Word has also indicated the number of occurrences of this search text in the document.

4   In the Search field, type: web for the new search criteria and press Enter. Then click the **Browse the results from your current search** tab in the Navigation pane.

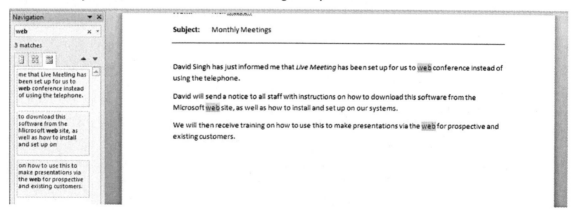

Notice how Word not only highlights each occurrence in the document, it also provides a list in the Navigation pane as a quick reference to how the search criteria are used. If this document had multiple pages, you could also click the **Browse by pages in your document** option to see where else the search criteria appear.

Suppose you want to find all occurrences of this word and replace them with another spelling.

5   Close the Navigation pane.

6   On the **Home** tab, in the **Editing** group, click **Replace**.

Word provides the last search criteria in the Find what field.

7 Click in the **Replace with** field and type: Web.

8 Click **Replace** to find and replace the first occurrence.

9 Click **Replace All** to find and replace any remaining occurrences.

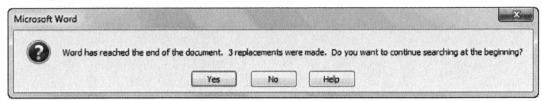

10 Click **Yes** to search from the beginning of the document for any occurrences prior to the first occurrence.

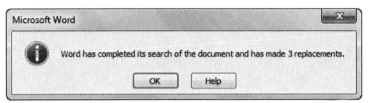

At this point, Word has found all occurrences of the search criteria and replaced them.

11 Click **OK** to complete this task.

12 Close the document without saving.

Lesson Summary

This lesson teaches you to create simple documents and introduces you to some file management tools available in Word. Upon completion of this lesson, you should be able to:

☑ change views

☑ select text

☑ use cut, copy and paste

☑ use the clipboard

☑ move text with drag-and-drop

☑ use Paste Options

☑ use Paste Special

☑ find text or items with Browse by

☑ replace text or items

Review Questions

MMM
Go online for Additional Review and Activities

1. Explain what the differences are between using the Print Layout and Draft view modes.

2. Discuss the difference between using Paste versus Paste Special.

3. How could you use the Paste Options for text you have copied?

4. Give an example of why you might want to collect multiple items to the Office Clipboard.

5. When might you use the **Browse the pages in your document** tab in the Navigation pane?

Microsoft®

Word 2010

Core Certification

Lesson 3: Formatting Content

Lesson Objectives

In this lesson, you will look at the various ways you can format a document. Formatting refers to the process of changing the appearance or position of text or objects in a document. On completion of this lesson, you should be able to:

☐ format text using bold, italics and underline

☐ change the font, font size and font color of text

☐ adjust the character spacing or position

☐ adjust text alignment

☐ indent paragraphs

☐ change line and paragraph spacing

☐ use the Format Painter

Formatting Characters

2.1

Character formatting refers to any feature that changes the appearance of characters on the screen and in print. You can use the following options for character formatting:

Font	Describes the typeface or appearance of characters on the screen and in print.
Font Size	Refers to the height of the characters; remember, as characters get taller, they also grow proportionally wider.
Character Formatting	Refers to the special stylized variations applied to plain characters to make them stand out from other text. They include bold, italics, underline, or color.
Effects	These are effects added to text i.e., strikethrough, superscript/subscript, shadow, small caps.

There are a number of ways of applying formatting to text characters:

- On the **Home** tab, in the **Font** group, click the appropriate formatting button, or
- use the formatting options in the Font dialog box, or
- press the appropriate keyboard shortcut for the formatting option you want to use, or
- right-click the text in the document, and then click **Font**, or
- click the appropriate option on the Mini toolbar.

Many common character formatting features are on the **Home** tab and in the **Font** group.

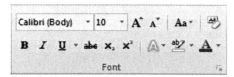

The Mini toolbar appears only when you select text. It contains specific, common character and paragraph formatting features.

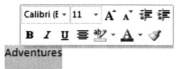

With most of these buttons, you can turn the feature on or off by clicking the button. When a feature is active, the button appears in a different color from the others. Buttons with an arrow contain more options for that feature. Notice how the **Font** group contains items for text formatting whereas the Mini toolbar contains features that also affect the position of the paragraph, e.g. centering text between the left and right margins or increasing or decreasing indents. The Mini toolbar contains the most frequently used formatting features. You can turn this feature off using the **Options** feature in Backstage.

You can apply formatting options as you type or, after the text is typed, by selecting the appropriate formatting option. Both methods offer advantages. Most users new to word processing find it easier to type the text first, save it, and then apply the formatting. Once you select text, you can apply as many formatting options as required. If you choose to apply formatting as you type, turn the feature on, type the text, and then turn the feature off before resuming typing. You can activate/deactivate as many features as required.

To remove all formatting options from selected text, on the **Home** tab, in the **Font** group, click **Clear Formatting**.

Learn the Skill

In this exercise, you will look at both methods of applying formatting features, using options from the **Font** group as well as the Mini toolbar.

1   Open *Tolano Adventures Employee List* and save the file as: Tolano Adventures Employee List – Student. Then select the first line, Tolano Adventures.

2   Click the **Home** tab, and in the **Font** group, click **Bold**.

3   With the text still selected, click the **Home** tab and, in the **Font** group, click the arrow for **Font** and then click **Cambria**.

4   Click the **Home** tab and, in the **Font** group, click the arrow for **Font Size** and then click **14**.

Tolano Adventures

New York

5   Select the New York line. Press (Ctrl) and select the Cape Town line.

6   Repeat step 5 with each location name in the list.

You should have six locations selected.

7   Press (Ctrl)+(B) to apply boldface to each of these titles.

8   Press (Ctrl)+(Home) to move quickly to the beginning of the document.

9   Select the Tolano title again and position the mouse cursor over the selection to view the transparent Mini toolbar.

10 Move the mouse cursor up slowly on the selection until the Mini toolbar is solid. Then click the arrow for **Font Color**.

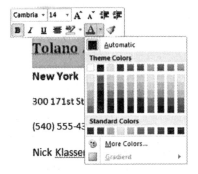

11 Click a color of your choice. Then click anywhere away from the selection.

The text is now in that color.

12 Save the document.

Using the Font Dialog Box

The Font dialog box contains basic formatting options and text enhancement options. Use this command when you want to access formatting options not available in the Font group or the Mini toolbar, or when you want to apply several options at the same time. Formatting options found in this command can also be applied to selected text or as you type.

To access the Font dialog box:

- On the **Home** tab, in the **Font** group, click **Font Dialog Box**, or
- press Ctrl + D , or
- right-click the selected text and then click **Font**.

There are a number of effects available in this option that you will not see in the Font group or the Mini toolbar. In addition to the effects in the Effects area, click **Text Effects** to view effects with further options for each effect:

Learn the Skill

In this exercise, you will practice formatting text using the Font command in the Tolano Adventures Employee List document.

1   Select the Tolano Adventures title again. Click the **Home** tab and in the **Font** group, click **Font Dialog Box**.

2   Click **Text Effects**.

3   Click **Shadow** and then click the arrow for **Presets**.

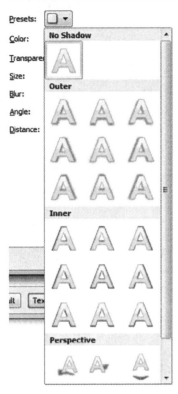

4   Point at the different options in the list and then click **Offset Right**.

5   Click the arrow for **Color** and then choose a medium black color such as Black, Text 1, Background 25%.

6   Click the up arrow for **Distance** twice to increase the distance of the shadow from the text. Click **Close**.

7   In the **Effects** area, click **All caps** and then click **OK**.

8   Click anywhere away from the selection to deselect the text.

TOLANO ADVENTURES

Based on the text color you chose, the total text effect may not be easy to read. You should also be careful not to select too much text with uppercase letters as this can be very distracting.

9   Select the title once more and press Ctrl+D to display the Font dialog box.

10 In the **Effects** area, click **All caps** to turn this effect off. Then click **Small caps** as an alternative for uppercase letters. Then click **OK**.

TOLANO ADVENTURES

Now apply a formatting feature for some common types of text that contain numbers.

11   In the New York address, select the "st" after 171.

12   Press ⌃Ctrl+⌃D to display the Font dialog box and in the **Effects** area, click **Superscript**. Then click **OK**.

300 171ˢᵗ Street, New York, NY 98032

13   Save the document.

Changing the Character Spacing

On occasion, you may want to adjust the spacing between the text characters. Proportionally spaced fonts use only as much space as needed for each character (an "I" takes up less space than a "W"), thereby giving text a pleasing look. Monospaced fonts were traditionally used on typewriters and dedicated word processing machines that gave each letter the same width. Take a look at the difference between a word using a proportional spaced font and a monospaced font.

Times New Roman is a proportionally spaced font.

`Courier is a monospaced font.`

Using proportionally spaced fonts can make reading large amounts of text easier. When used with the word wrap or Justify feature, the space between the words adjusts to fit as many words as it can on that line. However, there may be times when there is more white space between each of the words, as seen in the following:

Now is the time for all good people to come to the aid of their environment and help save the planet's resources.

Using a monospaced font gives text a different effect - as seen in the following which compares a Times New Roman and a monospaced font:

ENVIRONMENTAL ISSUES

ENVIRONMENTAL ISSUES

For a different text effect, adjust the spacing between words. Select character spacing options in the **Character Spacing** tab in the Font dialog box using one of the following methods:

- On the **Home** tab, in the **Font** group, click **Font Dialog Box**. Then click the **Advanced** tab to view the **Character Spacing** options, or

- press ⌃Ctrl+⌃D and click the **Advanced** tab to view the **Character Spacing** options, or

- right-click the text, click **Font**, and then click the **Advanced** tab to view the **Character Spacing** options.

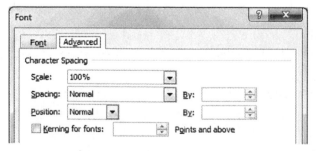

Scale	Alter the width of the selected text by a percentage amount.
Spacing	Adjust the amount of spacing used by each character in the selected text by the set amount. Expanding adds space between the characters; condensing reduces the amount of space used by each character.

Position	Raises or lowers the selected text from the normal position (base line) by the set amount. Press Ctrl+D and click the **Advanced** tab. ⟵— Normal/ Base Line
Kerning for fonts	Alters the amount of space between the selected text based on the characters in the selected text. For example, more space may be added between the "i" and "l" in the word "guild" to evenly space the characters.

Learn the Skill

In this exercise, you will adjust the character spacing for the title in this employee list.

1 Select the Tolano Adventures title once more and then press Ctrl+D to display the Font dialog box.

2 Click the **Advanced** tab and click the arrow for **Spacing**. Then click **Expanded**.

3 In the **By** field to the right of **Spacing**, click the arrow and change this to **1.5**.

4 Click **OK** and then click anywhere away from the selection.

TOLANO ADVENTURES

Notice how the title appears easier to read with the additional spacing between the characters.

5 Save the document.

Formatting Paragraphs

Formatting paragraphs refers to the process of applying a format that changes the position of the paragraph, such as alignment, tabs, or indents. These can be applied as you type or after all text has been typed. It may be easier to wait until all text has been typed or edited in the document before applying any formatting options. You must select the text before applying any text attributes, but it can save time as you don't need to remember to turn off or reset the feature to the original settings for text.

There are a number of ways of formatting paragraphs:

- On the **Home** tab, in the **Paragraph** group, click the appropriate formatting button, or
- use the formatting options in the Paragraph dialog box, or
- press the appropriate keyboard shortcut for the desired formatting option, or
- right-click the paragraph, and then click **Paragraph**, or
- on the Mini toolbar, click the appropriate option.

Many common paragraph formatting features are on the **Home** tab, in the **Paragraph** group. The Mini toolbar appears only when text is selected; it contains specific common character and paragraph formatting features.

If you want to remove all formatting options from selected text, click the **Home** tab and, in the **Font** group, click **Clear Formatting**.

Aligning Text

You can easily change the alignment of text for paragraphs in your document using one of the four types of paragraph alignment:

Align Left	Aligns text to the left margin with ragged right edges.
Center	Aligns text between the left and right margins.

| **Align Right** | Aligns text to the right margin with ragged left edges. |
| **Justify** | Aligns text so the left and right edges of the text are flush with both margins, except for the last line of a paragraph. |

Remember that any paragraph formatting affects the entire paragraph.

You can align text as you type or align existing text. If changing the alignment of existing text, make sure the cursor is positioned in the paragraph, and then choose the required alignment to affect the entire paragraph.

Select alignment options using one of the following methods:

- On the **Home** tab, in the **Paragraph** group, click **Paragraph Dialog Box**. Ensure you are viewing the **Indents and Spacing** tab. Click the arrow for **Alignment** and then click the appropriate alignment, or

- on the **Home** tab, in the **Paragraph** group, click the appropriate alignment button, or

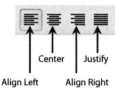

- press the corresponding keyboard shortcut for the appropriate alignment, or:

Align Left	Ctrl + L
Center	Ctrl + E
Align Right	Ctrl + R
Justify	Ctrl + J

- right-click the paragraph, click **Paragraph**, in the **Indents and Spacing** tab, click the arrow for **Alignment** and click the appropriate alignment.

Changing the Spacing

You can use spacing as a way of increasing the readability of a document, especially if it contains a large amount of text. Spacing can also be used to give a consistent look, regardless of whether the document is all text or a combination of text and illustrations.

Setting the Line Spacing

Line spacing refers to the standard space between lines of typed text, measured from one baseline to the next baseline of subsequent lines. Word can automatically adjust the amount of space between lines according to the size of characters being used.

You can specify line spacing to be set exactly to a specified point size. However, this setting will not adjust to accommodate larger text if the font size is changed.

You can increase or decrease line spacing by using **Paragraph** or shortcut keys. However, if you decrease line spacing too much, the lines of text may overwrite each other, or the text may not display.

Set the line spacing using one of the following methods:

- On the **Home** tab, in the **Paragraph** group, click **Line spacing**, or

3240-1 v1.00 © CCI Learning Solutions Inc.

- on the **Home** tab, in the **Paragraph** group, click **Paragraph Dialog Box**. Then in the **Indents and Spacing** tab of the Paragraph dialog box, click the arrow for **Line spacing** to choose the required line spacing, or

- press the shortcut key for the most commonly used line spacing options, or

Single	Ctrl + 1
One and a Half	Ctrl + 5
Double	Ctrl + 2

- right-click the paragraph, click **Paragraph**, click the arrow for **Line spacing** and click the appropriate spacing.

Setting Paragraph Spacing

Paragraph spacing refers to the amount of space between paragraphs. Most published documents use a set amount of space between each paragraph instead of a blank line created by pressing ⌐Enter⌐. This reduces the amount of white space used on a page and also sets consistency between styles used in a document.

By default, Word sets paragraph spacing of 10pt for every line of text in a new document. This may not be your preference or the standard required by your company.

To set or change the paragraph spacing, use one of the following methods:

- On the **Home** tab, in the **Paragraph** group, click **Paragraph Dialog Box**. Then, in the **Spacing** area, set the appropriate measurement for the spacing. You can set the spacing for **Before**, **After**, or both, or

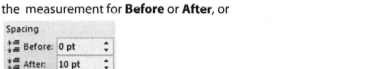

- on the **Page Layout** tab, in the **Paragraph** group, click the incremental buttons or type the measurement for **Before** or **After**, or

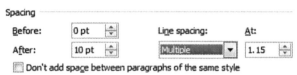

MMM
Applying
Formatting
Online
Exercise

- right-click the paragraph, click **Paragraph**, and in the **Spacing** area, choose the spacing for **Before**, **After**, or both.

Learn the Skill

This exercise will show you how to change the alignment on the title and then change the spacing for the paragraphs of text in the employee list.

1   Select the Tolano Adventures title once more. Click the **Home** tab, in the **Paragraph** group, click **Center**.

The title should now be centered between the left and right margin in this document.

2   Select from the New York heading to the end of the document.

3   Click the **Home** tab, and in the **Paragraph** group, click **Line Spacing**.

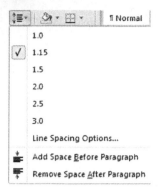

4 Click **1.0** for single spacing.

It appears as if nothing has changed in the document. This is because the paragraph spacing is set by default.

5 Click the **Page Layout** tab and, in the **Paragraph** group, click the down incremental button for **After** once.

New York
300 171st Street, New York, NY 98032
(540) 555-4321 (Head Office)
Nick Klassen
Vice President
nklassen@tolano.com
Madison Cowell
Travel Director
mcowell@tolano.com
Amar Boutros
Accountant
aboutros@tolano.com
Cape Town
#47 212 Pine Road, Cape Town 4002
555 456 1234

6 Move the cursor to Nick Klassen's name. Click the **Page Layout** tab and in the **Paragraph** group, click the up incremental button for **Before** to set this to 6pt.

New York
300 171st Street, New York, NY 98032
(540) 555-4321 (Head Office)

Nick Klassen
Vice President

7 Move the cursor to Madison Cowell's name and then on the Quick Access Toolbar, click **Repeat**.

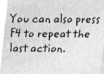

You can also press F4 to repeat the last action.

8 Repeat step 7 for every name and location in the document.

9 Save and close the document.

Indenting Paragraphs

An indented paragraph is a paragraph that wraps to a temporary left and/or right margin. Left and right indents are useful for emphasizing parts of a document or for quotations or sub-paragraphs. You can create indents using the ruler, the **Paragraph** group on the **Home** tab, the **Paragraph** command, the Mini toolbar, or with keyboard shortcuts.

The following screen shows various examples of indents that can be set:

Proposal for Haunted Adventure Tours

First Line Indent ———————→ Our preliminary research shows that the following tours are popular with travelers. These tours are broken down into adventure types:

Haunted Sites

Left Indent ———————→ The following buildings are known (with documented sightings) to be haunted:

- Borley Rectory, Britain
- The Whaley House, California, USA
- Edinburgh Castle, Scotland
- Monte Cristo Homestead, New South Wales

Hanging Indent with Left Indent ———————→
- Okiku's Well at Hameji Castle, Japan
- The Colosseum, Italy
- St. Francis Xavier University, Mount St. Bernard College, Antigonish, Nova Scotia, Canada

Celebrity Burial Sites

Many famous people (including some entertainers) are buried here:

- Arlington National Cemetery, Washington, DC, USA (US Presidents, Albert Einstein, Martin Luther King, National World War II Memorial, etc.)
- Tomb of the Unknown Soldier, Europe (Paris, London, Bucharest, Athens, etc.)
- Pierce Brothers Westwood Village Memorial Park Cemetery, Los Angeles, USA (Marilyn Monroe, Burt Lancaster, Jack Lemmon, Rodney Dangerfield, etc.)

Hanging Indent with Left & Right Indent ———————→
- Forest Lawn Hollywood Hills, Los Angeles, USA (Bette Davis, Lucille Ball, David Carradine, Stan Laurel, etc.)
- Pere Lachaise, Paris, France (Oscar Wilde, Gertrude Stein, Edith Piaf, Jim Morrison, etc.)

Left Indent	The entire paragraph is indented from the left margin. This type of indent is often used with bulleted lists.
Right Indent	The entire paragraph is indented from the right margin. When combined with a left indent, this type of indent is often used with quotations.
First Line Indent	Only the first line of the paragraph indents from the left margin, similar to pressing (Tab) but applies this indent measurement automatically for the first line of every following paragraph.
Hanging Indent	The paragraph indents from the left margin, leaving the first line "hanging" at the left margin. This type of indent is commonly used for bullets or numbered paragraphs, or for bibliographies.

The amount of indent is determined by the current tab settings.

Setting Indents on the Ruler

The ruler offers a quick and easy way of adjusting the indents by using the following indent markers:

Adjust the indent markers using the marker within the ruler, or select from the Tab Selector box. ScreenTips are available on the ruler to help identify the different indent markers. Place the mouse cursor over the marker to see a description for the marker.

To move or adjust an indent marker, use one of the following methods:

- drag the appropriate indent marker to indent the paragraph as desired, or
- click the Tab Selector until the appropriate indent marker is displayed, then click the ruler at the desired location for the indent.

Move, or click an indent marker on the ruler, a vertical line appears as a guide for the indent position.

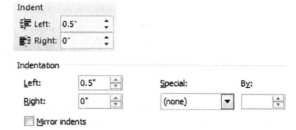

Using the Paragraph Group

You can set very precise paragraph indents by using one of the following two methods:

- On the **Page Layout** tab, in the **Paragraph** group, set the indent measurement from the **Left** or **Right** margin, or

- on the **Home** tab, in the **Paragraph** group, click **Paragraph Dialog Box**.

Left	Indents the text from the left margin, similar to using the ⊔ marker on the ruler.
Right	Indents the text from the right margin, similar to using the △ marker on the ruler.
Special	Displays a list where you can choose to set a First Line Indent, similar to using the ▽ marker on the ruler, or a Hanging Indent, similar to using the △ marker on the ruler. Once you select one of these items, **By** becomes available and you can set the required amount for the indentation.
Mirror indents	Adjust the left and right indents appropriately for odd and even pages.
Preview	View the effect of the indent measurements entered before finalizing the settings.

MMM
Indents Online
Exercise

Adjusting the Indents

Once the indent on text is activated, you can increase or decrease the amount of the indent on the ruler using the default tab stop at 0.5". On the **Home** tab and in the **Paragraph** group, click **Increase Indent** or **Decrease Indent**.

Learn the Skill

In this exercise, you will practice setting different types of indents for Proposal for Haunted Tour Adventures Flyer Draft - Student.

1   Open the *Proposal for Haunted Adventure Tours* and save this as: Proposal for Haunted Adventure Tours Flyer Draft - Student.

2   Select the text from Borley Rectory to St. Francis Xavier University.

3   On the ruler, position the cursor on the grey box (the Left Indent marker) below the other two indent markers and then drag to the 0.5" mark on the ruler, as seen below:

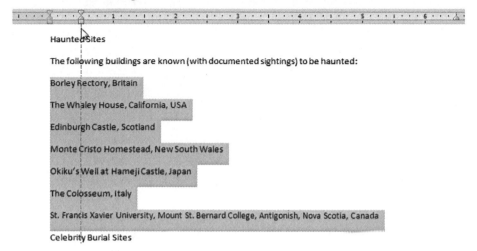

Notice how the ruler in Word shows that you are moving all the indent markers at the same time, and how the text will align once you release the mouse.

4   Release the mouse cursor.

The text is now indented at 0.5" from the left margin.

5   Position the cursor at the beginning of the paragraph, "The following buildings are known …".

6   On the ruler, position the mouse cursor on the Left Indent marker and then drag it to 0.5".

This paragraph should now line up with the beginning of all the tour locations .

7   Save the document.

8   Position the cursor at the beginning of the "Our preliminary research…" paragraph.

9   Click the **Home** tab and In the **Paragraph** group, click **Paragraph Dialog Box**.

10   In the **Indentation** area, click the arrow for **Special** and click **First Line.** In the **By** field, type: 0.75 and then click **OK**.

Proposal for Haunted Adventure Tours

Our preliminary research shows that the following tours are popular with travelers. These tours are broken down into adventure types:

Haunted Sites

The following buildings are known (with documented sightings) to be haunted:

Borley Rectory, Britain

The Whaley House, California, USA

11   Position the cursor at the beginning of the paragraph directly below the Celebrity Burial Sites.

12   Click the **Page Layout** tab, and in the **Paragraph** group, click in **Left** and type: 0.5.

This paragraph should now line up at the left indent set for the two paragraphs in the Haunted Sites area.

Now try adjusting an indent in one of the paragraphs.

13   Position the cursor at the first paragraph in the document, beginning with "Our preliminary research …".

14   Position the mouse cursor on the First Line Indent marker on the ruler and then drag to the 0.5" mark.

This paragraph now lines up with the other indented paragraphs in the document.

15   Save and close the document.

Using the Format Painter

Use the Format Painter to apply formatting from a piece of text to one or more pieces of text. This saves time from having to remember which formatting options were applied previously on text. The Format Painter can be used with styles or individual formatting applied to text. When active, the cursor shows as ▤Ⅰ.

- To apply formatting features from one piece of text to one other piece of text, select the text with the formatting features. On the **Home** tab, in the **Clipboard** group, click **Format Painter**. Move to the piece of text where you want to apply these formatting features, and select that text.

- To apply formatting features from one piece of text to multiple pieces of text, select the text with the formatting features. On the **Home** tab, in the **Clipboard** group, double-click **Format Painter**. As you click each piece of text, the formatting features are applied and the Format Painter stays active for further applications.

- To turn the Format Painter off, use one of the following methods:

    – On the **Home** tab, in the **Clipboard** group, click **Format Painter**, or

    – press Esc, or

    – click another command for another action.

Learn the Skill

In this exercise, you will apply similar formatting to a document used in previous exercises in the Lesson but now use the Format Painter to manage the consistent formatting for one or more selections of text.

1   Open the *Proposal for Haunted Adventure Tours* and save as Proposal for Haunted Adventure Tours Flyer Draft2 - Student.

2   Select the main title. Click the **Home** tab and in the **Font** group, click the arrow for **Font** and change this to **Arial Black**. Then click the arrow for **Size** and select **16**.

3   Select the next heading, Haunted sites. On the **Home** tab, in the **Font** group, click the arrow for **Font** and click **Arial Black**. Click the arrow for **Size** and click **12**. Click the arrow for **Font Color** and then click **Green**.

Proposal for Haunted Adventure Tours

Our preliminary research shows that the following tours are popular with travelers. These tours are broken down into adventure types:

Haunted Sites

The following buildings are known (with documented sightings) to be haunted:

4   On the **Home** tab, in the **Clipboard** group, click **Format Painter**.

Notice the new pointer for the cursor.

5   Move to the next subheading and then click in the selection bar at the left of the text.

Haunted Sites

The following buildings are known (with documented sightings) to be haunted:

Borley Rectory, Britain

The Whaley House, California, USA

Edinburgh Castle, Scotland

Monte Cristo Homestead, New South Wales

Okiku's Well at Hameji Castle, Japan

The Colosseum, Italy

St. Francis Xavier University, Mount St. Bernard College, Antigonish, Nova Scotia, Canada

Celebrity Burial Sites

Many famous people (including some entertainers) are buried here:

The subheading now has the same formatting as the first subheading. Notice also that the pointer no longer shows the Format Painter symbol. This is a result of clicking the Format Painter once.

6   Click the **Format Painter** once more and then click at the left of the Halloween subheading.

All three subheadings should have the same formatting.

7   Select all the buildings in the Haunted Sites, from Borley Rectory to St. Francis Xavier University.

8   Click the **Home** tab and in the **Paragraph** group, click **Bullets**.

9   On the **Home** tab, in the **Clipboard** group, double-click **Format Painter**.

10   Select the next set of points for the Celebrity Burial Sites (from Arlington to Pere Lachaise).

Word has now painted the same formatting from the previous bullet points to this selection of text. Notice also that the Format Painter tool is still active.

11   Select the points below the Halloween Theme section.

Your document should appear similar to the following:

Proposal for Haunted Adventure Tours

Our preliminary research shows that the following tours are popular with travelers. These tours are broken down into adventure types:

Haunted Sites

The following buildings are known (with documented sightings) to be haunted:

- Borley Rectory, Britain
- The Whaley House, California, USA
- Edinburgh Castle, Scotland
- Monte Cristo Homestead, New South Wales
- Okiku's Well at Hameji Castle, Japan
- The Colosseum, Italy
- St. Francis Xavier University, Mount St. Bernard College, Antigonish, Nova Scotia, Canada

Celebrity Burial Sites

Many famous people (including some entertainers) are buried here:

- Arlington National Cemetery, Washington, DC, USA (US Presidents, Albert Einstein, Martin Luther King, National World War II Memorial, etc.)
- Tomb of the Unknown Soldier, Europe (Paris, London, Bucharest, Athens, etc.)
- Pierce Brothers Westwood Village Memorial Park Cemetery, Los Angeles, USA (Marilyn Monroe, Burt Lancaster, Jack Lemmon, Rodney Dangerfield, etc.)
- Forest Lawn Hollywood Hills, Los Angeles, USA (Bette Davis, Lucille Ball, David Carradine, Stan Laurel, etc.)
- Pere Lachaise, Paris, France (Oscar Wilde, Gertrude Stein, Edith Piaf, Jim Morrison, etc.)

Halloween Theme/Haunted Tours

These tours include a ghostly theme which could be offered at Halloween:

- Ghost Tours of Southern Ontario, Canada
- Haunted Ghost Tours of England, UK
- Haunted Hollywood Tours, California, USA
- Hollywood Underground Tours, Los Angeles, USA
- Dracular Halloween Tours, Bucharest
- Halloween Haunting Tours, Mountfichet Castle, Essex, UK
- Paranormal Tours at Waverly Sanatorium, Kentucky, USA

Using the Format Painter can make formatting easier when you need to apply similar formatting in different parts of a document. It also maintains consistency for specific types of information such as subheadings or bullet styles.

12 Save and close the document.

Lesson Summary

In this lesson, you looked at the various ways to format a document using the Ribbon, shortcut keys, or dialog boxes. You should now be able to:

☑ format text using bold, italics and underline

☑ change the font, font size and font color of text

☑ adjust the character spacing or position

☑ adjust text alignment

☑ indent paragraphs

☑ change line and paragraph spacing

☑ use the Format Painter

Review Questions

MMM
Go online for
Additional
Review and
Activities

1. What does formatting characters refer to?

2. When would you want to change the character spacing?

3. What does paragraph formatting refer to?

4. When or why would you want to change the paragraph spacing?

5. Explain the different indent types and when or how you might use each.

Microsoft®

Word 2010
Core Certification

Lesson 4: Working with Tabs

Lesson Objectives

In this lesson, you will learn what tab stops are and how to use them with lists in documents. On completion of this lesson, you should be able to:

☐ understand what a tab stop is

☐ recognize the different types of tab stops

☐ set tab stops on the ruler as well as the Tabs dialog box

☐ set leaders for tab stops

☐ clear one or all tabs

☐ create bulleted or numbered lists

☐ create outline numbered lists

☐ customize lists

☐ work with multi-level lists

☐ create outlines

Setting Tab Stops

Tab settings (stops) are similar to text alignment; the difference is that setting tabs enables you to align information at specific points in the document and for setting up columns of text. When you create a tab stop, text aligns at the tab stop (similar to paragraph alignment):

Left Tab	Center Tab	Right Tab	Bar Tab	Decimal.Tab
T. Jones	VP, Computers	Data Processing		$65,082.3009
J. Martinez	VP, Supplies	Purchasing		64,376.08
A. Chan	VP, Manufacturing	Manufacturing		62,000.152
D. Arcosa	VP, Operations	Administration		$61,705.297

Left Tab	The default tab alignment - typed characters begin at the left and move right.
Center Tab	Text centers over the tab position. Use this type of alignment for column headings.
Right Tab	Typed characters begin at the right and move left. This type of alignment is used for short title lines, such as dates, case file numbers, or inventory numbers. It can also be used for aligning columns of numbers without decimal places.
Bar Tab	Set up a vertical line between the columns of text.
Decimal Tab	Align columns of numbers with decimal points. The typed numbers shift to the left (as with a right tab) until you type the decimal point; the text then moves right.

Each of the tab alignments can include leader characters to assist the reader in identifying data in that line. Leaders are commonly used for a table of contents, or large reports with multiple columns of data such as a stock analysis report or an annual budget.

There are two methods of setting tabs: on the ruler using the **Tab Selector**, or using the Tabs dialog box. To set leaders with your tab positions, you need to use the Tabs dialog box.

Note the following:

- The ruler is the fastest way of setting and adjusting tabs; however, use the Tabs dialog box for more precise tab positions or leaders.

- Align text using the appropriate tab alignment options instead of spaces.

- A tab stop is in effect from the paragraph location on. When you create another tab setting, the new tab setting takes effect.

- By default, there are Left tab stops every .5".

- Tab stops can be set before you begin typing or applied to existing text. For existing text, remember to select the text prior to adding or changing the tab stops.

- Press (Tab) to move from one column to the next when typing.

- Use the **Show/Hide ¶** feature to display → every time (Tab) was pressed. This can help you see why the text does not line up with the tab stops.

- For precise measurement of a tab setting on the ruler, press and hold (Alt) as you click the position of the tab setting on the ruler.

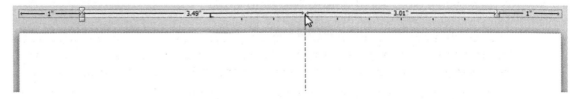

Setting Tabs on the Ruler

The advantage of setting tabs using the ruler is that, because the document window is visible, you can see where the tab is placed relative to your text. Use the ruler as a guide to where the tab position should be.

Different tab alignments are shown on the ruler in the following:

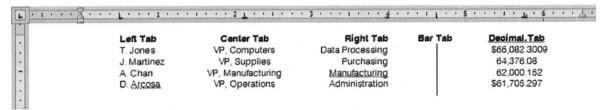

Left Tab	Center Tab	Right Tab	Bar Tab	Decimal Tab
T. Jones	VP, Computers	Data Processing		$65,082.3009
J. Martinez	VP, Supplies	Purchasing		64,376.08
A. Chan	VP, Manufacturing	Manufacturing		62,000.152
D. Arcosa	VP, Operations	Administration		$61,705.297

ScreenTips are available on the ruler to help identify the different tab stop markers. Place the mouse cursor over the tab marker (or the character box in the Tab Selector) to see a description for the tab stop marker.

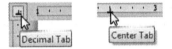

To choose a tab type, click the Tab Selector box until the required tab type appears. Each time you click the box, it moves forward to show the next tab type, as well as two indent markers. If you click past the tab type, keep clicking the Tab Selector until it displays the appropriate tab type.

Once you choose the tab type, you can click the ruler where the tab stop is to be placed. As you click the measurement on the ruler for the tab stop, you will see a line similar to the one below:

The best place to insert or add a tab stop is to click in the white area of the ruler just above the bottom blue line. You can also click in the bottom blue line of the ruler to insert the tab stop in the ruler.

When you need to adjust the tab position, click the tab character to drag it to the new measurement. As you drag the character, the line reappears to provide you with a guide to where the new tab stop can be placed.

Note the following options when working with tab stops on the ruler:

- To add a new tab stop, click the box in the Tab Selector to select the tab type and then click in the ruler at the approximate measurement.

- To delete an existing tab stop, click the tab character and then drag it off the ruler.

- To adjust an existing tab stop, click the tab character and drag it to where the tab stop is to be placed.

- You can check the tab stops set for individual lines of text by looking at the tab settings on the ruler as you move from one line to another. For example, if one line in your table shows text that does not line up with the rest of the table, click in that line to display the tab stops in the ruler. Once displayed, you will see which tab stops need to be adjusted on this line.

- If you select several lines in your table of text and the tab stops appear in grey on the ruler, this means there are different tab stops within the table. If you press Enter at the end of each line of text, you are creating paragraphs of text. You will need to adjust the tab stops for each paragraph line until every paragraph line has the same tab stops; only then will the tab stops appear in black.

  A method you can use to reduce the number of paragraph lines is to use a text wrapping or line break at the end of each text line. Press Shift + Enter instead of pressing Enter.

Learn the Skill

In this exercise, you will set tab stops on the ruler to align specific types of text, and then adjust a tab stop.

1   Create a new blank document, type: Popular Bicycling Tours for the title, press (Enter) and then save it as: Popular Bicycling Tours – Student.

2   At the far left of the ruler, click the box in the Tab Selector until you see the Right Align tab character.

3   On the ruler, click the cursor on the ruler at the **4.5" (11.4 cm)** mark and then click on the **6.0" (15.3 cm)** mark.

As you click on the measurement in the ruler, a dashed vertical line appears to show you where the tab position will be placed.

4   Press the (Tab) key and type: 2011.

5   Press the (Tab) key once more, type: 2010 and then press (Enter).

6   Type the rest of the document, pressing (Tab) to move from one column to another to enter the information:

Popular Bicycling Tours

	2011	2010
Bogota	250	200
Perth	175	150
Munich	200	180
Copenhagen	300	325

7   Save the document.

8   Select the title, click the **Home** tab, and in the **Font** group, click **Bold**. Click the arrow for **Size** and click **16**. Then, in the **Paragraph** group, click **Center**.

9   Select the line with the years (the column headings). Click the **Home** tab, and in the **Font** group, click **Bold**, click the arrow for **Size** and click **14.**

Popular Bicycling Tours

	2011	2010
Bogota	250	200
Perth	175	150
Munich	200	180
Copenhagen	300	325

You will now adjust a tab position and move the 2011 figures closer to the city names.

10   Select the text starting from the line with the years to the 325 figure.

11   On the ruler, click the right align character at 4.5" (11.4cm) and drag to 4.0" (10.2 cm).

As you drag the tab character, Word displays a vertical dashed line to confirm that you are moving this tab character.

12   Save and close the document.

Setting Tabs with the Tabs Dialog Box

Tabs can be set using the Tabs dialog box which displays a list of all the tab positions, but does not show the result of these settings until you click **OK**. The advantage of using this method is that you can set tabs with precise measurements and also select other tab options for the tab positions at the same time.

To display the Tabs dialog box, double-click any tab character on the ruler:

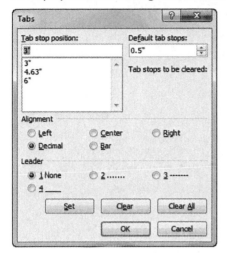

You can also display this dialog box by clicking **Tabs** in the Paragraph dialog box.

```
MMM
Using Tabs
Online
Exercise
```

Tab stop position	Enter the measurement for the new tab here. Once you click **Set**, the tab position displays in the list below the **Tab stop position** box.
Default tab stops	Displays the interval amount that the cursor moves to when you press (Tab). Change this when you want an equal amount of space between each column of text.
Tab stops to be cleared	Click the tab measurement to be removed and then click **Clear**.
Alignment	Select the alignment required for this tab position. These are the same options as found in the Tab Selector.
Leader	Select the character that will precede the text from one column to the next, giving the audience a visual guide when reading across a page.

Microsoft Office Word

Set	Use this after entering a new measurement or changing an existing measurement to set the tab stop.
Clear	Use this to clear or remove the selected tab measurement.
Clear All	Use this to clear all tab measurements in the list and reset to the default settings.

Learn the Skill

In this exercise, you will practice setting tabs with leaders for a report.

1   Create a new blank document and save this as Rock Climbing Tours – Student.

2   Type: Rock Climbing Tours as the title and then press (Enter).

3   Click the Tab Selector until it displays a right align tab character and then click the **3" (7.6 cm)** marker on the ruler.

4   Double-click this tab alignment character.

5   Ensure the tab position is highlighted in the topmost field. Ensure **Right** is selected in the Alignment area, and then click **2** for the style in the Leader area.

6   Click **Set**.

You have now successfully set the first tab position for this report.

7   Click in **Tab stop position** and type: 4.6" (11.7 cm).

8   Click **Right** for the alignment and click **Set**.

9   Click in **Tab stop position** and type: 6.13" (15.6 cm) for the third tab alignment character.

10 Ensure this last tab also has a right alignment and will use **2** for the leader.

11 Click **Set** and then click **OK**.

12 Begin typing the following text, pressing (Tab) between each of the columns.

Rock Climbing Tours

	Fee	Additional Fees	Group Size
	Fee	Additional Fees	Group Size
Kilimanjaro	$3,500	$1,000	4 – 16
Grand Teton Summit	1,300		3-6
Mt. Shasta	700		4-8
North Carolina	500		4-12
Tucson	350.00		4-6

Notice how the use of leaders makes it easier to read the numbers; however, the leaders for the first column may not be necessary.

13 Save the document again.

Now that you've entered the text, you want to adjust the leaders as well as the amount of space between the second and third columns.

14 Select all the text in the table and then double-click any tab character on the ruler.

15 When the Tabs dialog box appears, click the **6.13" (15.6 cm)** in the list and then click **Clear**.

16 Type: 6.25" (15.8 cm) as the new tab position, ensuring it is a **Right** alignment and has **2** for the leader set for this tab alignment character.

17 Click the **3" (7.6 cm)** measurement in the list of tab stops and click **1** in the Leader area. Then click **Set**.

Notice how you can make changes in any order to any of the tab stops.

18 Click the **4.6" (11.7 cm)** measurement in the list of tab stops and click 2 for the leader style. Click **Set** and then click **OK**.

Rock Climbing Tours

	Fee	Additional Fees	Group Size
Kilimanjaro	$3,500	$1,000	4 – 16
Grand Teton Summit	1,300		3-6
Mt. Shasta	700		4-8
North Carolina	500		4-12
Tucson	350.00		4-6

19 Save and close the document.

Organizing List Information

2.7

There are a number of different ways to emphasize or separate list information. Use bullets if there is no priority in a list, or apply numbers to prioritize a list. You can also use the Outline feature to show a progression of topics to discuss:

Popular Tours

- Cycling trips
- Whale watching
- Rock climbing
- Heli skiing
- Hot air ballooning
- Ice climbing

Popular Tours

1. Rock climbing
2. Cycling trips
3. Ice climbing
4. Whale watching
5. Heli skiing
6. Hot air ballooning

Popular Tours

1. Cycling trips
   a. Copenhagen
   b. Bogotá
2. Whale watching
   a. Victoria
   b. Perth
3. Rock climbing
   a. Kilimanjaro
   b. North Carolina
4. Heli skiing
   a. Rockies
   b. Colorado

Word provides a variety of bullet or numbering styles and displays the most commonly used styles. You can customize these styles for a different look.

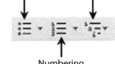

To apply a list style on text, on the **Home** tab, in the **Paragraph** group, click the arrow for the appropriate list button.

The selected bullet or number style that appears for the list style is the style that was used previously. To change it, click the area of the list style option and then click the style you want to use from the default options shown in the Library.

To remove a list style, click the corresponding button. Alternatively, if you are entering items for the list and no longer need the list style, press (Enter) twice. You can also use Clear Formatting to remove any formatting on the list items.

Use the automatic list feature to organize information when you need to move or copy items. Word reorganizes the information and adds the appropriate bullet or number or, in the case of a numbered list, will renumber the list.

Learn the Skill

In this exercise, you will add bullets and numbering to text, as well as apply some formatting to help emphasize the lists.

1 Open *Proposal for Haunted Adventure Tours* and save it as Proposal for Haunted Adventure Tours List – Student.

2 Select the list starting from Borley Rectory to St. Francis Xavier University.

3   Click the **Home** tab, and in the **Paragraph** group, click **Bullets**.

The following buildings are known (with documented sightings) to be haunted:

- Borley Rectory, Britain
- The Whaley House, California, USA
- Edinburgh Castle, Scotland
- Monte Cristo Homestead, New South Wales
- Okiku's Well at Hameji Castle, Japan
- The Colosseum, Italy
- St. Francis Xavier University, Mount St. Bernard College, Antigonish, Nova Scotia, Canada

Celebrity Burial Sites

Now try a different list option to see which style is most appropriate for this report.

4   Select the list starting with Arlington to Pere Lachaise.

5   Click the **Home** tab, in the **Paragraph** group, click **Numbering**.

Many famous people (including some entertainers) are buried here:

1. Arlington National Cemetery, Washington, DC, USA (US Presidents, Albert Einstein, Martin Luther King, National World War II Memorial, etc.)
2. Tomb of the Unknown Soldier, Europe (Paris, London, Bucharest, Athens, etc.)
3. Pierce Brothers Westwood Village Memorial Park Cemetery, Los Angeles, USA (Marilyn Monroe, Burt Lancaster, Jack Lemmon, Rodney Dangerfield, etc.)
4. Forest Lawn Hollywood Hills, Los Angeles, USA (Bette Davis, Lucille Ball, David Carradine, Stan Laurel, etc.)
5. Pere Lachaise, Paris, France (Oscar Wilde, Gertrude Stein, Edith Piaf, Jim Morrison, etc.)

Halloween Theme/Haunted Tours

To identify which areas are affected, apply simple formatting to selected text.

6   Select the title, Haunted Sites. Press (Ctrl), select Celebrity Burial Sites and then select Halloween Theme/Haunted Tours.

7   Press (Ctrl)+(B) to apply bold to these titles.

8   With the titles still selected, click the arrow for the **Size** and then click **14**.

9   Now select the list starting from Ghost Tours to Paranormal Tours and on the **Home** tab, in the **Paragraph** group, click **Bullets**.

With the three areas set up to appear as lists, you can see the effect the list style has on the document. The purpose of this report is to provide a list of different areas of interest for this proposed new adventure. As this is a proposal, with no priority or preference in the items listed, you can change the numbered list to bullets.

10 Select the numbered list and then on the **Home** tab, in the **Paragraph** group, click **Bullets**.

11 Save the document.

Customizing the Lists

Using Bullets or Numbering applies the last style of bullets or numbers used. You may want to change a specific style for the bullets or numbers.

Once the bullet or numbering feature is applied, you can change the default bullet or numbering style by using the options in the Library.

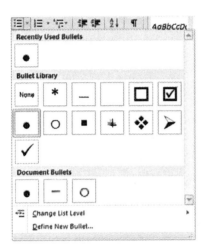

The list style shown in the Preview may differ if the samples were customized by another user. Select each bullet or numbering sample and click **Reset** (if available) to set the default.

Alternatively, you can define a new style for the bullet or numbering.

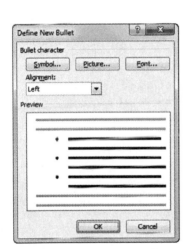

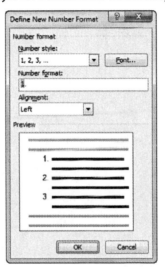

When you want to customize the existing list style, use **Change List Level**, or if using numbers, click **Define New Number Format**. For instance, if you need to change the numbering or the indent on a list item, you can increase the number accordingly or use **Continue from previous list** to have Word apply consecutive numbering for the list.

Learn the Skill

In this exercise, you will customize the bullets and numbers in the Proposal for Haunted Adventure Tours – Student document to distinguish between the three lists.

1   Select the list in the Celebrity Burial Sites. Click the **Home** tab, and in the **Paragraph** group, click the arrow for **Bullets**.

2   In the list of bullets, click the **four-diamonds** bullet.

Celebrity Burial Sites

Many famous people (including some entertainers) are buried here:

❖ Arlington National Cemetery, Washington, DC, USA (US Presidents, Albert Einstein, Martin Luther King, National World War II Memorial, etc.)

❖ Tomb of the Unknown Soldier, Europe (Paris, London, Bucharest, Athens, etc.)

❖ Pierce Brothers Westwood Village Memorial Park Cemetery, Los Angeles, USA (Marilyn Monroe, Burt Lancaster, Jack Lemmon, Rodney Dangerfield, etc.)

❖ Forest Lawn Hollywood Hills, Los Angeles, USA (Bette Davis, Lucille Ball, David Carradine, Stan Laurel, etc.)

❖ Pere Lachaise, Paris, France (Oscar Wilde, Gertrude Stein, Edith Piaf, Jim Morrison, etc.)

You have now applied a different bullet using one of the pre-defined bullet styles provided with Word.

3   Select the list in the Halloween Theme/Haunted Tours area. On the **Home** tab, in the **Paragraph** group, click the arrow for **Bullets** and then click **Define New Bullet**.

4   Click **Symbol**.

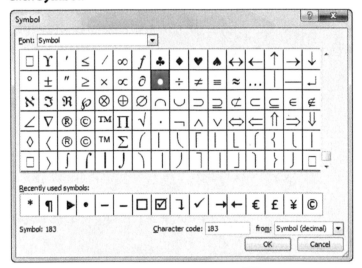

5   Click the arrow for **Font** and then press Ⓦ to move quickly to the first font that begins with this character. Scroll in the list to click **Wingdings**.

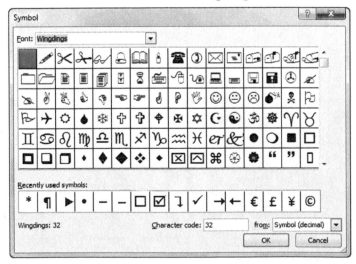

6   Click the candle symbol in the first row (eighth character), and then click **OK**.

7   Click **Font** in the Define New Bullet dialog box.

You should now be viewing the Font dialog box.

8   In the **Size** list, click **14** as the new size. Click the arrow for **Font Color** and choose a color.

9   Click **OK** to exit the Font dialog box and click **OK** again to exit the Define New Bullet dialog box.

These tours include a ghostly theme which could be offered at Halloween:

- Ghost Tours of Southern Ontario, Canada
- Haunted Ghost Tours of England, UK

10 Save and close the document.

Now try applying and customizing numbering in a document.

11 Open *Staff Retreat Presentation Notes* and select the Revenues text.

12 Click the **Home** tab and in the **Paragraph** group, click **Numbering**.

Staff Retreat – December 7th

Tolano Environmental Consulting (TEC)

1. Revenues

It's been a tough year and, like so many companies, we have felt the impact of the international

13 Repeat step 12 for the next subheading, Upcoming Business.

14 Repeat step 12 for the Revenues subheading under Tolano Adventures.

Tolano Adventures

3. Revenues

In our second year of business, we saw a significant increase in revenues, especially internationally. The economic downturn has forced consumers to spend their money more wisely with an emphasis on becoming, or staying, green.

Word has applied the numbering option but it is continuous from the previous text. In this case, you want to numbering to start at 1 again for this division of the company.

15 With Revenues still selected, click the arrow for Numbering and then click **Define New Number Format**.

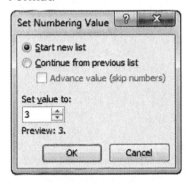

16 In the **Set value to** field, click the incremental button to change the number to 1. Then click **OK**.

Tolano Adventures

1. Revenues

In our second year of business, we saw a significant increase in revenues, especially internationally. The economic downturn has forced consumers to spend their money more wisely with an emphasis on becoming, or staying, green.

Word has now adjusted the numbering to better suit the purpose of using numbers in this report.

17 Close the document without saving.

Creating a Multilevel List

You can create a list with levels of topics using bullets, numbering, or a combination of both. This is useful when list items are not titles or headings, but you want to prioritize the topics. This formatting style can be applied either to existing text or as you type. To apply multilevel list numbering, on the **Home** tab, in the **Paragraph** group, click **Multilevel List**.

To choose a different numbering style for the list, click the style from the displayed list. You can also define your own list or style; the ones provided are commonly used in business documents.

To change the text for only one level using one list style, first select the text and then on the **Home** tab, in the **Paragraph** group, click **Multilevel List** and click **Change List Level**. Then click the list style you want to apply.

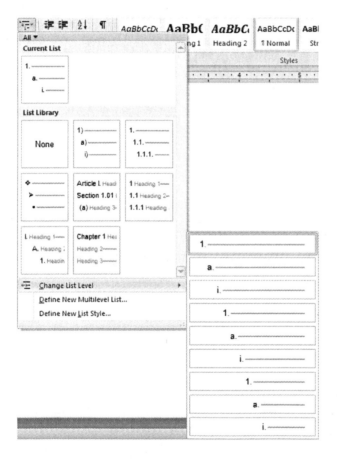

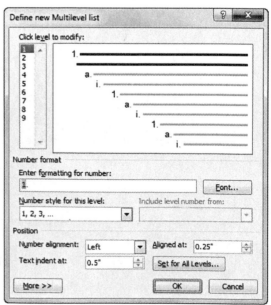

To customize a level used in one of the list styles, on the **Home** tab, in the **Paragraph** group, click the arrow for **Multilevel List**. Then click **Define New Multilevel List**.

For Word to apply the appropriate numbering to existing text, tabs must be used with the text to denote the different levels, similar to pressing Tab to demote text or Shift + Tab to promote text.

Learn the Skill

In this exercise, you will learn how to apply a multilevel numbering list to text in the Staff Agenda document.

1   Open *Staff Agenda* and then save as Staff Agenda – Student.

2   Select the text starting from Current status to Opportunities.

3   Click the **Home** tab, and in the **Paragraph** group, click **Multilevel**. Then click the **1. a. i.** style.

9:00   President's Welcome

1.   Current status

2.   Environmental Consulting

3.   Revenues

4.   Upcoming Business

5.   Adventures

6.   Strengths & Weaknesses

7.   Open session

8.   December 8th

9.   Vision for the Future

10. Open session in groups

11. Sales

12. Strategies

13. Opportunities

Word has applied the numbering to all the items although there are no sublevels. This is because all the items were at one level prior to applying the multilevel numbering style.

4   Position the cursor at the beginning of Environmental Consulting and press ⌈Tab⌉.

9:00   President's Welcome

1.   Current status

    a.   Environmental Consulting

2.   Revenues

5   Repeat step 4 for the next three items.

1.   Current status

    a.   Environmental Consulting

    b.   Revenues

    c.   Upcoming Business

    d.   Adventures

2.   Strengths & Weaknesses

3.   Open session

Suppose you realize that Revenues and Upcoming Business are subtopics within the Environmental Consulting division.

6   Select the Revenue and Upcoming Business lines, and then press ⌈Tab⌉.

    1. Current status

        a. Environmental Consulting

            i. Revenues

            ii. Upcoming Business

        b. Adventures

7 Position your cursor at the beginning of December 8th, click the **Home** tab and, in the **Paragraph** group, click **Numbering** to turn this feature off.

8 Set the levels for the rest of the text:

December 8th

    4. Vision for the Future

        a. Open session in groups

    5. Sales

        a. Strategies

        b. Opportunities

9 Save and close the document.

Creating Outlines

Outline numbering is useful when you need several levels of numbering to show a progression. For example, if you want to organize your ideas for a presentation, or if you want to show headings and subheadings in a report, similar to a draft table of contents. Choose from a variety of preset outline numbering styles for each level or customize the style for each level.

When you use the outline feature in Word, the numbering styles can be set before you begin typing, or select the text after it has been typed and apply the appropriate outline numbering style. To switch to Outline view:

- On the **View** tab, in the **Document Views** group, click **Outline**; or
- click **Outline** from the View modes on the Status bar.

Then use items in the **Outlining** tab to set up the text levels:

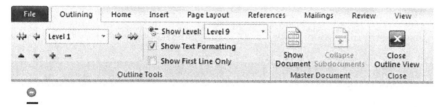

Promoting or Demoting Text   Moving, Expanding or Collapsing Text

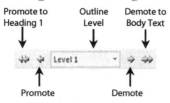

- To promote the text to a higher level, click **Promote** or press (Shift)+(Tab).
- To demote the text to a lower level, click **Demote** or press (Tab).
- Each time you use Promote or Demote, the text moves forward or backward one level at a time.
- To add text at the same level, press (Enter) at the end of that line and then type the new text.

- To demote the selected text to the Body Text style level, click **Demote to Body Text**.
- To promote the selected text to the Heading 1 style level, click **Promote to Heading 1**.
- To view or change the level applied for the current line, use **Outline Level**.
- The ⊕ and ⊖ symbols at the left of the levels work in a similar manner to file management in Windows. Double-click the ⊕ symbol to expand this line and display the text below whereas the ⊖ symbol indicates all text at this level has been expanded and you can collapse the levels by clicking this symbol.
- You can also click **Expand** or **Collapse** to show more or less text for the outline.
- The text between the ⊕ symbols is referred to as a "family of text". Click **Move Up** or **Move Down** to move a family of text, or click and drag the ⊕ symbol to the new location. Individual levels can be moved as needed without affecting the "family".

As you enter the content for your outline, you can use other tools to help you view different parts of the document in the Outline view:

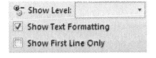

- Use **Show Level** to display only text at that level.
- Use **Show Text Formatting** to change the display of text from formatted or regular. Displaying the unformatted text enables you to see more of the outline and focus on the text.
- Use **Show First Line Only** to display only the first line of multiple lines of text for a level.

When you switch to Draft or Print Layout view, the text displays with the default styles set for the level. This is your guide to identifying the headings and subheadings for your report. Outlining helps you formulate the flow of content and adjust the text as you insert or delete items.

Note that any tabs set will determine the outline numbering style for that line, including the default tab settings at every 0.5" (1.3 cm). The outline numbering styles work with hanging indents.

Learn the Skill

In this exercise, you will create an outline for Nick Klassen to organize topics for discussion at the Staff Retreat.

1   Create a new blank document and save this as Staff Retreat Notes for Nick – Student.

2   On the Status bar, click **Outline**.

You can now enter the "table of contents" for the items Nick wants to discuss at the Retreat.

3   Type: Revenues and press Enter.

Word inserts the text and places you at the main level. Nick has already given you information on these main titles so you can add them to the outline.

4   Press Tab to move to a sub-level and type: steady increase in all adventures. Press Enter.

Notice how Word puts the new topic at the same level assuming that you want to enter more topics at this level.

5   Type the following information and press (Tab) on the blank line below Better economy …:

   ⊕ **Revenues**
       ⊖ Steady increase in all adventures
       ⊖ Tour costs remain same
       ⊕ Better economy means more travel
           ⊖

   You are now indicating to Word that you have topics to be discussed for the "Better economy means more travel" topic.

6   Type the following information, pressing (Enter) at the end of the last item:

   ⊕ Better economy means more travel
       ⊖ Australia had largest increase
       ⊖ More group tours being booked
       ⊖ Resurgence in climbing adventures

7   Click the **Outlining** tab and, in the **Outline Tools** group, click ⬆ **Promote** twice to return to the main level for the next major topic.

8   Type the remaining items for the outline, using (Tab):

   ⊕ **Upcoming Business**
       ⊖ Haunted Tours
       ⊖ More Eco Tours
   ⊕ **Strengths & Weaknesses**
       ⊖ Heli skiing accidents
       ⊖ More resources to explore tours
       ⊖ Economy to improve customer spending
       ⊖ New vendors want to partner with us

9   Save the document.

After reviewing these notes, Nick wants some sub-topics to moved to another part of the outline.

10 Click at the end of Strengths and press (Enter). Then delete the extra characters so Weaknesses is at the left margin.

   ⊖ **Strengths**
   ⊕ **Weaknesses**
       ⊖ Heli skiing accidents
       ⊖ More resources to explore tours
       ⊖ Economy to improve customer spending
       ⊖ New vendors want to partner with us

11 Select More resources to explore tours item and then drag it to the beginning of Weaknesses.

   ⊕ **Strengths**
       ⊖ More resources to explore tours
   ⊕ **Weaknesses**   📋 (Ctrl) ▾
       ⊖ Heli skiing accidents
       ⊖ Economy to improve customer spending
       ⊖ New vendors want to partner with us

   Notice how Word moved this item into a new location.

12 Repeat step 11 with the New vendors item.

Suppose the next move is for an entire set of items in another part of the notes.

13 Position the mouse cursor on the ⊕ at the left of the Better economy means more travel item in the Revenues area.

   ⊕ **Revenues**
       ⊖ Steady increase in all adventures
       ⊖ Tour costs remain same
       ⊕ Better economy means more travel
           ⊖ Australia had largest increase

14 Drag this item to the line between New vendors and Weaknesses.

○ **Strengths**
  ⊖ More resources to explore tours
  ⊖ New vendors want to partner with us
○ **Weaknesses**   (Ctrl) ▾
  ⊖ Heli skiing accidents
  ⊖ Economy to improve customer spending
  ⊖

15 Release the mouse when you see the corresponding line to verify the location.

○ **Revenues**
  ⊖ Steady increase in all adventures
  ⊖ Tour costs remain same
○ **Upcoming Business**
  ⊖ Haunted Tours
  ⊖ More Eco Tours
○ **Strengths**
  ⊖ More resources to explore tours
  ⊖ New vendors want to partner with us
  ○ Better economy means more travel
    ⊖ Australia had largest increase
    ⊖ More group tours being booked
    ⊖ Resurgence in climbing adventures
○ **Weaknesses**
  ⊖ Heli skiing accidents
  ⊖ Economy to improve customer spending

You have successfully moved a "family" of items to a new location.

16 Save and close the document.

Lesson Summary

In this lesson, you looked at tab stops and how they can be used with different types of lists in documents. You should now be able to:

☑ understand what a tab stop is

☑ recognize the different types of tab stops

☑ set tab stops on the ruler as well as the Tabs dialog box

☑ set leaders for tab stops

☑ clear one or all tabs

☑ create numbered lists

☑ create bulleted lists

☑ customize lists

☑ work with multi-level lists

☑ create outlines

Review Questions

MMM
Go online for
Additional
Review and
Activities

1. Explain what a tab stop is and why you should use tab stops for aligning text.

2. When would you use the Tabs dialog box and how do you access it?

3. Why would you apply numbering to a list of items instead of using bullets?

4. Why would you set up a multilevel list?

5. Explain the purpose of the Promote or Demote features when working on an outline.

Microsoft®
Word 2010
Core Certification

Lesson 5: Formatting Documents

Lesson Objectives

In this lesson, you will look at ways of formatting a document such as changing the margins, paper size, or orientation. On successful completion of this lesson, you should be able to:

☐ work with document formatting

☐ change the paper size

☐ change the orientation

☐ change the margins

☐ insert page breaks

☐ insert page numbers

☐ insert headers or footers

☐ customize headers or footers

☐ work with odd/even pages

☐ apply backgrounds or themes

Setting up the Document

Each time you request a new blank document, Word creates one using default options that can include settings such as letter size, margins, etc. You can change these at any time. New documents created from templates also include specific settings for that template that you can adjust as needed.

You can view all options to set up the document by clicking the **Page Setup Dialog box launcher** on the **Page Layout** tab.

Changing the Paper Size

The default paper size is determined by your computer settings. The default size we are using for this courseware is Letter 8½ by 11" (21.59 x 27.94 cm). This can be changed at any time using the **Page Layout** tab. To change the paper size on a document:

- On the **Page Layout** tab, in the **Page Setup** group, click **Size**, or

- double-click anywhere in the darker area of the ruler, and then click the **Paper** tab.

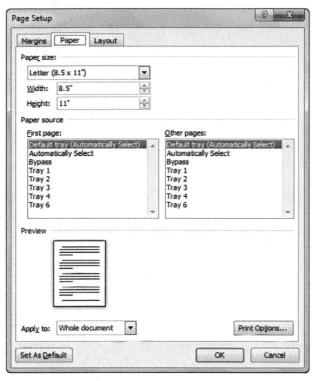

Paper size	Choose a standard paper size such as Letter or Legal (commonly used in North America), or A4 and B5 (commonly used in Europe and Australia). You can also specify a variety of envelope sizes. To specify a new size, click Custom size and type the horizontal and vertical measurements for the custom paper, e.g. personalized note paper.
Paper source	Select the tray containing the paper for this document. You can set a different tray for the first page (e.g. letterhead) and subsequent pages in the document (e.g. page 2 forward for the letter or proposal to use plain paper). The number of trays available depends on your printer type.
Preview	Displays how the document will look when changes are accepted. Use Apply to indicate whether the changes are for the entire document, just one section, selected text, or from this point forward.
Print Options	Set options for how the printer handles printing of documents.

Changing the Orientation

Orientation refers to the printed text layout: **Portrait** refers to vertical orientation, while **Landscape** refers to horizontal orientation. To change the document orientation:

- On the **Page Layout** tab, in the **Page Setup** group, click **Orientation**; or

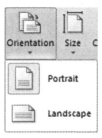

- double-click a darker area of the active ruler, click the **Margins** tab and then the orientation to use.

Orientation

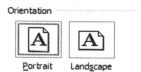

Portrait   Landscape

Changing the Margins

Margins are the amount of space between the edge of the paper and the printed text area. You can adjust the margin settings for the entire document or for different parts of the document.

When setting margins using the ruler, you must be in Print Layout view before the arrows to adjust the margins will appear on the horizontal and vertical rulers. The Draft view does not include the vertical ruler.

The margin boundaries for the top and bottom margins are easy to see as they appear as the divider line between the lighter (inside margins) and darker (outside) shades on the ruler. When you position the cursor at the divider line, a ScreenTip appears:

The margin boundaries for the left and right margins appear on the top ruler; however, the indent markers may obscure the left margin. You can access the left margin marker by pointing precisely between the left and first line indent markers. You can access the right margin marker by pointing above the right indent marker.

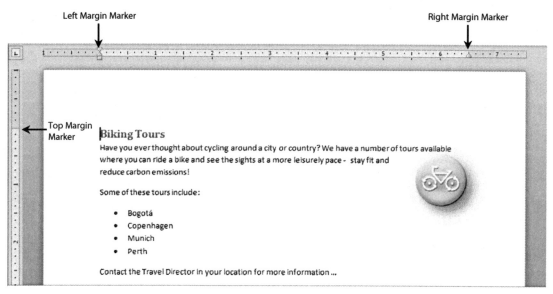

Ways to adjust your margins:

- On the **Page Layout** tab, in the **Page Setup** group, click **Margins**, or

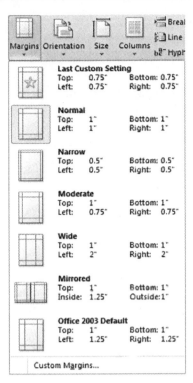

- point the mouse at the margin to adjust on the ruler and, when the appropriate arrow appears, drag to the measurement for the margin, or

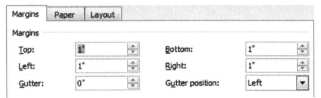

- double-click one of the darker areas of the horizontal or vertical ruler.

Top	The amount of space from the top edge of the paper to where the text begins vertically.
Bottom	The amount of space from the bottom edge of the paper to where the text ends for each page.
Left	The amount of space from the left edge of the paper to where text starts on the left side.
Right	The amount of space from the right edge of the paper to where text wraps at the right side.
Gutter	The amount of white space added to the top or side margin if the document is to be bound e.g. coil, 3-hole binder, card stock folders with metal fasteners.

Gutter position	Sets the gutter or binding position for the document, e.g. left, top, inside margin for double-sided pages.

Each method allows you to change some or all margins at the same time. The **Margins** command lists the most common measurements, but you can also click **Custom Margins** to set different measurements. When using the **Page Setup** dialog box, you can type the measurements for the margins in the appropriate boxes, or click the incremental buttons to select the measurements.

When you click in the ruler to adjust the left or right margin, you should see the ⟷ symbol with the appropriate ScreenTip before dragging to the new measurement for the margin. The top or bottom margin marker will appear as ↕. To set a precise measurement, hold (Alt) while dragging a margin boundary to display the margin measurement.

```
┌─────────────────┐
│      MMM        │
│    Popular      │
│  Tours Online   │
│    Exercise     │
└─────────────────┘
```

Biking Tours

Learn the Skill

In this exercise, you will learn how to change the margins in the Tour Prices Breakdown report.

1   Open *Tour Prices Breakdown*.

Although the table lists the information, there is a lot of text in the first column. This report may be easier to read if the orientation was changed.

2   Click the **Page Layout** tab and, in the **Page Setup** group, click **Orientation** and then click **Landscape**.

The report now displays in the new page width.

3   Click the **Page Layout** tab, in the **Page Setup** group, click **Margins** and then click **Narrow**.

Word has adjusted the width of the report to accommodate the narrower margins.

4   Position the mouse cursor on the line between the dark and light area on the vertical ruler. Drag down approximately **1" (2.5 cm)**.

Notice you can adjust a margin for the report using the ruler.

5   Close this document without saving.

Inserting Page Breaks

Although Word automatically paginates the document as you type, there may be occasions when you want to end a page somewhere other than where Word has determined it should end, such as when you are typing a title page containing only a few lines of text.

When Word calculates that enough text fills the page, a soft page break is inserted. In Draft view, when the non-printing characters (e.g. ¶) display, the soft page break appears as:

....

When you choose to break the page at a desired location, you do so by inserting a manual page break. Avoid pressing (Enter) continuously until at a new page as this makes editing awkward and time consuming. A manual page break line appears at the indicated location (visible only when the ¶ display) as:

...............Page Break...............¶

Ways to enter a manual or hard page break:

- On the **Insert** tab, in the **Pages** group, click **Page Break**, or
- press Ctrl + Enter , or
- on the **Page Layout** tab, in the **Page Setup** group, click **Breaks** and then click **Page**.

A manual page break code works in a similar manner to text characters. It can be deleted using Delete or Backspace , depending on where the cursor is at the time you want to remove the code. For instance, if the cursor is at the beginning of the next page, press Backspace to delete the code; alternatively, if you are at the end of the paragraph where the page break code was inserted, press Delete to delete the code. You may want to display the formatting characters to see the code.

Learn the Skill

In this exercise, you will practice how to add and remove page breaks.

1   Open *Staff Retreat Presentation Notes* and save this as Staff Retreat Presentation Notes – Student.

2   Scroll down the first page to view the contents.

You should notice that information for Tolano Environment Consulting and Tolano Adventures are on one page. It would be preferable to have these on separate pages.

3   Position the cursor at the beginning of Tolano Adventures and then press Ctrl + Enter .

> **Tolano Adventures**
>
> **Revenues**
> In our second year of business, we saw a significant increase in revenues, especially internationally. The

The text for Tolano Adventures now starts on a new page.

Suppose you are then asked to move the Upcoming Business text to another page as there will be more text and a table from that division.

4   Position the cursor at the beginning of Upcoming Business. Click the **Page Layout** tab, and in the **Page Setup** group, click **Breaks** and then **Page**. Repeat for Strength & Weaknesses.

5   Look at the left of the Status bar to verify you have more than two pages in total for this report.

6   Press Ctrl + G to activate the Go To feature and type: 4 as the page number you want Word to move to quickly.

7   Scroll up to view the bottom of page 3 and the top of page 4. Then click the **Home** tab, and in the **Paragraph** group, click **Show/Hide ¶**.

Notice the number of paragraph marks at the bottom of page 3. This is why you have four pages in the document.

8   Move the cursor to the first blank line near the bottom and delete two blank lines that follow.

The document should now have only three pages in total.

Suppose you now decide that Upcoming Business does not need to be on a new page, which means you can now remove the page break.

9 Move to the bottom of page 1 and then position the cursor at the beginning of the Page Break code.

10 Press (Delete) to remove the code and move the text back to the previous page.

11 Save the document.

Working with Section Breaks

A section break separates formatting that changes within a document, such as margins, page orientation, headers and footers, and page number sequences.

To insert a section break, on the **Page Layout** tab, in the **Page Setup** group, click **Breaks**. Then from the Section Breaks area, choose the type of section break you want to insert into the document:

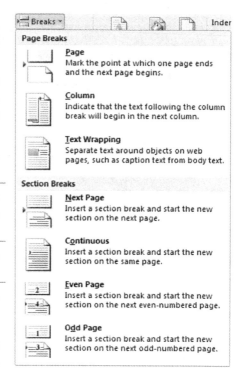

Next Page	Starts a new section on the next page, e.g. landscape orientation, different header or footer.
Continuous	Starts a new section on the same page, e.g. set up a three column format, go back to a single column format (regular text entry).
Even Page	Starts a new section on the next even page, e.g. the left side of an open book.
Odd Page	Starts a new section on the next odd page, e.g. the right side of an open book.

A section break code appears at the indicated location (visible only when the ¶ display) with the appropriate type shown in brackets:

···Section Break (Next Page)···

···Section Break (Continuous)···

···Section Break (Even Page)···

···Section Break (Odd Page)···

MMM
11 x 17 Map
Online
Exercise

You can remove a section break in the same way as a page break. Be careful when deleting section breaks as they may cause the formatting in your document to change to another layout, e.g. if you delete the section break just before the landscape orientation for a financial table in your report, the entire document may change to landscape orientation. Display the formatting characters to see the Section Break code so you can then delete the code.

Learn the Skill

In this exercise, you will insert a front page and insert a section break to change the page orientation in the Staff Retreat Presentation Notes – Student document.

1 Position the cursor at the beginning of Tolano Adventures on page 2.

2 Click the **Page Layout** tab, and in the **Page Setup** group, click **Orientation** and then click **Landscape**.

Notice how the entire report is now in landscape orientation. If you only want this for the Tolano Adventures area, you need to insert a section break to tell Word you want to set up something different on this page.

3   On the Quick Access Toolbar, click **Undo**.

4   Scroll up to see the page break code on page 1, delete the code and the blank line.

5   Click the **Page Layout** tab and, in the **Page Setup** group, click **Breaks** and then click **Next Page**.

With·the·expansion·of·services·to·the·public·through·our·Adventures·division,·another·strategy·is·to· establish·specific·branding.¶

¶···Section Break (Next Page)···

6   Repeat step 2 with your cursor at the top of page 2.

This time only this page changed the orientation to landscape. Notice also that the orientation is from this point forward; however, Strengths & Weaknesses should be on a new page and have portrait orientation.

7   Position the cursor at the beginning of Strengths & Weaknesses. Click the **Page Layout** tab and, in the **Page Setup** group, click **Breaks** and then click **Next Page**.

8   Then on the **Page Layout** tab, in the **Page Setup** group, click **Orientation** and then click **Portrait**.

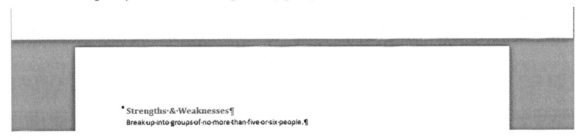

Strengths·&·Weaknesses¶
Break·up·into·groups·of·no·more·than·five·or·six·people.¶

Page 3 should now be in portrait mode.

Suppose you now decide to add a blank page at the beginning of the report for a future title page.

9   Press (Ctrl)+(Home) to go quickly to the first page.

10   Press (Ctrl)+(Enter) to insert a new page break.

Notice how you just inserted a Page Break code and not one for a Section Break.

11   Save the document again.

Working with Columns

Use the **Columns** feature to set up to three "newspaper style" columns for a document; the number of columns in a document depends on factors such as column width, margins, paper size and orientation, font size, or document layout such as for a Web page. In newspaper style columns, the text from the bottom of one column flows to the top of the next, making it an ideal layout for documents such as newsletters or reports.

When working with multiple columns, Draft view displays the appropriate column widths; however, the columns do not display side by side. To view columns side by side, use Print Layout view.

Consider the following in regards to working with columns:

- You can apply columns to text before or after you have typed it. However, you may find it easier to type the text first, and then apply multiple column formatting.

- To break a column manually and force the text to continue in the next column, on the **Page Layout** tab, in the **Page Setup** group, click **Breaks** and then click **Column**. Alternatively, press (Ctrl)+(Shift)+ (Enter) where the column break should be placed.

- To insert a page break, move to where you want the page break to be, and then on the **Insert** tab, in the **Pages** group, click **Page Break**, or press Ctrl + Enter.

- To set a new set of columns on a page where columns have already been set up, you need to insert a **Continuous** section break between the two different column layouts.

- When you change the column layout of a document, the entire document is affected unless you specify otherwise. If you want to change only the column layout for a portion of the document, you should make that portion a separate section by inserting section breaks in the appropriate places.

To create columns, on the **Page Layout** tab, in the **Page Setup** group, click **Columns**.

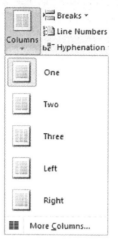

To set up more options for the columns, click **More Columns**.

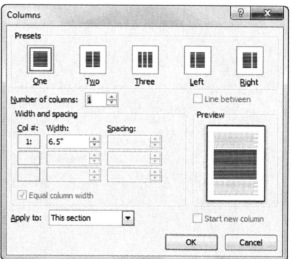

Presets	The **One**, **Two**, or **Three** options provide columns of equal width initially and are generally used for newspaper style columns. The Left or Right column layouts can be used for Web pages or manuals where a banner appears on one side, usually for a table of contents.
Number of columns	Enter the number or use the incremental buttons to set the number of columns to be applied in the document.
Width and spacing	Alter the width and spacing between this column and the next in these fields. Use **Equal column width** to have columns of equal width; if set, options for column 1 display only as any changes made there will affect the others equally.
Apply to	Select which text to apply the column structure (as defined here), e.g., Whole document, From this point forward, or Selected text.
Line between	Word will automatically insert a vertical line between each of the columns in the document.

Start new column	Only becomes available when you apply the columns from this point forward, similar to inserting a section break after entering some text in order to start a new format.

Once columns have been set to text, you can make changes to the columns, as required. Consider the following when making changes to text in columns:

- To change the number of columns, select the text and use the **Columns** command to set the new number.

- To adjust the width of each column or the spacing between each column, use the Columns dialog box or drag the appropriate markers in the ruler for each side of a column to be adjusted (e.g., ↔ for the left or right margins for the document, or the ▦ marker for the left margin of each inside column).

- Each column has its own indent markers that can be adjusted.

To insert or turn off vertical lines between each column, in the Columns dialog box, click **Line between**.

Learn the Skill

In this exercise you will apply columns in a document.

1   Open *Staff Retreat Presentation Notes* and save as Staff Retreat Presentation Notes Report – Student.

2   Select the paragraphs below Revenues for Tolano Environmental Consulting.

3   Click the **Page Layout** tab and in the **Page Setup** group, click **Columns**. Then click **Three**.

Tolano Environmental Consulting (TEC)

Revenues

It's been a tough year and, like so many companies, we have felt the impact of the international economic downturn. Although we expected a decrease in revenues, we hoped to avoid serious impact given that our

services are so environmentally friendly.

We have seen a slight improvement following some of the Environmental Conferences during the year, especially in Southern Asian

and Australia where we have worked hard to expand the business.

The following shows the revenues for last year and anticipated revenues for the next quarter:

Word has applied the specific layout to the selected text with the default settings. You change these easily.

4   Click **Columns** and then click **More Columns**.

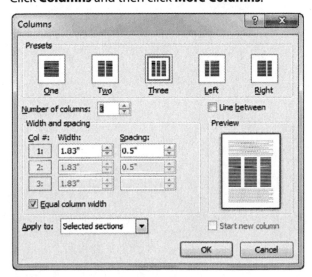

5 In the Width and spacing area, click the incremental button to reduce the **Spacing** between the three columns to be **0.2"** (0.51cm).

6 Click **OK**.

Tolano Environmental Consulting (TEC)

Revenues

It's been a tough year and, like so many companies, we have felt the impact of the international economic downturn. Although we expected a decrease in revenues, we hoped to avoid

serious impact given that our services are so environmentally friendly.

We have seen a slight improvement following some of the Environmental Conferences during the year, especially in

Southern Asian and Australia where we have worked hard to expand the business.

The following shows the revenues for last year and anticipated revenues for the next quarter:

By reducing the amount of spacing between the columns, there are more words per line and thereby reduces the amount of space the columns use in the report.

Suppose you decide you want two columns instead.

7 With the text still selected, on the **Page Layout** tab, in the **Page Setup** group, click **Columns** and then click **Two**.

Revenues

It's been a tough year and, like so many companies, we have felt the impact of the international economic downturn. Although we expected a decrease in revenues, we hoped to avoid serious impact given that our services are so environmentally friendly.

We have seen a slight improvement following some of the Environmental Conferences during

the year, especially in Southern Asian and Australia where we have worked hard to expand the business.

The following shows the revenues for last year and anticipated revenues for the next quarter:

Your text has now changed from three columns to only two. At this point you may decide to edit the text or add a picture to balance the columns of text. The choice you make depends on the message you want to convey in the report.

8 Click the **Home** tab, and in the **Paragraph** group, click **Show/Hide ¶**.

Revenues¶━━━━━━━━━━━━━━━━━━━━━━━Section Break (Continuous)━━━━━━━━━━━━━━━━━━━━━━━

It's·been·a·tough·year·and,·like·so·many· companies,·we·have·felt·the·impact·of·the· international·economic·downturn.·Although·we· expected·a·decrease·in·revenues,·we·hoped·to· avoid·serious·impact·given·that·our·services·are·so· environmentally·friendly.¶

We·have·seen·a·slight·improvement·following· some·of·the·Environmental·Conferences·during· ·¶

the·year,·especially·in·Southern·Asian·and· Australia·where·we·have·worked·hard·to·expand· the·business.¶

The·following·shows·the·revenues·for·last·year· and·anticipated·revenues·for·the·next·quarter:¶

Notice the Continuous section break codes in the document: Word inserted these automatically when you applied a column layout to selected text.

9 Turn the Show/Hide feature off.

10 Apply a two column format to the remaining paragraphs so your report appears similar to the following:

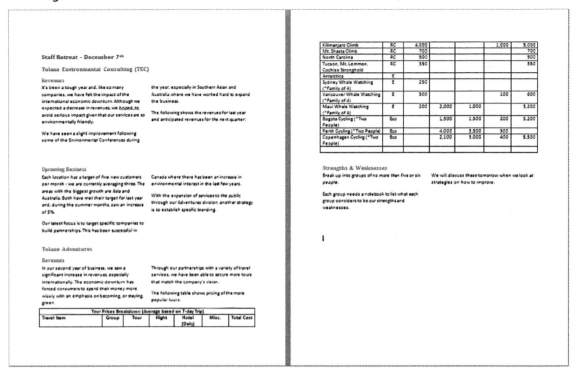

11 Save the document.

Controlling the Text Flow

Two features you can activate to control text flow is to set how hyphenation works in Word. This can be advantageous when you work with features such as columns where you have shorter line lengths.

To set the hyphenation, on the **Page Layout** tab, in the **Page Setup** group, click **Hyphenation**.

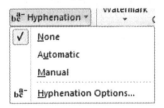

You can choose how you want this feature to work; some business standards do not allow for hyphens to break words at the right margin; however, hyphens can help to reduce large amounts of white space between words in a line of text.

You can also select more options for hyphens by using the Hyphenation Options feature:

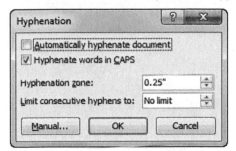

Learn the Skill

In this exercise, you will look at how you can apply hyphenation rules in a report.

1   With the *Staff Retreat Presentation Notes Report – Student* active on the screen, click the **Page Layout** tab, in the **Page Setup** group, click **Hyphenation** and then click **Automatic**.

Revenues

It's been a tough year and, like so many companies, we have felt the impact of the international economic downturn. Although we expected a decrease in revenues, we hoped to avoid serious impact given that our services are so environmentally friendly.

We have seen a slight improvement following some of the Environmental Conferences during the year, especially in Southern Asian and Australia where we have worked hard to expand the business.

The following shows the revenues for last year and anticipated revenues for the next quarter:

Word automatically applies hyphens in the document based on the words used.

2   Save and close the document.

Using Headers and Footers

3.5

Headers are text or graphics that appear at the top of a page and footers are text or graphics that appear at the bottom of a page. The header and footer can contain simple information such as the document title, page number, or author's name; or it can contain sophisticated graphics (such as a company logo or product design).

Headers and footers can be the same on every page, or you can alternate different headers and footers on even and odd numbered pages. By dividing your document into sections, you can use different headers and footers for each section of the document. You can also have different headers and footers on the first page of your document or a section.

The header prints within the top margin area and the footer prints within the bottom margin area. You can adjust how close the header and footer are to the document text.

Inserting Page Numbers

Page numbers are inserted into a header or footer, based on the cursor position at the time the page number feature is activated. You can also insert a page number without adding any other text for a header or footer.

To insert page numbers only into a document, on the **Insert** tab, in the **Header & Footer** group, click **Page Number**. Each of these displays more options for the layout and design of the page number.

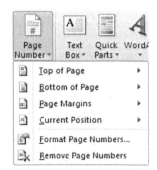

Top of Page	Choose the style you want to use for adding page numbers at the top of the page, or in the header area.
Bottom of Page	Choose the style you want to use when adding page numbers at the bottom of the page, or in the footer area.

Page Margins	Choose the margin position for the page number.
Current Position	Choose a style for the page number using the current location or position.
Format Page Numbers	Choose a different numbering style (i.e., alpha, lowercase Roman numerals, etc.), include a chapter number, or to have the page numbers start at a different number (instead of 1).
Remove Page Numbers	Remove the page numbers from the document.

Inserting the Date or Time

Another piece of information you may want to include in a header or footer is the date or time, although this feature can be used without needing to set up a header or footer.

To insert the date or time in a location of the document, on the **Insert** tab, in the **Text** group, click **Date & Time**.

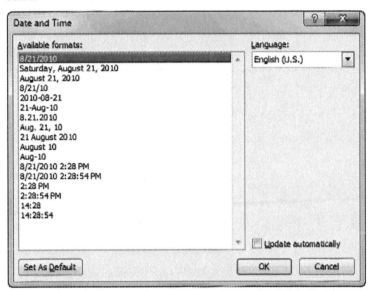

Word provides you with a number of formats for the date or time based on the standards required in your organization, school, or your own preference. Once you select a format, you can click **Set As Default** so this format is used whenever you want to insert the date or time. You can also set the date or time to always show the current date and time, regardless of when you are viewing the document, by using **Update automatically**.

Creating Headers and Footers

Create headers and footers using the **Insert** tab or in the **Header & Footer** group. You can insert a style for the header or footer initially. Remember that headers appear across the top of the page whereas footers appear at the bottom of the page.

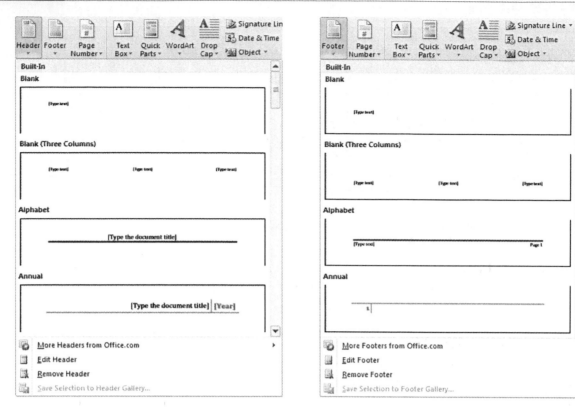

Once selected, Word displays the **Header & Footer Tools** Ribbon for further modifications to the header or footer.

In the document, a dashed line with an identifier appears at the top or bottom of a page for you to enter or modify the text or images inside the header or footer.

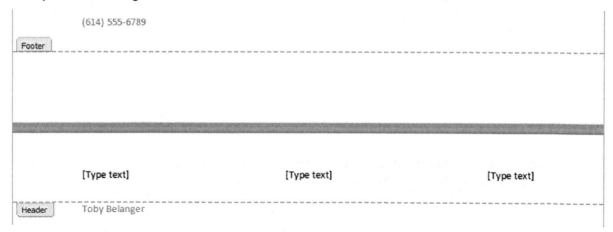

In a document where there are section breaks, Word identifies the different sections in the header or footer. This is helpful if you only want to print specific sections or need to check where changes may be required in your document. You can print sections of text by entering *s#*, where s represents the section and # is the number of the section, in the **Pages** box of the **Print** dialog box.

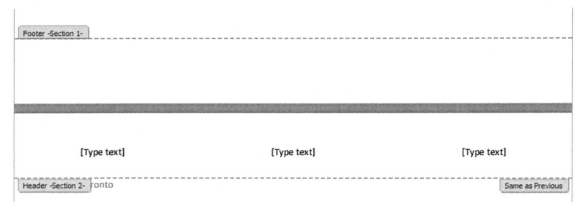

The **Link to Previous** option gives you the opportunity to use the same header or footer from the previous section. If you turn this feature off, you can have a different header or footer in the current section.

Some styles include tab stops set up for the header or footer. In general, one tab stop centers the text and the other right aligns it; you can adjust these tabs as required. You can also change text alignment, insert indents or apply formatting.

Headers and footers usually contain no more than two or three lines of text. While you can insert pictures into a header or footer, be careful how much information the header or footer contains. Use the screen display to help identify the top or bottom edge of the paper – the dashed line indicates the margin. Word displays the margins used for the header or footer in the Position group of the Header & Footer Ribbon as reference.

To edit an existing header or footer, double-click the header or footer area to activate the feature, and then make the modifications.

 **Learn the Skill**

In this exercise, you will learn how to create headers and footers, including adding page numbers, to Staff Retreat Presentation Notes - Student.

1   Ensure the cursor is at the beginning of page 1. Click the **Insert** tab and, in the **Header & Footer** group, click **Footer**.

2   Scroll in the list and then click **Pinstripes**.

Notice how the footer was inserted into the document with a specific font and design. You can add or remove items in the footer. Note that Word inserted a blank header for you at the same time.

3   In the footer, click in **[Type text]**, type: Draft1.

4   In the Selection bar area, click to select this entire line. Then click the **Home** tab and, in the **Font** group, click the arrow for **Font** and change this to **Calibri**. Click the area for the **Size** and change this to **9pt**.

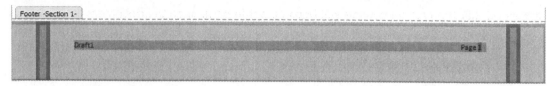

Now adjust the margin for the footer.

5 Under the Header & Footer Ribbon, click the **Design** tab and in the **Position** group, click the down arrow for **Footer from Bottom** twice to reduce the bottom margin.

6 Scroll to the bottom of page 2 to view the footer.

7 In the **Design** tab, click **Close Header and Footer**.

8 Save the document.

Alternating Headers and Footers

Use alternating headers and footers when you want to have different header or footer information on odd- and even-numbered pages in your document (e.g. manuals, large proposals, or reports).

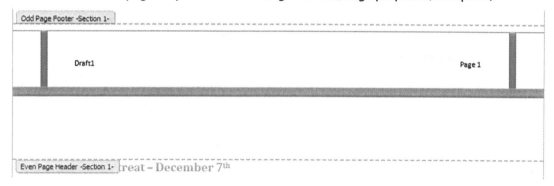

You can set odd and even pages, a different first page, or both. An example of this can be seen with this courseware. The first page of this book does not contain a header or footer, but every subsequent page has a header and footer. These headers and footers vary slightly from the odd and even pages, as well as with each Lesson. Notice that the odd page number occurs with the pages on the right, not the ones on the left, as this is how a book is traditionally read, starting with page 1 or the title page on the right side.

Once you set up the headers and footers to be different, you will have to use the **Link to Previous** feature carefully to decide which headers and footers are to be different.

Learn the Skill

In this exercise, you will learn how to alternate headers and footers in Staff Retreat Presentation Notes - Student.

1 Double-click anywhere in the footer area at the bottom of page 2.

The footer should become active and available for modifications; the Header & Footer Ribbon should also be active on the screen.

It may be that the first blank page will become a title page once the document content is finalized. You may also want to set up double-sided printing for the report to comply with corporate policy and also enable others to read the report as if reading a book.)

2   Click the **Design** tab and, in the **Options** group, click **Different First Page** and **Different Odd and Even Pages**.

3   Scroll to the bottom of page 1 to view what changes were made to the document.

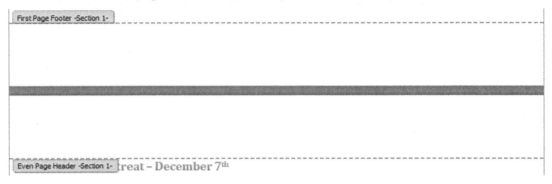

Notice that the page number is gone from page 1 and that there is a new identifier for the footer area.

4   Scroll to the bottom of page 2 to check the footer.

Notice that there is nothing in the footer area. This is because you have changed the layout to be alternating which, in this scenario, means the page numbers will sit over each other when the report is closed.

5   Click the **Design** tab and, in the **Header & Footer** group, click **Footer** and then click **Blank (Three Columns)**.

6   Click the first [Type text] and then on the **Design** tab, in the **Header & Footer** group, click **Page Number**.

7   Click **Current Position** and then **Accent Bar 1**.

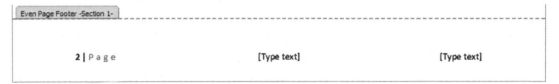

8   Click the middle [Type text] and press (Delete). Click the last [Type text] and type: Draft1.

Now change the footer text for the odd pages.

9   Scroll to the bottom of page 3, click in the Selection Bar area to select this footer and then press Delete.

10   On the **Design** tab, in the **Header & Footer** group, click **Footer** and then click **Blank (Three Columns)**.

11   Click the first [Type text] and then type: Draft1.

12   Click the middle [Type text] and press (Delete). Click the last [Type text] and then on the **Design** tab, in the **Header & Footer** group, click **Footer**, click **Current Position,** and click **Accent Bar 2**.

Word has now inserted the new header and footer styles, although you need to make some modifications to the page for the Draft text as well as the position of the page number on page 3.

13 Scroll up and down in the document to view the footers for the odd and even pages.

Notice how the page numbers will overlap each other when the report is closed. Notice that the footer for the even pages is slightly higher than the first page.

14 Scroll to the footer on page 2 or page 4 and then, on the **Design** tab, and in the **Position** group, click the down arrow twice to reduce the bottom margin.

15 Scroll to the footer on page 3 and repeat step 14 to ensure the margin here matches the other two sections.

16 In the **Design** tab, click **Close Header and Footer**.

17 Save and close the document.

Working with Document Backgrounds

Backgrounds can be used to enhance online documents, e-mail documents or Web pages. Backgrounds use colors, patterns, pictures, gradients, textures, or watermarks to make your documents more interesting. They can be an informative logo or a decorative texture.

To add a background to a document, on the **Page Layout** tab, in the **Page Background** group, click the type of background you want to apply.

Adding Watermarks

Watermarks can be text, graphics, shapes, or pictures that appear behind text. Watermarks appear paler than regular graphics.

Watermarks are used for printed documents while other backgrounds are for online documents. Watermarks anchor to a header or footer as their point of reference. Watermarks print with the document.

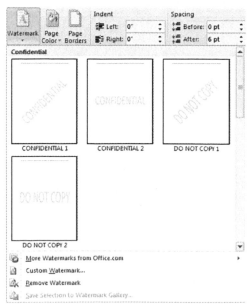

You can choose a watermark from the gallery list, customize it for your own purposes, or remove it. You can also save a watermark design to the gallery. For example, if you need to use Draft Copy Only as a watermark on several documents, you can create this text as a watermark on a blank document and then save it to the Watermark Gallery.

Using Page Color

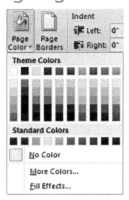

Use background colors for online documents or Web pages, as they do not print with the document text.

Be careful about the background effect as it can detract from the message in the document. For instance, how easy is it for your audience to read the text if you use a dark background with a light text color? If you use a picture for the background, will the audience focus on the picture rather than the message? Make a habit of changing the views once you apply a background to look at it from different perspectives, e.g. is the background more suitable for a Web page?

This option has a live preview available so you see the effect of choosing this color immediately on the document. This is useful when comparing the background color with watermark text, changing the font colors, or for any pictures that may also be inserted in the document.

Use **More Colors** to fine-tune the color to be used in the background.

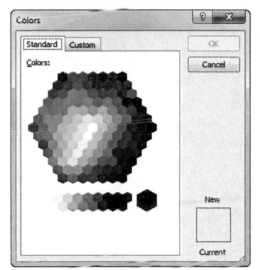
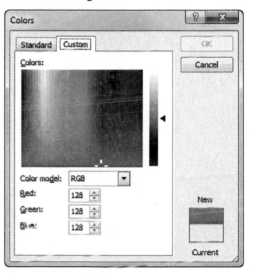

Use **Fill Effects** to set a gradient, pattern or texture:

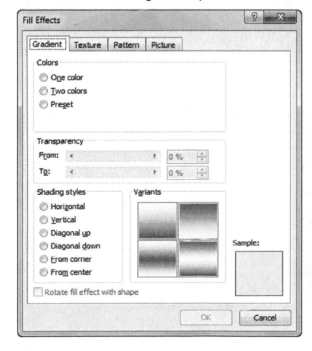
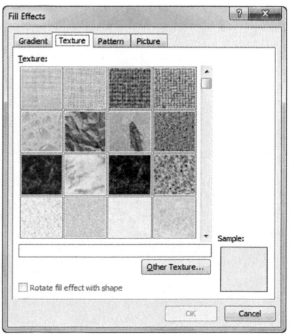

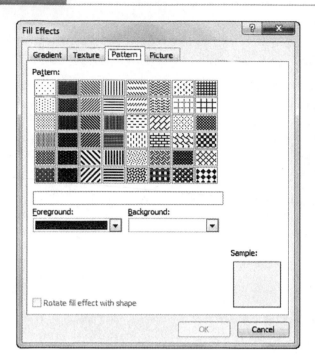

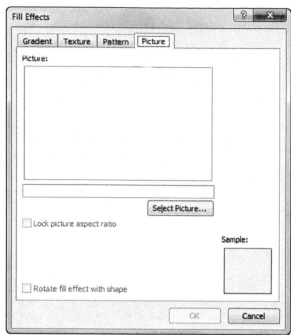

Applying Page Borders

Page borders are an effective way to draw the reader's eye to the document, especially if set up to emphasize items in the document. A page border appears on every page unless a section break is inserted and the page border removed for that section.

As with watermarks and page colors, be careful about the colors you use or the size of the borders. These should be enhancements to a focal point, which generally is the text.

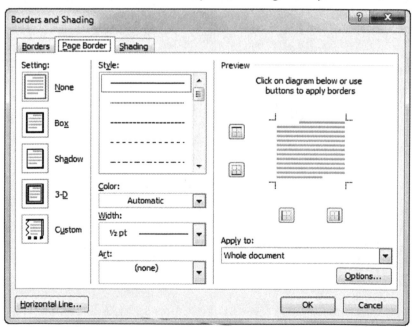

Setting	List of existing types of border settings, e.g. to have border appear on all four sides, click Box.
Style	Line style for the border.
Color	Color of the border.

Width	Width of the border.
Art	Use art shapes instead of lines; click the down arrow to choose from the large variety.
Preview	Displays a preview of all settings selected, with buttons to turn specific border sides on or off.
Apply to	Which part of the document will have these borders applied.
Options	Set other options i.e., amount of space between the border and text, whether the border is measured from the edge of the page or the text.
Horizontal Line	Choose from a list of horizontal lines provided by Microsoft to insert a different line style than currently available in the Style or Art lists.

Learn the Skill

In this exercise, you will learn how to add different types of backgrounds to a corporate profile report that will be sent to Travel Directors for review. This document will also be viewed online, either from the company intranet or the company Web site.

1   Open *Corporate Profile* and save as Corporate Profile - Student.

2   Click the **Page Layout** tab and, in the **Page Background** group, click **Watermark**.

3   Click **Custom Watermark**.

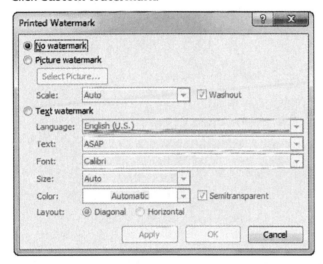

4   Click **Text watermark**. Then click the arrow for **Text** and click **DRAFT**.

5   Leave all other items as set and then click **OK**.

Tolano Adventures provides eco-friendly travel services to a growing market. All our tours meet stringent requirements to ensure these adventures have the lowest carbon footprint and are environmentally friendly. At Tolano, we are pleased to be achieving our goal to "go green" at every opportunity.

Tolano Adventures is a division of Tolano Environment Consulting, based in New York. We also have Travel Directors at international locations to serve you better.

We work with a number of international vendors and are always looking for new and exciting adventures. Each new adventure is reviewed by our Site Assessor along with the Travel Director to ensure it meets our standards for being ecological while offering maximum enjoyment and opportunities for participation.

We review all our tours annually to ensure that:

- they have a low environmental impact (particularly the more popular ones)
- there is no significant change in their environmental impact compared to the previous year
- guests are still getting maximum enjoyment from them
- the cost is reasonable compared to the number of bookings and environmental impact

Occasionally we will also review a tour if there has been some noticeable change or danger such as in the case of avalanches, earthquakes, or other natural disasters.

Some of the more popular tours we offer include:

- Rock or Ice Climbing
- Heli-skiing
- Hot Air Ballooning
- Whale Watching
- Cycling

For more information about the exciting tours we offer, visit us at www.tolanoadventures.com.

This marks the report with a watermark so everyone reading it knows this is a draft.

As the report will be viewed online, try adding background color.

6   Click the **Page Layout** tab and in the **Page Background** group, click **Page Color**.

7   Point at different colors to see how they change the appearance of the document.

This is an example of why you need to be careful when choosing colors for a document, regardless of whether it is the background or within the document. Note how darker colors emphasize the gold star bullets, but may make the text harder to read; however, some lighter colors also make the text difficult to read.

8   Click a color that you consider suitable for the text.

9   Save the document.

Using Themes

3.2

Themes are sets of integrated document designs that make your online documents attractive and effective. A theme provides a look for the document by using colors, fonts and graphics. Each theme has options such as background color or graphics, body and heading styles, bullets, horizontal lines, hyperlink colors and table border colors. You can apply a theme to achieve a professional and well-designed document for viewing in Word, in an e-mail, or on the web.

Themes are best used for Web pages, HTML documents, e-mail documents and online documents. Theme options such as styles, lines and graphics appear when printed, but backgrounds and animated graphics will not appear when the document is printed. To see the animation of theme graphics, view the document using the Web Layout view mode or in a web browser.

You can apply a new theme, change or remove a theme. You can also customize an existing theme or create your own.

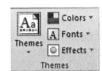

Applying Themes

Applying a theme to a document is a matter of matching a theme to the message. Word includes a live preview of the theme and its options so you can decide quickly whether the theme is appropriate for the message in the document.

To apply a theme to a document, on the **Page Layout** tab, in the **Themes** group, click **Themes**.

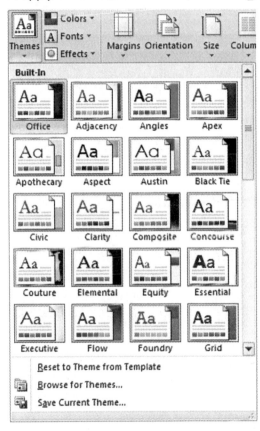

Customizing Themes

You can customize a theme to suit the message in your document. You can change the color scheme by using one from another theme, or create your own colors such as those used in your company logo. You can also change the fonts or effects for a theme.

- To change the colors used in a theme, on the **Page Layout** tab, in the **Themes** group, click **Colors**.

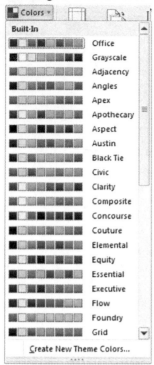

- To change the fonts used in a theme, on the **Page Layout** tab, in the **Themes** group, click **Fonts**.

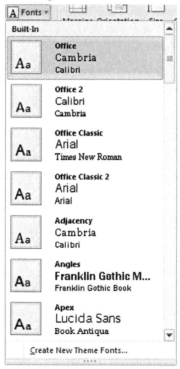

- To change the effects used in a theme, on the **Page Layout** tab, in the **Themes** group, click **Effects**. These affect any lines or fill effects used in your document.

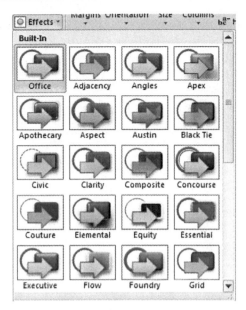

If these choices still do not meet your requirements, you can customize these and save the new theme. After making your choices for colors, fonts or effects, on the **Page Layout** tab, in the **Themes** group, click **Themes** and then **Save Current Theme**. Note that, while you cannot create your own themes, you can choose one of these to be included in your own theme.

Learn the Skill

In this exercise, you will learn how to apply a theme to the draft online corporate profile, and then modify certain parts of the theme.

1   Click the **Page Layout** tab and then in the **Themes** group, click **Themes**.

2   Point at the different themes to preview effects on the document.

Notice how each theme has its own set of designs including font, size, and colors.

3   Click the **Foundry** theme.

Tolano Adventures provides eco-friendly travel services to a growing market. All our tours meet stringent requirements to ensure these adventures have the lowest carbon footprint and are environmentally friendly. At Tolano, we are pleased to be achieving our goal to "go green" at every opportunity.

Tolano Adventures is a division of Tolano Environment Consulting, based in New York. We also have Travel Directors at international locations to serve you better.

We work with a number of international vendors and are always looking for new and exciting adventures. Each new adventure is reviewed by our Site Assessor along with the Travel Director to ensure it meets our standards for being ecological while offering maximum enjoyment and opportunities for participation.

Suppose you like the color previously set and the new font size but want a different font for the document.

4   Click the **Page Layout** tab and then in **Themes** group, click **Fonts**.

5 Point at different themes to see the font change and then click **Thatch**.

Tolano Adventures provides eco-friendly travel services to a growing market. All our tours meet stringent requirements to ensure these adventures have the lowest carbon footprint and are environmentally friendly. At Tolano, we are pleased to be achieving our goal to "go green" at every opportunity.

Tolano Adventures is a division of Tolano Environment Consulting, based in New York. We also have Travel Directors at International locations to serve you better.

We work with a number of international vendors and are always looking for new and exciting adventures. Each new adventure is reviewed by our Site Assessor along with the Travel Director to ensure it meets our standards for being ecological while offering maximum enjoyment and opportunities for participation.

6 Save and close the document.

Lesson Summary

In this lesson, you looked at different features you can use to format a document such as changing the margins, the paper size, or the orientation. You should now be able to:

- ☑ work with document formatting
- ☑ change the paper size
- ☑ change the orientation
- ☑ change the margins
- ☑ insert page breaks

- ☑ insert page numbers
- ☑ insert headers or footers
- ☑ customize headers or footers
- ☑ work with odd/even pages
- ☑ apply backgrounds or themes

Review Questions

MMM
Go online for Additional Review and Activities

1. Explain the purpose of setting margins for a document.

2. Explain the difference between a soft and manual page break.

3. Explain what the different section breaks are and how you might use each one.

4. Explain what a header or footer is.

5. How can you use themes?

Microsoft®

Word 2010

Core Certification

Lesson 6: **Getting Ready to Print**

Lesson Objectives

In this lesson, you will explore different ways to prepare your document for printing, including proofing and previewing the document. On completion of this lesson, you should be able to:

☐ check the spelling

☐ check the grammar

☐ check for contextual text errors

☐ use AutoCorrect

☐ add comments for review

☐ preview the document

☐ print the document

Proofing Your Document

5.1

Before printing your document, you should proof it for spelling or grammatical mistakes, contextual errors, or repetitive text. Word provides tools to help automate some of the proofing so you can concentrate on the document flow instead of the data entry. Word also displays visual hints when it encounters items that should be reviewed prior to finalizing the document:

Texr	Red wavy lines indicate a word that is not recognized in the dictionary set for Word.
move the	Green wavy lines indicate a grammatical or structural error in this sentence.
what to where	Blue wavy lines indicate a possible contextual text error.

Checking the Spelling and Grammar

The Spelling and Grammar feature provides options for checking spelling and grammatical errors, and offers the option of creating custom dictionaries.

- The spelling portion of the feature checks for incorrect spelling, duplicate words, and incorrect capitalization.

- The grammar portion of the feature uses natural language grammar to detect sentences with grammatical errors or weak writing style, based on standards set in the language used to check your spelling and grammar.

The automatic Spelling and Grammar feature works in the background to check for spelling and grammatical mistakes as you type. Using this feature enables you to correct the mistakes immediately, or to wait until you have finished creating the document. To activate the Spelling and Grammar feature:

- On the **Review** tab, in the **Proofing** group, click **Spelling & Grammar**, or
- press F7.

When Word finds the first misspelled word in the document, the word is displayed in the Spelling and Grammar dialog box in red - the same color as the wavy lines in the document.

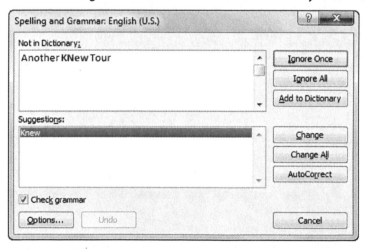

Not in Dictionary	Displays the misspelled word, the grammatical or contextual error. Use one of the options to change or ignore the item, or click in the box to make a change directly.
Suggestions	Displays a list of suggestions for the misspelled word. If the correct word is in the list, click it and then click **Change**. Alternatively, you can double-click the word in the list to change it immediately.
Ignore Once	Ignore this occurrence, but continue to find other occurrences of words with the same spelling.

Ignore All	Ignore all occurrences of words with this spelling, e.g. person's name or specialized industry terminology.
Add to Dictionary	Add the word to the custom dictionary. Word uses a custom dictionary in addition to the regular dictionary to check the spelling in your documents.
Change	Change this occurrence with the selected word in the **Suggestions** box.
Change All	Change all words with this spelling to the selected word in the **Suggestions** box.
AutoCorrect	Add this item to the AutoCorrect list so it will be corrected every time you misspell it.
Check grammar	Choose whether to have Word check the grammar at the same time as the spelling.
Options	Choose how the spelling and grammar options should work.
Undo	Click this button to undo the spelling or grammatical change recently made.
Undo Edit	Click this button to undo the spelling or grammatical change recently made. This button only appears if you make a change directly in the Not in Dictionary box.
Resume	Click this button to continue with the spelling and grammar check after making a change directly in the Not in Dictionary box.

You may also notice that the Proofing tool on the status bar changes in appearance if there is a potential error in the document. A ![icon] icon means Word is beginning the check; ![icon] means there are no errors whereas ![icon] indicates there is at least one item you need to check in the document.

To view the first error in the document, click the ![icon] icon on the status bar. Word then moves to the error location and displays a list of suggestions for the misspelled word. If one of these words is the correct spelling, click it.

Grammatical errors appear in the same green color in the Spelling and Grammar dialog box as in the document.

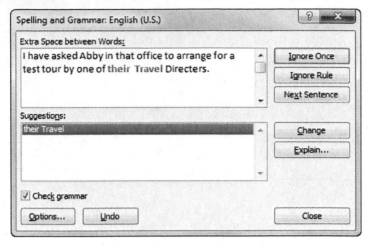

[Rule] box	Displays the reason why the text was marked with the green wavy line. The rule will change with the grammatical error.
Suggestions	Provides a list of suggestions on how to correct this error.
Ignore Once	Ignore this occurrence and continue to show other occurrences of the same grammatical error.
Ignore Rule	Ignore the rule for the entire document.
Next Sentence	Move to the next sentence containing a grammatical error.
Change	Change the noted error in the top box with the highlighted option in the **Suggestions** box.
Explain	Provides an explanation for the error and how to correct it.
Options	Choose how the spelling or grammar options should work.

Contextual errors refer to words that have the same sound, but different spellings and meanings. Examples of common contextual errors are:

- there (refers to a place), their (possessive form), or they're (contraction for they are), or
- its (possessive form) and it's (contraction for it is), or
- where (refers to a location) and wear (attire or clothing), or
- bear (the animal, or to endure or support) and bare (plain or empty), or
- to (going somewhere) and two (number) and too (include this).

Contextual errors appear in blue text in the Spelling and Grammar dialog box, the same color as the wavy line in the document.

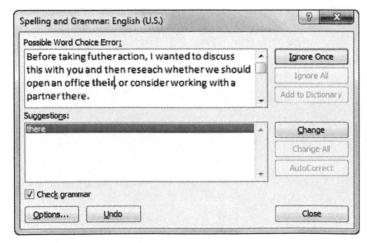

MMM
Invitation to
Weekend
Event Online
Exercise

Learn the Skill

In this exercise, you will correct spelling mistakes in a memo using the automatic spelling and grammar option.

1   Open *Camel Tours* and save this as Camel Tours – Student.

2   Click the **Review** tab and, in the **Proofing** group, click **Spelling & Grammar**.

3   Ensure *New* is selected in the **Suggestions** box and then click **Change**.

4   Continue changing the incorrect spelling in the document. When you see Taroudant in the list, click **Ignore Once** as this is the correct spelling for this city.

5   Continue making the appropriate changes for the spelling errors, including:

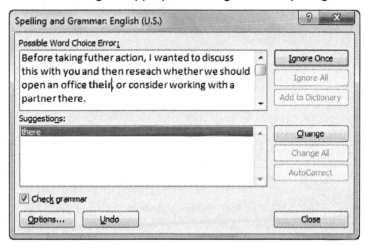

6   Make the appropriate choice for Nick Klassen's last name.

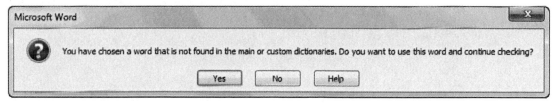

7   Click **Yes** and make the final change for Nick's title.

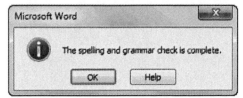

8   Click **OK** and then save the document.

Using AutoCorrect

5.2

Use this feature to have Word automatically correct common spelling, punctuation and capitalization errors as you type. When you make an error Word recognizes, Word automatically replaces the mistake with the appropriate correction (such as capitalizing the first letter of the word at the beginning of a sentence). You can also use AutoCorrect to expand abbreviated words or create specific symbols such as the copyright symbol ©.

To access the AutoCorrect option, click the **File** tab, click **Options**, and then in the **Proofing** category, click **AutoCorrect Options**.

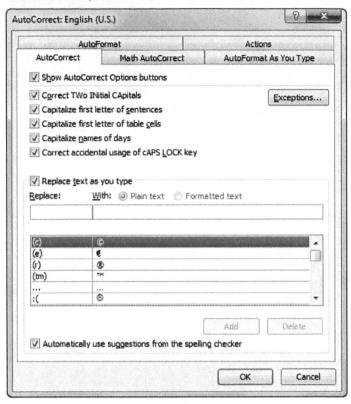

Notice that the first five options Microsoft provides help you concentrate on entering the text, not how you enter it. For example, after you type a period at the end of sentence, you can continue typing as Word automatically capitalizes the first letter of the next sentence.

Occasionally you may see items where Word did not apply the AutoCorrect option. This may be a result of an exception rule set in place for text. Use **Exceptions** to enter text where you do not want AutoCorrect to change the text based on these rules.

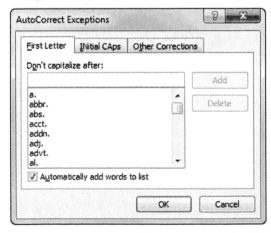

AutoCorrect may not change the text because the last word in the sentence is a number or, if you have edited the text at that point several times, Word recognizes you do not want this change.

When making entries into AutoCorrect, use **Replace text as you type** to help you focus on entering the text. Consider the following:

Replace	Enter the text you want Word to replace with the corresponding item in the **With** box. This can be commonly misspelled words, phrases, abbreviations, or special characters.
With	Enter the replacement for the entry in the **Replace** box.
Add	Once you enter the item in the **Replace** and **With** boxes, you must click this button to add the new items to the list.
Delete	Select the item from the list and then use this button to remove the entry from the list.
Automatically use suggestions from the spelling checker	Word provides suggestions when it finds an "incorrect" spelling first, it will then look in the list of AutoCorrect replacement items which contain many of the most commonly misspelled words, symbols or abbreviations.

Once you make an entry in the AutoCorrect list, each time you type the **Replace** entry incorrectly, Word automatically replaces this entry with the item you put into the **With** list when you press the ⬚Spacebar⬚ or another character that Word recognizes as non-text such as a period, comma, semi-colon, or quotation mark. A small blue box will also appear below the item to indicate this item exists in AutoCorrect.

as shown in ©

When you place the cursor over this box, it displays the **AutoCorrect Options** button.

as shown in ©

MMM
AutoCorrect
Entry Online
Exercise

You can then click the box or click the down arrow for this button to see the options available for this text entry.

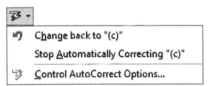

You can also press BACKSPACE to change the AutoCorrect entry back to the original text entered.

Note that, while these options may save time in text entry, you are still required to visually proof your document. There are exceptions to every rule (e.g. a period after a date like January 01st will not automatically have the next character capitalized); always double-check your document or ask someone else to review the document before finalizing it.

Learn the Skill

In this exercise, you will work with the AutoCorrect feature to set up shortcuts for the company names and then use this during text entry.

1   Create a new blank document, type: Tolano Environmental Consulting and press ⬚Enter⬚.

2   On the next line, type: Tolano Adventures and press ⬚Enter⬚.

3   Click the **File** tab and then click **Options** in the left panel of Backstage.

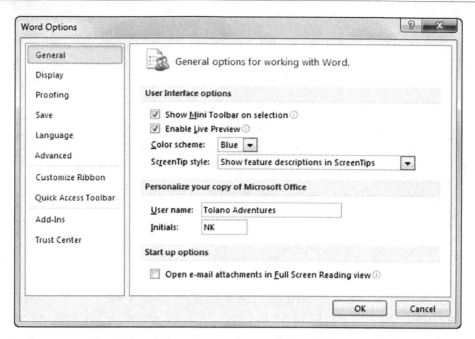

4   In the pane at the left, click **Proofing** and then click **AutoCorrect Options**.

5   Click in the **Replace** text box, type: tec and then click in the **With** text box to type: Tolano Environmental Consulting.

6   Click **Add**.

7   Click in the **Replace** text box, type: ta and then click in the **With** text box to type: Tolano Adventures. Then click **Add**.

8   Click **OK** to close the AutoCorrect and Word Options windows.

9   Switch to the *Camel Tours – Student* document and below Vice President, type: ta plus a space.

     Tolano Adventures should appear as soon as you press the (Spacebar).

10   Save the document.

Using Comments

5.3

When working with documents, you may find that you require advice on the document content or layout; or you may want to insert reminders to yourself regarding text or formatting changes. The **Comment** feature can be used in as the same way as sticky notes. Comments are inserted into the document in balloon objects, making it easy to identify who made the comment and to move from one comment to the next. Comments only display on the screen; they will not be printed as part of your document, unless you choose to.

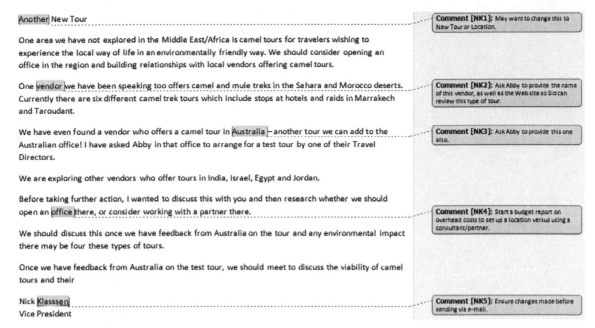

The **Review** tab provides the following options in the **Comments** group:

To insert a comment, on the **Review** tab, in the **Comments** group, click **New Comment**.

To view the comments, on the **Review** tab, in the **Comments** group, click **Previous** or **Next**.

To delete a comment, click the comment to be deleted and then on the **Review** tab, in the **Comments** group, click **Delete**.

Learn the Skill

In this exercise, you will insert comments into the Camel Tours document as reminders.

1   Press (Ctrl)+(Home) to move quickly to the beginning of the document.

2   Select the title, click the **Review** tab and in the **Comments** group, click **New Comment**.

3   Type: May want to change this to New Tour or Location.

4   In the One vendor we have ... paragraph, select vendor and then on the **Review** tab, click **New Comment**.

5   Type: Ask Abby to provide the name of this vendor, as well as the Web site so Sid can review this type of tour.

6   Add the following comments for the selected text:

Text	Location	Comment
Australia	4th paragraph	Get Abby to provide this one also.
Office	6th paragraph	Start a budget report on overhead costs to set up a location versus using a consultant/partner.
Klassen	Closing salutation	Ensure changes made before sending via e-mail.

7   Save the document.

Preparing to Print

Once you are satisfied with the document content, you may want to preview it for overall page layout. Although the screen gives an accurate view of how the document will print, you may still want to check the document before you use the Print command. For example, you may want to check this is if you create and modify your document in the office, but then want to print it at home, as the margins may change based on the printer type. A laser printer allows for margins usually to a minimum of 0.25" whereas an inkjet printer may have a minimum of 0.55". By previewing the document with the current printer selected, you can check whether you need to make any other changes before printing.

With Word 2010, when you activate the Print command, you have a preview of the document in Backstage. You can also select which options you may need to change for the printer, what you want to print along with the document, or add properties to the file.

In this view, the document appears as it will when printed. All headers, footers, multiple columns and page numbers appear in their appropriate locations. You can also make changes to the layout such as margins, paper size, or orientation – similar to activating the Page Setup dialog box.

To preview or print a document:

- Click the **File** tab and click **Print**, or
- press Ctrl + P.

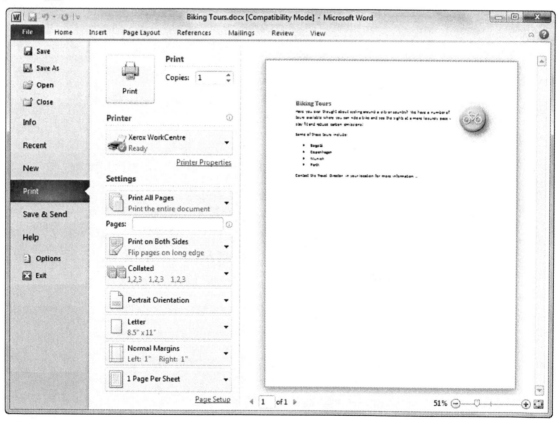

Use the status bar at the lower right to zoom in or out of the previewed document. The above sample is a preview of a one page document with comments; if this was a multiple page document, you could use the scroll bar at the right to move to different pages or the page navigator at the bottom left of the preview.

You can choose to print the document in this format or without the comments using the print options at the left of the preview. All print options are available in this area:

Print	Click to send the document to print using options set.
Copies	Specify the number of copies to be printed.
Printer	Indicates which printer is active. To change settings for the printer (e.g. print in color), click **Printer Properties**.
Print All Pages	Set print options for the document:

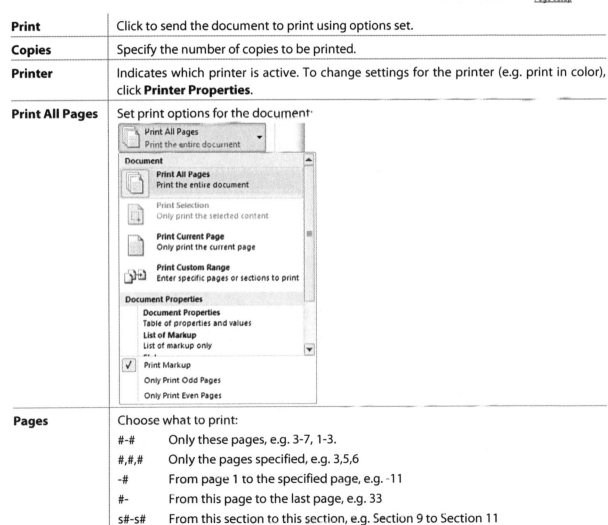

Pages	Choose what to print:
	#-# Only these pages, e.g. 3-7, 1-3.
	#,#,# Only the pages specified, e.g. 3,5,6
	-# From page 1 to the specified page, e.g. -11
	#- From this page to the last page, e.g. 33
	s#-s# From this section to this section, e.g. Section 9 to Section 11

Print on Both Sides	Set how the double-sided option will print the document: long or short edge. 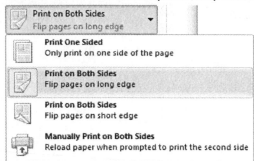
Collated	Set how multiple copies of the document will be printed, as all copies of page 1, then page 2, and so on, or print the entire document for each copy requested. 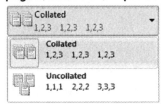
Portrait Orientation	Change the orientation here, as needed. 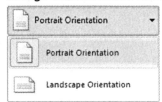
Letter	Change the paper size, as needed. 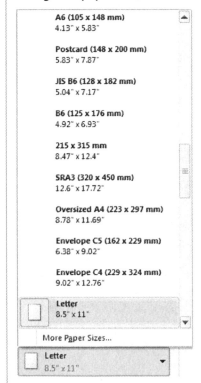

                                                                                    3240-1 v1.00 © CCI Learning Solutions Inc.

Normal Margins	Change the margins as needed. 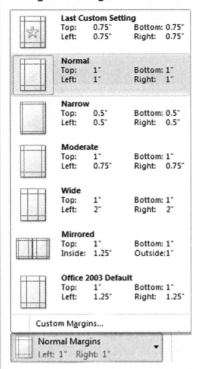
1 Page per Sheet	Set how many pages of the document will print on each sheet of paper; this is very useful for printing a draft of the layout of the document on the minimum number of pages. 
Page Setup	Activate the Page Setup dialog box to make other page layout changes to the document, as needed.

You should save your document prior to printing so that, if problems occur during printing, you will not lose your work.

Learn the Skill

In this exercise, you will preview a document, make some changes to how it will print, and then send it to print. Check with your instructor regarding the printer to use.

1   Open *Biking Tours*. Then click the **File** tab and click **Print** from the panel at the left.

2   Click **Portrait Orientation** and then click **Landscape Orientation**.

3   Click **Normal Margins** and then click **Wide**.

    Notice how the document preview changes with each change you make.

4   Click **Print** to print the document.

5   Close the document without saving.

6   With the *Camel Tours – Student* document active on the screen, click the **File** tab and then click **Print**.

7   Click **Print All Pages** and then click **Print Markup** to turn this feature off.

    The comments will not print now; if you chose to print with the comments, the text size in the document will reduce to accommodate the comments within the width of the paper size selected.

8   Click **Print All Pages** and then click **Print Markup** to display the comments again.

9   Click **Print** to print the document.

10 Close the document without saving.

Lesson Summary

In this lesson, you explored different ways to prepare your document for printing. You should now be able to:

☑ check the spelling   ☑ add comments for review

☑ check the grammar   ☑ preview the document

☑ check for contextual text errors   ☑ print the document

☑ use AutoCorrect

Review Questions

MMM
Go online for
Additional
Review and
Activities

1.   Explain the difference between spelling errors, grammatical errors, and contextual text errors.

2.   Explain how you could use the AutoCorrect feature to help with entering text characters.

3.   When might you add comments to a document?

4.   Discuss why you might want to preview the document before printing.

5.   Give examples of why you might want to change the print options for a document.

Microsoft®
Word 2010
Core Certification

Lesson 7: Using Tables

Lesson Objectives

In this lesson, you will look at tables and how they can be used to align text in a document. You will also learn how to format a table and its contents. On successful completion of this lesson, you should be able to:

☐ create tables

☐ enter items into tables

☐ adjust rows and columns

☐ merge and split cells

☐ insert and delete cells, rows and columns

☐ format tables

☐ modify table properties

Working with Tables

2.5

One of the quickest and easiest ways to arrange columns of text and numbers in Word is to use the Table feature. You can also use this feature to group paragraphs side by side and create many types of forms by adding borders and shading.

The Table feature is similar to a spreadsheet program such as Microsoft Excel, as it makes use of cells, rows and columns to arrange text and graphics. You can insert spreadsheets from Excel into your Word document, and then make changes to column widths or borders. Similarly, you can insert tables you created in Word into an Excel worksheet. Excel treats the data like any other spreadsheet data.

Note the following when you are working with tables:

- Each horizontal line in a table is called a row. Rows are numbered consecutively downward (e.g. 1, 2, 3, 4, etc.).

- Each vertical line is called a column. Columns are listed alphabetically from left to right (e.g. A, B, C, D, etc.).

- The intersection of a row and column is called a cell. The cell uses the column letter and row number as its identification. For example, B5 means you are in the second column across, and five rows down.

You can create tables using one of the following methods:

- Drag from the top corner of the grid in the Table command to specify the number of columns and rows you want in the new table. Word displays the number of columns by the number of rows above the grid as confirmation of your selection.

- Use **Insert Table** to display a dialog box to specify options for the table. Word creates the table in a way that is similar to using the grid option, but includes any settings specified in the Insert Table dialog box.

- Use **Draw Table** to draw the outside border as well as the borders for each row or column to be inserted in a table. This feature can also be used to draw rows, columns, or cells within an existing table.

- Text set up with tab alignments can be converted to tables; you must select the text before activating the Table option.

- Use the displayed grid as your guide to how wide the columns are, how high the rows are, or how text or objects appear in the table.

- You can enter text, numbers or graphics into a cell. If you type more than one line of information in a cell or press Enter within the cell, the height of the cell automatically increases. When you enter more text than can fit on a line in the cell, the text wraps to the next line.

- You can create a table before or after you type the text. Depending on the table information, you may find it is easier to create the table before you type the text. As you enter the text, you will see where you have long lines of text, and which column widths or row heights need to be adjusted.

- Before you type the text, design the overall appearance and layout of the table. You can make adjustments to exact cell size later to accommodate the longest line of text for the rows or columns.

- By default, Word adds a single line border to the table; border lines and shading can be adjusted as required. You can also choose to show or hide the gridlines that appear when you remove borders in a table.

- The gridlines for a table work in the same way as non-printing characters. They do not print, but show on the screen where the edges of your columns and rows are.

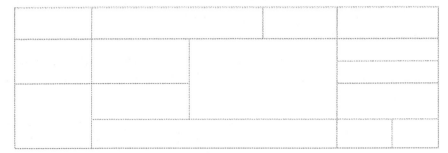

- Display end of cell markers ¤ to show where you are in the table, or to help you determine how text appears in the cells. When entering text in a complex table or if you want to see the finished document, you may want to hide the markers. To show or hide these markers, on the **Home** tab, in the **Paragraph** group, click **Show/Hide ¶.**

- You can apply alignment and formatting to the cell contents, as well as aligning the text vertically at the top, center or bottom of a cell.

- Adjacent cells can be merged horizontally and vertically.

- Text can be rotated by 90° in a cell. You can also insert WordArt in a cell instead of text for a different effect.

- A new table uses the default settings unless set otherwise.

- You can move the table to any position on the document by dragging the Table Selector ⊞ symbol, which appears when you point the cursor in or near the table.

- The Table Tools Ribbon appears when your cursor is in a table. There are two tabs with specific commands you can use to manipulate the table:

Inserting a Table

The **Insert Table** command is best used when you want to create a simple table. This command enables you to specify even column width and row height. These can be adjusted at any time during or after text entry.

There are two ways to insert a table with equal column width and row height:

- On the **Insert** tab, in the **Tables** group, click **Table**.

  Starting from the topmost box in the drop-down, drag to specify the number of columns and rows you want. As you drag across and down, Word displays the number of columns and rows for reference in the title area of this list. This is useful when creating a table with a maximum of 10 columns by 8 rows.

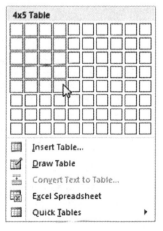

- If you need a larger table, you will need to use the **Insert Table** feature from within this menu. You can also set the following:

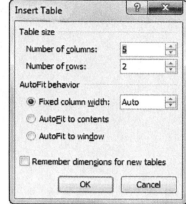

Table size	Enter the number of columns and rows directly in the box or use the increment buttons.
AutoFit behavior	Select how you want text or items entered into the cells of the table. For example, if every column should be 1" in width, ensure *Auto* is active for the *Fixed column width* option.
Remember dimensions for new tables	Select this option as the default for all your new tables. You can adjust column widths or row heights after creating the table.

Learn the Skill

In this exercise, you will learn how to create a simple table to use as a directory for Tolano Adventure employees.

1 Create a new document and save as Directory – Student.

2 Click the **Insert** tab and then in the **Tables** group, click **Table**.

3 Starting at the top box in the grid, drag in the grid for a table with **4** columns and **5** rows.

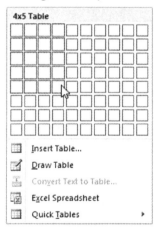

Your new table should be similar to:

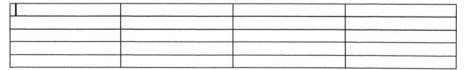

4 Save the document.

Drawing a Table

The **Draw Table** feature enables you to draw a table of any size, creating rows, columns and cells of any height and width. You can also create wider cells or more cells for the table.

To activate the Draw Table feature:

- On the **Insert** tab, in the **Tables** group, click **Table** and then click **Draw Table**, or
- Under **Table Tools**, on the **Design** tab, in the **Draw Borders** group, click **Draw Table**.

The Draw Table feature is active and changes the cursor to the ℓ symbol for drawing. This is similar to using a pencil to draw the lines or borders.

Once you see this symbol, consider the following when ready to draw the table:

- Start by drawing the outside border for the box. Click at approximately where you want the top left corner of the table to begin, and then drag down to where you want the lower right corner of the table to be. Word will display a ⊤ℓ symbol when you drag the mouse as a guide to indicate that you are creating the outside border of the table. The guides on the horizontal or vertical rulers help you determine the measurements for the top left corner or the bottom right corner of the table.

- To draw a horizontal border, click at the location where you want the left side of the border to begin and then drag across to where the end of the border will be. Where there are no vertical borders within the table, Word will display a full border from the left to the right of the outside borders, as seen here.

- To draw a vertical border, click at the location where you want the top of the border to begin and then drag to where the end of the border will be. If there are no horizontal borders within the table, Word displays a full border from the top to the bottom of the outside borders. In the first diagram below, notice how Word draws a border to create a cell once it encounters a horizontal border. In the second diagram, Word has drawn a longer border to create a full column when the cursor was dragged down past the horizontal border.

- To draw a diagonal border, click at the top corner of the cell and then drag diagonally to the lower corner of the cell. A diagonal line can be created from any one corner to another.

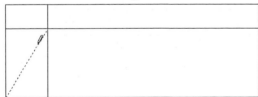

- Use the **Eraser** tool to erase borders in the table in the same way as when you were drawing the borders i.e., click at the beginning of the border to be erased and drag to where you want to finish erasing the border. Word displays the ⌀ symbol to show that you are in Erase instead of Draw mode. As with drawing a border, you can determine how much of a border you want to erase. For instance, the first example shows only the vertical border in this row will be erased, leaving a larger cell. The second example shows how you can erase all the highlighted borders by dragging to select those borders to be erased.

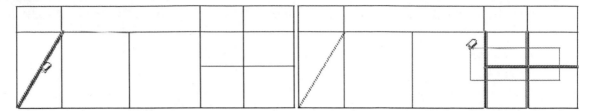

- To turn off the **Draw Table** or **Eraser** tools, click the button again.

Learn the Skill

In this exercise, you will learn how to draw another simple table using the Draw Table feature.

1   Create a new blank document and save it as New Client Requests – Student.

2   Click the **Insert** tab, and in the **Tables** group, click **Table** and click **Draw Table**.

3   Using the rulers as a guide, drag the outside border for a table that is **6.5" (16.5 cm)** in width and **3.5" (8.9 cm)** in height.

4   Using the vertical ruler as a guide, draw horizontal borders at **1" (2.5 cm)**, **2" (5 cm)** and **3" (7.6 cm)**.

5   Using the horizontal ruler as a guide, draw a vertical border at **1.5" (3.8 cm)** and **5" (12.7 cm)**.

6   Save and close the document.

Creating a Quick Table

You can also create a new table using a feature called **Quick Tables**. These are pre-designed tables created by Microsoft based on commonly used document layouts.

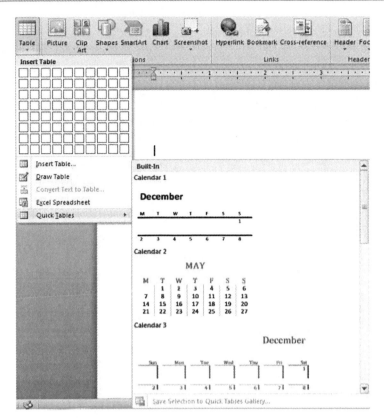

You can also create a table with specific formats and layouts that can be saved to this list. This means you do not have to recreate the table next time you want to use the same format.

Learn the Skill

In this exercise you will create a quick table.

1   Create a new blank document and save as Monthly Calendar – Student.

2   Click the **Insert** tab, and in the **Tables** group, click **Table** and then **Quick Tables**.

3   Scroll through the list to see the different styles available and then click Calendar 2.

    The month that appears is based on the date when you complete this exercise.

4   Save and close the document.

Working with Text

Once you have created a table layout, Word places the insertion point in the first cell of the table so that you are ready to begin typing.

You can move within a table by:

- Pressing (Enter) to add more lines of text in the same cell. This will increase the row height.
- Using the arrow keys to move through the text in the cell.
- Using (Tab) to move forward to the next cell.
- Using (Shift)+(Tab) to move backward to the previous cell.
- If you need to insert a tab or indent, press (Ctrl)+(Tab).
- If you need additional rows to enter text, in the last cell in the last column, press (Tab).

Once text has been entered into a table, you can format it in a similar manner to regular text. You must select the text before making any changes.

Although you may be tempted to format the text as you type, consider waiting until you have entered all the text. This will give you a better idea of what needs to be changed, e.g. column width, row height, length of text or font size.

┌─────────────┐
│   MMM   │
│ Create a   │
│ Calendar Online │
│ Exercise   │
└─────────────┘

Learn the Skill

In this exercise, you will insert text into the table created in the *Directory – Student* document.

1 Click in the first cell of the table and type: Location. Then press (Tab) to move to the next cell to the right.

2 Type: Travel Director in the second cell and then press (Tab).

3 In the third column, type Admin. Assistant and press (Tab).

4 In the last column, type: Phone # and press (Tab) to move to the first cell of the second line.

5 Enter the rest of the table:

Location	Travel Director	Admin. Assistant	Phone #
New York	Madison Cowell		540-555-4321
Cape Town	Jamie Gibson	Robin Black	555-456-1234
Toronto	Toby Belanger	Pauline Hernandez	614-555-6789
London	Andrew McSweeney	Kyla McGill	032 7654 826
Tokyo	Kanda Yamoto	Christie Akira	04 3456 17555
Sydney	Lawrence Jang	Abigail Colby	04 5555 1234
	Curtis Gorski		

6 After entering Curtis Gorski, press (Tab) twice to go to the last cell in the table.

7 Press (Tab) to create a new row.

8 Type: Nick Klassen, Vice President, is in the New York office.

Location	Travel Director	Admin. Assistant	Phone #
New York	Madison Cowell		540-555-4321
Cape Town	Jamie Gibson	Robin Black	555-456-1234
Toronto	Toby Belanger	Pauline Hernandez	614-555-6789
London	Andrew McSweeney	Kyla McGill	032 7654 826
Tokyo	Kanda Yamoto	Christie Akira	04 3456 17555
Sydney	Lawrence Jang	Abigail Colby	04 5555 1234
	Curtis Gorski		
Nick Klassen, Vice President, is in the New York office.			

Don't worry about the length of the text and how it wraps within one cell. This demonstrates how Word handles the text content in a cell, wrapping it when text is longer than the width of the cell. You will change this later.

9 Save the document.

Manipulating Tables

2.6

Text and other objects (e.g. pictures, drawings) can be inserted into a table; however, when you want to change the text or the object, you must select it first.

Selecting Items in the Table

To make changes in the table, you need to select the item. There are some fast methods of selecting items in a table:

- To select an entire column, move the cursor to the top of the column until you see ↓. Click to then select the entire column.
- To select an entire row, move the cursor to the selection bar (i.e. the left margin) and click to select the entire row.
- To select multiple columns or rows, click and drag across the columns or rows.
- To select one cell, move the cursor to the lower left corner of that cell until you see ↗. Then click to select the entire cell.
- To select multiple adjacent cells, click and drag across those cells.
- To select multiple non-adjacent cells, select the first cell, and then press (Ctrl) as you click each subsequent cell to select.
- To select the entire table, click the ⊞ symbol at the top left corner of the table. This symbol appears whenever the mouse cursor is pointing anywhere in a table.
- Under **Table Tools**, on the **Layout** tab, in the **Table** group, click **Select** and then click the appropriate selection.

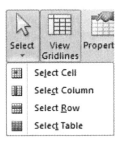

Adjusting the Width or Height

You can adjust the width of each column, the height of each row, and the alignment of the table. You can also evenly space selected rows or columns in a table.

Use one of the following methods to adjust the column width or row height:

- Under **Table Tools**, on the **Layout** tab, in the **Cell Size** group, change the width or height as required, or
- place the cursor on a vertical border on either side of the column to be adjusted. When you see ↔, click and drag the border left or right to the desired column width, or
- place the cursor on the top horizontal border for the row to adjust. When you see ↕, click and drag the border up or down to the desired row height, or
- click the ▦ in the ruler representing the right border of the column to adjust, and drag to the desired width, or
- under **Table Tools**, on the **Layout** tab, in the **Table** group, click **Properties**. Then in the Table Properties dialog box, click the appropriate tab to change the row height, column width, or cell width.

If the cursor is not active in any cell of the table, you will not see the column markers in the ruler for the table. This is a visual clue to check where your cursor is in the document. Only when the cursor is in the table will you be able to activate any options from the Table Tools ribbon for the table.

To distribute the width for each column or height of each row evenly, under **Table Tools**, on the **Layout** tab, in the **Cell Size** group, click **Distribute Rows** or **Distribute Columns**.

Inserting Rows, Columns or Cells

You can easily insert, delete or move rows or columns once you have created a table. However, remember to select the appropriate rows or columns before performing any of these actions.

When inserting multiple rows, columns or cells at once, you must select the appropriate number of units in the table to insert the same number of rows, columns or cells.

To insert a row or column, position the cursor in a cell where you want to insert the row or column and then:

- Under **Table Tools**, on the **Layout** tab, in the **Rows & Columns** group, click the appropriate option to insert, or

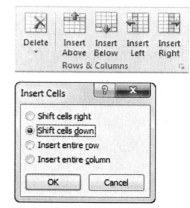

- under **Table Tools**, on the **Layout** tab, in the **Rows & Columns** group, click the **Dialog box launcher**. Then click the appropriate item to insert from the Insert Cells dialog box, or

- in the last cell of the last row in a table, press (Tab) to quickly insert a new row at the bottom of the table, or

- right-click a row or column to display the shortcut menu and then click **Insert**.

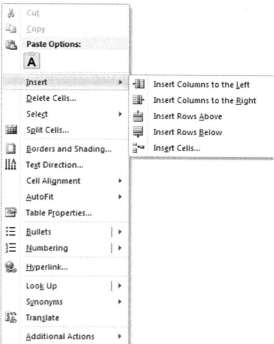

Deleting Rows, Columns or Cells

To delete a row, column or cell, use the same procedure as to insert a row, column or cell. Select the table item to be deleted, and then use one of the following methods:

- Under **Table Tools**, on the **Layout** tab, in the **Rows & Columns** group, click **Delete**, or

- right-click a row or column and then click **Delete Row** or **Delete Column**, or
- if you click **Delete Cells**, the following dialog box appears:

Merging and Splitting Cells

Table cells can be merged to create a single cell, or a cell can be split into more columns or rows as required. Merging is particularly useful when creating a title row. This is an example of why you may want to consider entering the text into the table first before making any changes to the table. Once the text is in the table, you can see, at a glance, which cells should be merged and which just need the width adjusted.

To merge cells, select the cells and then:

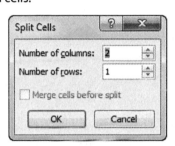

- Under **Table Tools**, on the **Layout** tab, in the **Merge** group, click **Merge Cells**, or
- right-click and then click **Merge Cells**, or
- under **Table Tools**, on the **Design** tab, in the **Draw Borders** group, click **Eraser** to remove the borders from appropriate cells to create larger or merged cells.

To split cells, select the cell to be split and then:

- Under **Table Tools**, on the **Layout** tab, in the **Merge** group, click **Split Cells**, or
- right-click and then click **Split Cells**, or
- under **Table** Tools, on the **Design** tab, in the **Draw Borders** group, click **Draw Table** to add borders in the cell to create or split this cell.

Learn the Skill

In this exercise, you will insert and delete rows in the Directory table.

1   Move the mouse pointer to the left of the first row (in the Selection Bar).

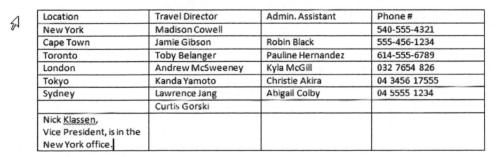

Location	Travel Director	Admin. Assistant	Phone #
New York	Madison Cowell		540-555-4321
Cape Town	Jamie Gibson	Robin Black	555-456-1234
Toronto	Toby Belanger	Pauline Hernandez	614-555-6789
London	Andrew McSweeney	Kyla McGill	032 7654 826
Tokyo	Kanda Yamoto	Christie Akira	04 3456 17555
Sydney	Lawrence Jang	Abigail Colby	04 5555 1234
	Curtis Gorski		
Nick Klassen, Vice President, is in the New York office.			

2   Click to select the entire row.

3   Under **Table Tools**, click the **Layout** tab, and in the **Rows & Columns** group, click **Insert Above**.

Location	Travel Director	Admin. Assistant	Phone #
New York	Madison Cowell		540-555-4321
Cape Town	Jamie Gibson	Robin Black	555-456-1234
Toronto	Toby Belanger	Pauline Hernandez	614-555-6789
London	Andrew McSweeney	Kyla McGill	032 7654 826
Tokyo	Kanda Yamoto	Christie Akira	04 3456 17555
Sydney	Lawrence Jang	Abigail Colby	04 5555 1234
	Curtis Gorski		
Nick Klassen, Vice President, is in the New York office.			

4   With the cells in this row still selected, in the **Merge** group, click **Merge Cells**.

You should now have one large cell here for the title of the table.

5   In this cell, type: Staff List.

6   Select the first two rows in the table and then press ⌃Ctrl+ B and ⌃Ctrl+ E to bold and center the text in these rows.

7   Select the Location row only and then, in the **Rows & Columns** group, click **Insert Below**.

Staff List			
Location	**Travel Director**	**Admin. Assistant**	**Phone #**
New York	Madison Cowell		540-555-4321
Cape Town	Jamie Gibson	Robin Black	555-456-1234
Toronto	Toby Belanger	Pauline Hernandez	614-555-6789
London	Andrew McSweeney	Kyla McGill	032 7654 826
Tokyo	Kanda Yamoto	Christie Akira	04 3456 17555
Sydney	Lawrence Jang	Abigail Colby	04 5555 1234
	Curtis Gorski		
Nick Klassen, Vice President, is in the New York office.		nklassen@tolano.com	

8   Select the first two cells in the last row of the table and then in the **Merge** group, click **Merge Cells**.

9   Repeat step 8 for the remaining two cells in this row.

10   Click in the second cell and type: nklassen@tolano.com.

11   Save the document.

At this point, the table could be considered complete as all the data has been entered. However, you can improve the readability of the table by adjusting the column widths or choosing other options to enhance the contents.

12   Point the mouse cursor at the lower left corner of the e-mail cell.

13   Point the mouse cursor at the vertical border between the two columns in the last row. When you see ╫ drag the border to the right until the text in the first cell is on one line.

	Curtis Gorski		
Nick Klassen, Vice President, is in the New York office.		nklassen@tolano.com	

14   Point the mouse cursor at the vertical border at the right of the Location column. Drag this to the left to reduce the column width by approximately 0.5" (0.2 cm).

15   Point the mouse cursor at the vertical border at the left of the Phone # column. Drag this to the right to reduce the column width by approximately 0.5" (0.2 cm).

Staff List			
Location	Travel Director	Admin. Assistant	Phone #
New York	Madison Cowell		540-555-4321
Cape Town	Jamie Gibson	Robin Black	555-456-1234
Toronto	Toby Belanger	Pauline Hernandez	614-555-6789
London	Andrew McSweeney	Kyla McGill	032 7654 826
Tokyo	Kanda Yamoto	Christie Akira	04 3456 17555
Sydney	Lawrence Jang	Abigail Colby	04 5555 1234
	Curtis Gorski		
Nick Klassen, Vice President, is in the New York office.		nklassen@tolano.com	

16 Select the blank row below the column headings. In the **Rows & Columns** group, click **Delete** and then **Delete Rows**.

17 Increase the size of the title to be **16** and the column headings to be **12**.

18 Save the document.

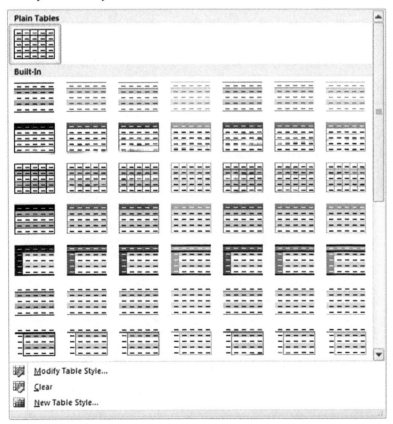

> MMM
> Modify a Table
> Online
> Exercise

Using Table Styles

Table Styles are similar to Quick Styles but are pre-designed formats that can be applied to a table. This is a quick and easy way to enhance a table using a commonly used standard style. Word provides a gallery that can be accessed under **Table Tools**, on the **Design** tab, in the **Table Styles** group, click **More** to display a variety of table styles.

This option also includes a live preview so you can view the effect of this style on the table. You can also modify an existing table style or create your own and save it on the list for easy access.

Learn the Skill

In this exercise, you will apply a table style to the Directory report.

1   Under **Table Tools**, click the **Design** tab and, in the **Table Styles** group, click **More** to display the gallery.

2   Point at the different styles to preview the style for the table; then click **Medium Grid 1 – Accent 3**.

Staff List			
Location	Travel Director	Admin. Assistant	Phone #
New York	Madison Cowell		540-555-4321
Cape Town	Jamie Gibson	Robin Black	555-456-1234
Toronto	Toby Belanger	Pauline Hernandez	614-555-6789
London	Andrew McSweeney	Kyla McGill	032 7654 826
Tokyo	Kanda Yamoto	Christie Akira	04 3456 17555
Sydney	Lawrence Jang	Abigail Colby	04 5555 1234
	Curtis Gorski		
Nick Klassen, Vice President, is in the New York office.		nklassen@tolano.com	

The biggest advantage of table styles is the ability to quickly add colors and other formatting to enhance the look of the table; however, there may be occasions when there is something in the table style that you don't want to use. For example, in this exercise, the color and theme has a professional look, but you don't want the items in the first column to be bold.

3   Select Location and then apply bold to this column heading. Also bold the title in the table.

4   Remove the bold formatting from the rest of the items in the first column, including the note about Nick Klassen.

5   Select the cell with Sydney and also the blank cell below it.

6   Under **Table Tools**, click the **Layout** tab and in the **Merge** group, click **Merge Cells**.

7   Repeat step 6 for the Sydney office phone number and the blank cell below it.

Your table should look like this:

Staff List			
Location	Travel Director	Admin. Assistant	Phone #
New York	Madison Cowell		540-555-4321
Cape Town	Jamie Gibson	Robin Black	555-456-1234
Toronto	Toby Belanger	Pauline Hernandez	614-555-6789
London	Andrew McSweeney	Kyla McGill	032 7654 826
Tokyo	Kanda Yamoto	Christie Akira	04 3456 17555
Sydney	Lawrence Jang	Abigail Colby	04 5555 1234
	Curtis Gorski		
Nick Klassen, Vice President, is in the New York office.		nklassen@tolano.com	

8   Save the document.

Modifying the Borders and Shading

When Word creates a table for the first time, it is automatically created with single line borders for every cell. The borders in a table can be modified to appear with different colors, styles, widths, or turned off completely for individually selected cells. They can also be changed after applying a table style.

Under **Table Tools**, on the **Design** tab, in the **Table Styles** group, click the arrow for **Borders**.

You can change the look by adding shading effects, similar to those available with specific Table Styles. Under **Table Tools**, on the **Design** tab, in the **Table Styles** group, click the arrow for **Shading**.

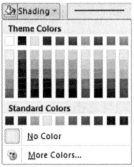

You can draw or modify the properties for borders in a table using features in the **Draw Table** group. Under **Table Tools**, on the **Design** tab, in the **Draw Borders** group, click the appropriate option to draw borders into the table.

 Learn the Skill

In this exercise you will modify the borders for the Directory table.

1   Click the Table Selector to select the entire table.

2   Under **Table Tools**, on the **Design** tab, in the **Draw Borders** group, click the arrow for **Pen Colors**.

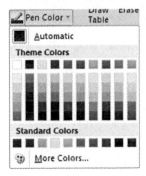

3   Click the **green** in the first row of colors below **Theme Colors**.

4   In the **Draw Borders** group, click the arrow for **Line Weight**.

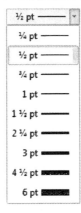

5   Click **2 ¼**.

The mouse pointer should now be a pen and not an arrow.

6   Starting at the left of the top border, begin to draw across to the right side of that border only.

Notice as you begin to draw across, Word displays the full line guide for you:

Staff List			
Location	**Travel Director**	**Admin. Assistant**	**Phone #**
New York	Madison Cowell		540-555-4321
Cape Town	Jamie Gibson	Robin Black	555-456-1234
Toronto	Toby Belanger	Pauline Hernandez	614-555-6789
London	Andrew McSweeney	Kyla McGill	032 7654 826
Tokyo	Kanda Yamoto	Christie Akira	04 3456 17555
Sydney	Lawrence Jang	Abigail Colby	04 5555 1234
	Curtis Gorski		
Nick Klassen, Vice President, is in the New York office.		nklassen@tolano.com	

You have now changed the top border by drawing the border again with the new style options.

Suppose you now want to have this border around the entire table. You can choose to draw each side or use Borders to choose this option.

7   In the **Table Styles** group, click the arrow for **Borders** and then click **Outside Border**.

Staff List			
Location	**Travel Director**	**Admin. Assistant**	**Phone #**
New York	Madison Cowell		540-555-4321
Cape Town	Jamie Gibson	Robin Black	555-456-1234
Toronto	Toby Belanger	Pauline Hernandez	614-555-6789
London	Andrew McSweeney	Kyla McGill	032 7654 826
Tokyo	Kanda Yamoto	Christie Akira	04 3456 17555
Sydney	Lawrence Jang	Abigail Colby	04 5555 1234
	Curtis Gorski		
Nick Klassen, Vice President, is in the New York office.		nklassen@tolano.com	

On reviewing the table, you decide you like the thicker outside border and now want the inside borders to be more noticeable, but not as thick as the outside borders.

8   In the Draw Borders group, click the arrow for **Line Weight** and then click **1 pt**.

9   In the **Table Styles** group, click the arrow for **Borders** and then click **Inside Borders**.

The borders will disappear from the table as you wish to change them.

10   In the **Table Styles** group, click the arrow for **Borders** and then click **Inside Borders** again to apply the **1 pt** borders.

Staff List			
Location	Travel Director	Admin. Assistant	Phone #
New York	Madison Cowell		540-555-4321
Cape Town	Jamie Gibson	Robin Black	555-456-1234
Toronto	Toby Belanger	Pauline Hernandez	614-555-6789
London	Andrew McSweeney	Kyla McGill	032 7654 826
Tokyo	Kanda Yamoto	Christie Akira	04 3456 17555
Sydney	Lawrence Jang	Abigail Colby	04 5555 1234
	Curtis Gorski		
Nick Klassen, Vice President, is in the New York office.		nklassen@tolano.com	

11   Save the document.

Manipulating Text in Cells

Word can format text in a table as with regular text and can align the text vertically in a cell. You can also change the text direction for a different effect.

To change the horizontal or vertical alignment, under **Table Tools**, on the **Layout** tab, in the **Alignment** group, click the appropriate command.

Changing the alignment of the table refers to the position of the table relative to the left and right margins for the document. The alignment alters how the text aligns within each selected cell; to change the alignment for the table, you need to change the table properties.

To change the direction of text in a cell, under **Table Tools**, on the **Layout** tab, in the **Alignment** group, click **Text Direction**. Each time you click this command, it rotates the text and the other alignment options to match the rotation.

You cannot turn text upside down; this text effect can only be achieved using WordArt (will be discussed in this courseware).

Learn the Skill

In this lesson, you will apply vertical alignment to a couple of cells in the Directory table.

1   Select the Sydney cell.

2   Under **Table Tools**, click the **Layout** tab, and then in the **Alignment** group, click **Align Center Left**.

Staff List			
Location	Travel Director	Admin. Assistant	Phone #
New York	Madison Cowell		540-555-4321
Cape Town	Jamie Gibson	Robin Black	555-456-1234
Toronto	Toby Belanger	Pauline Hernandez	614-555-6789
London	Andrew McSweeney	Kyla McGill	032 7654 826
Tokyo	Kanda Yamoto	Christie Akira	04 3456 17555
Sydney	Lawrence Jang	Abigail Colby	04 5555 1234
	Curtis Gorski		
Nick Klassen, Vice President, is in the New York office.		nklassen@tolano.com	

3   Repeat step 2 for the Sydney phone number.

4   Save and close the document.

Converting Text to a Table

You can convert text separated by tab characters, commas or paragraph marks into a table. Word uses these characters to place the text into individual cells. Be careful about the number of tabs between the columns as Word reads each tab character (➔) as a new column in the table.

To convert text information to a table format, select the text and then on the **Insert** tab, in the **Tables** group, click **Table** and click **Convert Text to Table**.

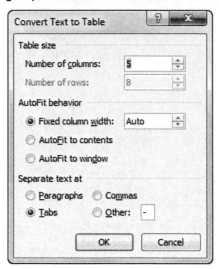

You can also select the text and on the **Insert** tab, in the **Tables** group, click **Insert Table** to quickly create a table.

Learn the Skill

In this exercise, you will learn how to convert a document formatted with tabs to a table.

1   Open *Popular Tours Breakdown* and save it as Popular Tours Breakdown Table - Student.

2   Select the entire document.

3   Click the **Insert** tab, in the **Tables** group, click **Table** and then click **Convert Text to Table**.

4   Accept all the defaults and click **OK**.

Popular Tours				
	2011	2010	2009	2008
Rock Climbing	250	200	150	225
Ice Climbing	175	150	100	125
Whale Watching	350	250	100	260
Hot Air Ballooning	105	60	25	45
Heli Skiing	95	85	70	125
Cycling (Cities)	75	70	65	110

5   Save the document.

Converting a Table to Text

A table can be converted to text with specified separators between the columns of text. This could be beneficial when you want to convert a table created in Word that will then be used in another program such as a spreadsheet or database program.

To convert a table into a text format, click anywhere in the table. Then under **Table Tools**, on the **Layout** tab, in the **Data** group, click **Convert to Text**.

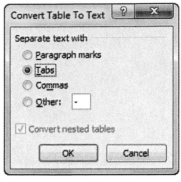

Paragraph marks	Insert a paragraph mark between each column of text, which results with data from each column being on a single line.
Tabs	Insert a tab character between each column of text, resulting in the data appearing as if you had set tab stops for each piece of data.
Commas	Insert a comma between each column of text, resulting in a file that can be imported into a spreadsheet or database program using a common character to identify where columns should be inserted.
Other	Insert another character to separate each column of text. This option is generally used for similar purposes as with commas wherein the file will be imported into another program that requires this special character.

Learn the Skill

In this exercise you will learn how to convert a table of values to one that has commas between the data values so the file can later be imported into Access or Excel.

1   With *Popular Tours Breakdown Table – Student* active, save this as Popular Tours Breakdown (commas) – Student.

2   Place your cursor anywhere within the table.

3   Under **Table Tools**, click the **Layout** tab, in the **Data** group, click **Convert to Text**.

4   Click **Commas** and then click **OK**.

Popular Tours˯,,,

, 2011, 2010, 2009, 2008

Rock Climbing, 250, 200, 150, 225

Ice Climbing, 175, 150, 100, 125

Whale Watching, 350, 250, 100, 260

Hot Air Ballooning, 105, 60, 25, 45

Heli Skiing, 95, 85, 70, 125

Cycling (Cities), 75, 70, 65, 110

5   Save and close this document.

Sorting Lists of Data

You can quickly arrange text by sorting it alphabetically or numerically. The **Sort** command can be used to sort paragraphs, lists created with tab characters, commas, or rows in a table. This feature is particularly useful when arranging a data source before performing a merge, especially if the records need to be in a specific order, or if you want to sort inventory items set up in a table.

You can sort data using up to three different columns as the criteria and then select the order the columns are sorted.

When sorting data in a table, Word will sort by the first column of data unless otherwise specified. Word identifies each column heading making it easier to specify which information to sort.

To sort regular text, on the **Home** tab, in the **Paragraph** group, click **Sort**.

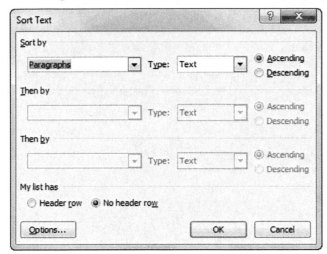

To sort text in a table, under **Table Tools**, on the **Layout** tab, in the **Data** group, click **Sort**.

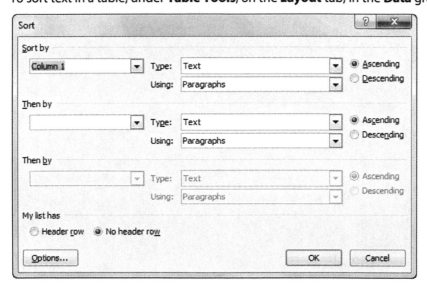

Sort by	Choose which data you want Word to sort the information by first; if the data has column headings, these display when you click the arrow for the list.
Type	Choose the type of data, e.g., text, number, or date.
Using	Select how the data for each row in the table is separated, e.g., paragraphs.
Order	Select whether the data is to be sorted in ascending (A-Z, 0-9) or descending (Z-A, 9-0) order.

Then by	Select the next priority to sort the information by.
My list has	Select whether the information has titles for each of the columns, called a header row.
Options	Select how the data is organized if it is not regular text or table format.

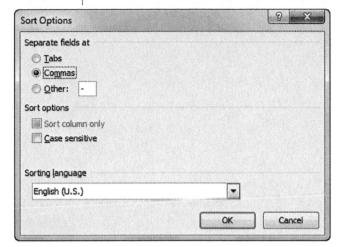

Learn the Skill

In this exercise, you will learn how to sort text and then sort text in a table.

1 Open *Proposal for Haunted Adventure Tours* and then select from Borley House to St. Francis.

2 Click the **Home** tab, and in the **Paragraph** group, click **Sort**.

3 Accept the default settings here and click **OK**.

Borley Rectory, Britain

Edinburgh Castle, Scotland

Monte Cristo Homestead, New South Wales

Okiku's Well at Hameji Castle, Japan

St. Francis Xavier University, Mount St. Bernard College, Antigonish, Nova Scotia, Canada

The Colosseum, Italy

The Whaley House, California, USA

The sites listed for this area are now sorted in ascending alphabetical order.

4 Open *Tour Prices Breakdown* and select every row in the table except for the title row.

5 Under **Table Tools**, click the **Layout** tab, and in the **Data** group, click **Sort**.

6 At the lower left corner of the Sort dialog box, click **Header Row** to indicate you have column titles for the table.

Word has now replaced Column 1 with Travel Item, the heading for the first column.

7 Click the arrow for the **Then by** and click **Total Cost** in the list. Leave both options in ascending order. Click **OK**.

Tour Prices Breakdown (Average based on 7-day Trip)						
Travel Item	Group	Tour	Flight	Hotel (Daily)	Misc.	Total Cost
Antarctica	E					
Bogota Cycling (*Two People)	Eco		1,500	1,500	200	3,200
Copenhagen Cycling (*Two People)	Eco		2,100	3,000	400	5,500
Kilimanjaro Climb	RC	4,000			1,000	5,000
Maui Whale Watching (*Family of 4)	E	200	2,000	1,000		3,200
Mt. Shasta Climb	RC	700				700
North Carolina	RC	500				500
Perth Cycling (*Two People)	Eco		4,000	3,500	500	
Sydney Whale Watching (*Family of 4)	E	250				
Tucson, Mt. Lemmon, Cochise Stronghold	RC	350				350
Vancouver Whale Watching (*Family of 4)	E	500			100	600

Now try a different sort order where the total costs will be the first priority for sorting.

8   With the same rows still selected, click **Sort** once more.

9   Ensure **Header row** is selected and then set the options to the following:

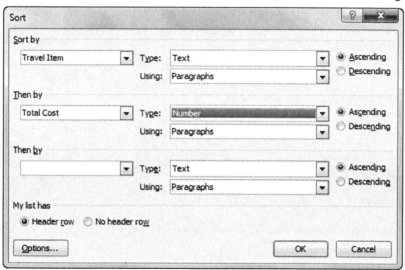

10   Click **OK**.

3240-1 v1.00 © CCI Learning Solutions Inc.

Tour Prices Breakdown (Average based on 7-day Trip)						
Travel Item	Group	Tour	Flight	Hotel (Daily)	Misc.	Total Cost
Copenhagen Cycling (*Two People)	Eco		2,100	3,000	400	5,500
Kilimanjaro Climb	RC	4,000			1,000	5,000
Bogota Cycling (*Two People)	Eco		1,500	1,500	200	3,200
Maui Whale Watching (*Family of 4)	E	200	2,000	1,000		3,200
Mt. Shasta Climb	RC	700				700
Vancouver Whale Watching (*Family of 4)	E	500			100	600
North Carolina	RC	500				500
Tucson, Mt. Lemmon, Cochise Stronghold	RC	350				350
Antarctica	E					
Perth Cycling (*Two People)	Eco		4,000	3,500	500	
Sydney Whale Watching (*Family of 4)	E	250				

11   Close all documents without saving.

Lesson Summary

In this lesson, you looked at tables and how they are used to align text in a document. You also looked at table formatting and content. You should now be able to:

☑ create tables

☑ enter items into tables

☑ adjust rows and columns

☑ merge and split cells

☑ insert and delete cells, rows and columns

☑ format tables

☑ modify table properties

Review Questions

MMM
Go online for Additional Review and Activities

1.   Explain the difference in appearance from a border and the gridline on a table.

2.   How can you create a new table?

3.   If you want to insert a row between the title and the column headings in the following table, in which row would you place the cursor?

Tour Prices Breakdown (Average based on 7-day Trip)						
Travel Item	Group	Tour	Flight	Hotel (Daily)	Misc.	Total Cost
Kilimanjaro Climb	RC	4,000			1,000	5,000

4.   Provide an example of when you would merge a cell.

5.   What alignment options are available for text when working with tables?

Microsoft®

Word 2010

Core Certification

Lesson 8: **Working with Illustrations**

Lesson Objectives

In this lesson, you will look at the different types of illustrations such as pictures, object shapes, text boxes, and diagrams that you can insert into a document, as well as what types of modifications or enhancements can be applied to these illustrations. On successful completion of this lesson, you should be able to:

☐ insert or modify pictures or Clip Art

☐ insert, modify and enhance text boxes

☐ insert and modify WordArt objects

☐ use screenshots

☐ create, arrange and enhance shapes

☐ create a drop cap

☐ add or remove captions

☐ insert and modify SmartArt diagrams

Inserting Pictures

You can insert pictures into any document from various sources such as the Clip Organizer, graphics files, scanned photographs, or online from the Microsoft Clip Art and Media Web site. With Microsoft it is possible to insert picture files in a variety of file formats, in addition to the commonly used Windows Metafile (*.wmf), JPEG File Interchangeable format (*.jpg, *jpeg), Portable Network Graphics (*.png), Windows Bitmap (*.bmp), or Graphics Interchange format (*.gif).

To insert a picture, position the cursor approximately where you want the picture to be placed and, on the **Insert** tab, in the **Illustrations** group, click **Picture**.

Notice how Word displays a dialog box to select the picture file, similar to opening a text file. Navigate to where the picture file is located and then insert it into the document.

You can insert a picture from a Web page by copying it from the Web page and pasting it into the Word document. This picture can also be set as a hyperlink to the Web page, if preferred.

Learn the Skill

In this exercise, you will insert pictures into the Staff Agenda document.

1   Open *Staff Agenda* and save as Staff Agenda (final) – Student.

2   At the top of the document, click the **Insert** tab and then in the **Illustrations** group, click **Picture**.

3   Navigate to where the student data files are located and then select *Tolano logo*.

Staff Retreat

Word has now inserted the picture on the same line as the title.

4   Press the right arrow once to move the cursor and then press ⌈Enter⌋.

The picture should now be on a separate line from the title.

5   Save and close the document.

Inserting Clip Art

4.3

Microsoft provides a number of clip art graphics with Office. Clip art images are usually drawn using vector-based shapes. Clip art and other graphics can be downloaded to your computer from the Microsoft Office Online Web site. To insert a clip art image, position the cursor approximately where you want to place the graphic and, on the **Insert** tab, in the **Illustrations** group, click **Clip Art**.

Once you access the command to insert a clip art image, Word displays the Clip Art window.

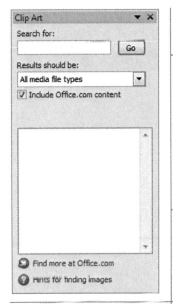

Search for

Enter text for Word to search for specific clip art images.

Results should be

Specify where Word should search for matching clip art images:

All media file types	Everything
Illustrations	Only clip art images
Photographs	Only photographs
Video	Only video files
Audio	Only audio files

Include Office.com content

Include any pictures from Office.com that match the search criteria. If this is deselected, Word displays only those files that have been saved on the local computer or network (specified in the Word options).

Find more at Office.com	Go to the Microsoft Clip Art and Media Web site to search for specific clip art images, view the newest images, or to search for specific media files such as video or audio clips.
Hints for finding images	Displays a Help window with information and tips on how to obtain the best results for the images you want to find.

To insert a clip art image in the results list at the cursor location:

- Click the image in the list, or

- point at the graphic and then click the down arrow for the graphic:

Insert	Insert the image.
Copy	Copy this image into the Office Clipboard for pasting later.
Delete from Clip Organizer	Delete this image from any category where it appears in the Clip Organizer.
Make Available Offline	Copy this image to a specific collection for future use when not connected to the Internet for access to the Microsoft Office Online Web site.
Move to Collection	Move this image from its current location to a specific collection.
Edit Keywords	Edit the keywords used to identify this image for future searches.
Preview/ Properties	Display a larger preview of this image as well as general information for the image, e.g. size of the image, keywords to find this image, name of the image, etc.

To determine whether this image is suitable for your document, point the cursor at the image - a screen tip appears with some keywords included as reference. This is useful when you want to search for other pictures that may be more applicable to your document.

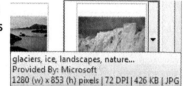

glaciers, ice, landscapes, nature...
Provided By: Microsoft
1280 (w) x 853 (h) pixels | 72 DPI | 426 KB | JPG

Learn the Skill

In this exercise, you will add some pictures to a document.

1   Open *Experiencing Antarctica* and save as Experiencing Antarctica – Student.

2   Position the cursor at the beginning of the first paragraph, Antarctica - a mysterious …

3   Click the **Insert** tab, and then in the **Illustrations** group, click **Clip Art**.

4   Click in the search field of the Clip Art task pane, type: Antarctica and press (Enter) (or click **Go**).

5 Scroll in the list until you see the map of Antarctica and click the picture to insert it into the document:

The position and size of the picture can be changed later in this Lesson. If you don't have this picture in the list, choose another picture in your list. The purpose of this exercise is to demonstrate how to insert and manipulate the picture in the document.

6 Move the cursor to the end of the document and then click the following image:

If you don't have this picture, insert another one from the list.

7 Click the ☒ to close the Clip Art task pane.

8 Save the document.

Manipulating Pictures

Once a picture has been inserted into a document, you can make changes to it, e.g. size, placement, text wrap, brightness and contrast. The picture must be selected before you can make changes. When the picture is selected, the **Picture Tools** ribbon appears with features for manipulating the picture.

These tools enable you to change the position or enhance the appearance of graphics in the document. To edit the actual picture, you must use a dedicated graphic design program such as Adobe Photoshop, Adobe Illustrator, or CorelDRAW. These graphic design programs provide more flexibility for editing pictures than Word, and are beyond the scope of this courseware.

By default, Word inserts graphics using the *in line with text* layout. This means the image inserts with the bottom of the picture lining up with the bottom of the text line. You can then treat this image as with text characters, e.g. center it or press (Tab) to line up the image with the next tab position.

The other layout option is to turn the image into a *floating* image, with text wrapping around it.

When the image is inserted, it is selected automatically. An image is selected when it shows eight small boxes and circles around its perimeter. These boxes or circles are called *handles* and enable you to manipulate the selected image.

All graphics have eight handles around the picture with a green circular handle at the top, as seen in the image at the right. Use the handles to show that the picture is selected or to adjust the size; use the green top handle to rotate the picture.

You can reset the picture to its original image by using **Reset Picture** in the Adjust group of the Format tab in the Picture Tools ribbon.

Sizing a Picture

When you insert a picture into a document, the scale used in the original picture is maintained. However, you can resize and/or scale the picture to any required proportions.

You must select the picture before making any adjustments. Note the following when using the handles to adjust the picture size:

- Point the cursor on one of the horizontal handles (top or bottom) to adjust the height of the picture. The cursor will change to show ↨.

- Point the mouse cursor on one of the vertical handles (left or right side) to adjust the width of the picture. The cursor will change to show ↔.

- Point the mouse cursor on one of the corner handles to adjust the height and width of the picture proportionately at the same time. The cursor will change to show ⌀.

- To size the picture proportionately from its center, press and hold the (Ctrl) key as you drag the appropriate handle.

Scaling the Picture

If you want to resize the picture to a more precise measurement, use the Size dialog box to set up these measurements. To activate this option, under **Picture Tools**, on the **Format** tab, in the **Size** group, click the **Advanced Layout: Size Dialog box launcher**.

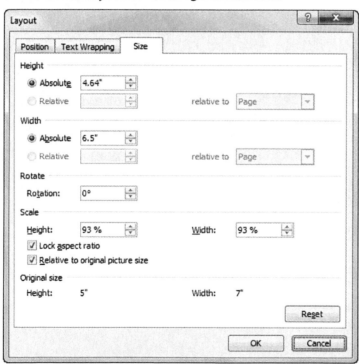

When a picture is inserted, or as you size it using the mouse, Word adjusts the size and scaling of the picture based on default options. You can change these in this dialog box, setting different or standard measurements as needed. Notice how Word also displays the original size of the picture at the bottom of the dialog box for reference.

If you want to change all the settings back to the original, click **Reset**.

Cropping the Picture

The Crop tool enables you to cut away certain portions of the picture, similar to using scissors. You can crop a picture to affect the height or width of the picture, fit it to a shape, or set options for the cropped picture:

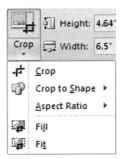

To crop a picture horizontally or vertically, select the picture and then:

- Under **Picture Tools**, on the **Format** tab, in the **Size** group, click **Crop**. Then crop the picture using the appropriate crop handle.

  When you have finished cropping the picture, click the button to turn this feature off; to remove the crop handles, click anywhere away from the picture; or

- under **Picture Tools**, on the **Format** tab, in the **Picture Styles** group, click the **Format Shape Dialog box launcher**, click **Crop** at the left, and then in the **Crop** area, enter the appropriate crop measurements.

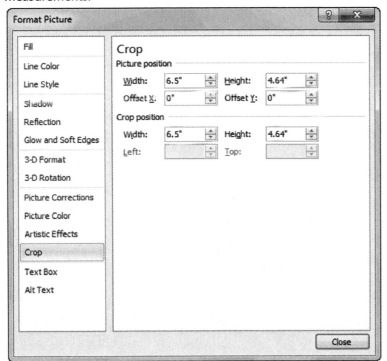

To crop a picture to a shape, select the picture and, under **Picture Tools**, on the **Format** tab, in the **Size** group, click the arrow for **Crop** and then click **Crop to Shape**.

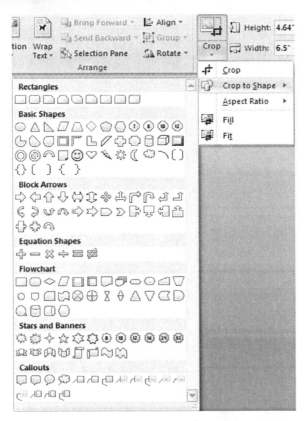

As you crop the picture, the portion being cropped appears in shadow so you can see what has been cropped. This makes it easy to decide how much of the picture should be cropped. You will be able to see this shadow if you activate the Crop command once more.

Rotating the Picture

You can rotate pictures by 90° at a time, or you can set the rotation to a specific angle. Each object rotates based on its center point. Note that not all images can be rotated. When you select an image, if there is a green circle at the top of the image you can rotate the picture to any angle required.

To rotate a picture, select it and then:

- Drag the green circular handle to rotate the object. When you point at the handle, Word displays a circular arrow to show this is the rotation direction. As you click the handle, it displays a circular motion on the symbol as a reminder, or

3240-1 v1.00 © CCI Learning Solutions Inc.

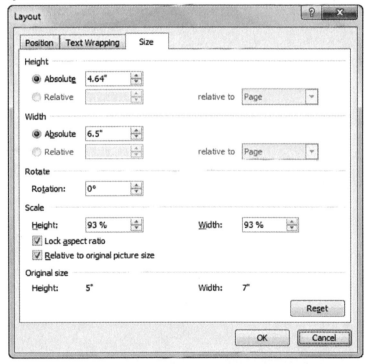

To rotate the object by 15° at a time, press the SHIFT key as you drag the object.

- under **Picture Tools**, on the **Format** tab, in the **Arrange** group, click **Rotate**, or

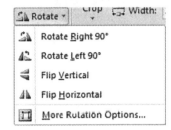

- under **Picture Tools**, on the **Format** tab, in the **Arrange** group, click **Rotate** and then **More Rotation Options**. In the **Rotation** area, enter the measurements for the rotation.

To set a more specialized rotation using 3-D effects, under **Picture Tools**, on the **Format** tab, in the **Picture Styles** group, click **Picture Effects** and then **3-D Rotation**.

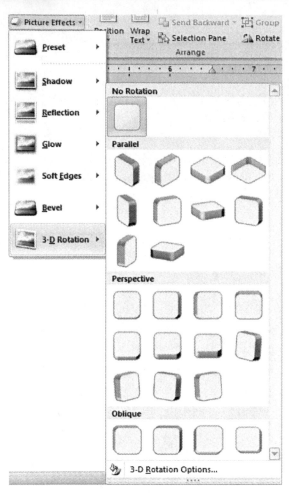

Alternatively, to further customize the rotation, click **3D Rotation Options**.

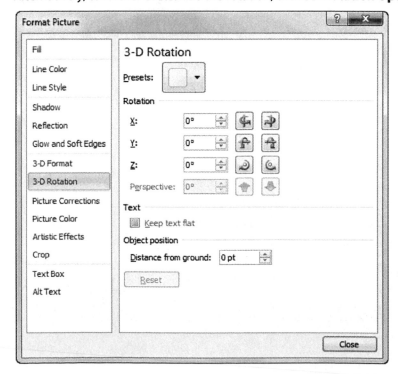

Wrapping Text Around a Picture

Wrapping styles affect the way the text flows around pictures and change how the pictures are positioned in relation to the surrounding text.

By default, the picture wrapping style is *In Line with Text*, which places the graphic at the insertion point on a line of text in the document. The graphic then moves with the text, so that if text is added before the graphic, the graphic moves down to make room for the new text.

Changing the wrapping style can give the document a completely different look and enables the picture to "float" or be positioned anywhere in the document. Word provides a number of tools to achieve this effect including a method that uses the most common types of layout for pictures in a document.

To change the text wrapping style for a picture object, after selecting the picture use one of the following methods:

- Under **Picture Tools**, on the **Format** tab, in the **Arrange** group, click **Position** to select a specific position where the graphic is to be placed and the appropriate text wrapping style, or

- under **Picture Tools**, on the **Format** tab, in the **Arrange** group, click **Wrap Text** to choose the appropriate text wrapping style.

You can also click **More Layout Options** to display a dialog box showing advanced options for adjusting the picture position or text wrapping style.

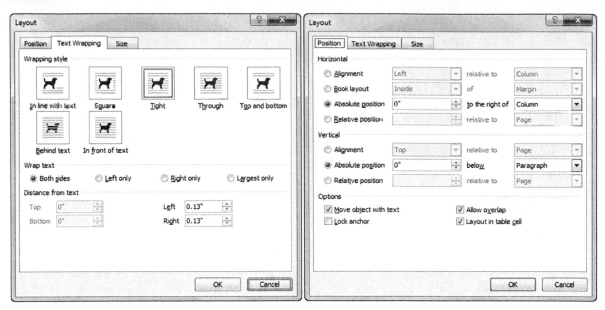

These settings can be used to customize the text wrapping position, such as the amount of white space between the margin and the picture. Options in the **Picture Position** tab do not become available until you change the text wrapping style from *In Line with Text* to another wrapping style.

Each text wrapping style provides a different effect for the picture and the text in the document. Use the previews as a guide to which text wrap style is suitable for the picture and the document. You can also use a combination of these methods to achieve the desired effect.

Moving a Picture

Pictures can be moved in the document using drag-and-drop along with a transparent preview of the picture to show where the picture can be placed. There is a subtle difference in the mouse cursor when you try to move an inline graphic versus a floating graphic, as noted below:

- This is how the mouse cursor appears if you move an *In Line with Text* graphic. The cursor looks the same as if you were dragging text to another location.

- This is how the mouse cursor appears if you move a floating graphic. Not only does the mouse cursor change to ⬚, but a copy of the image appears as you drag this picture to its new location.

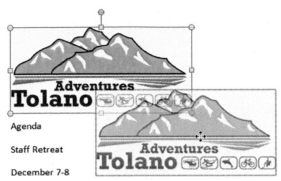

Once a picture has been moved, you can continue to adjust the location by moving it on the screen. You can also use the arrow direction keys to make minor adjustments to the location. This is called "nudging" the picture.

Learn the Skill

In this exercise, you will learn to size, crop and wrap text around pictures in the Experiencing Antarctica – Student document.

1 Click the first picture in the document.

2 Position the cursor at the top right corner of the picture, and then drag down and to the left by approximately 1" (2.5 cm).

Notice how Word begins to change the picture size although it is not exactly 1" at the right side. When you use a corner handle to resize a picture, you are asking Word to resize the picture in proportion to the original size. Once you release the mouse button, the text flows to the picture on the same line; this indicates the image is an inline graphic.

3 With the picture still selected, under **Picture Tools**, click **Format**, in the **Arrange** group, click **Wrap Text** and then click **Square**.

The text then wraps around the picture. Now that you have changed the wrapping style, you can move the picture to a different location.

4 Position the cursor inside the picture; when you see , drag the picture to the right side of the paragraph. Line up the top of the picture with the first line of text as follows:

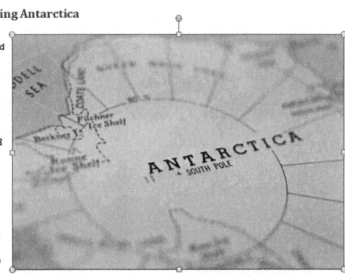

The size of the picture seems right for the size of the paragraph; however, in this case, you want the audience to focus on the text, not the image.

5   Click a corner handle and drag to resize the picture to appear similar to the following.

Experiencing Antarctica

Antarctica - a mysterious land virtually untouched by civilization. Antarctica's biggest challenge is global warming and possible extinction of rare species. This tour is a once-in-a-lifetime opportunity to experience all that Antarctica has to offer!

Our package includes:

- An experienced Antarctica tour guide

6   Save the document.

7   Move to the end of the document to view the second picture.

8   Click the picture to select it. Under **Picture Tools**, click **Format**, and in the **Size** group, click **Crop**.

9   Drag the middle bottom handle up to reduce the amount of water for the picture.

10   Click anywhere away from the picture to view it.

11   Save the document.

Applying Quick Styles

Quick Styles are pre-designed effects that can help create a specific mood for the document message. For example, inserting a picture of your latest product in a promotional flyer may be effective, but adding a style that makes the picture appear to reflect on a shiny surface may capture the reader's eye.

You can apply a wide variety of effects to a picture before or after a style has been selected. You can also apply these effects in place of a picture style. These design features are under **Picture Tools**, on the **Format** tab, in the **Picture Styles** group.

- Use the **Picture Styles Gallery** to affect the look of the picture:

MMM
Sailboat
Picture Online
Exercise

- Use **Picture Border** to apply a border style around the picture:

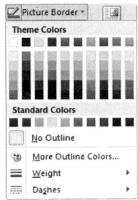

- Use **Picture Effects** to apply a special effect to the picture:

Adjusting the Picture's Color

You can change the brightness or contrast of pictures, sharpen or soften the picture, or add an artistic effect. Use this when you need to adjust the quality of a photograph, but don't have a dedicated graphics program to assist you. Word provides tools to correct the appearance of a photograph, although these do not offer the same level of detail as dedicated graphics programs. In general, brightness applies more light while contrast makes the picture sharper.

- To adjust the clarity of the picture, under **Picture Tools**, on the **Format** tab, in the **Adjust** group, click **Correction**.

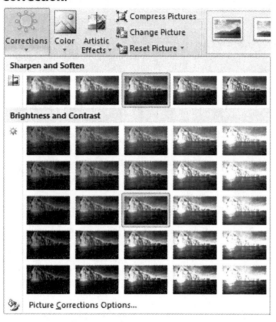

- To change the color of the picture, under **Picture Tools**, on the **Format** tab, in the **Adjust** group, click **Color**. Use this option when you want to follow a simple color scheme using a specific color for pictures and black for text. For example, a memo regarding recycling could have all pictures in a shade of green while the text remains black.

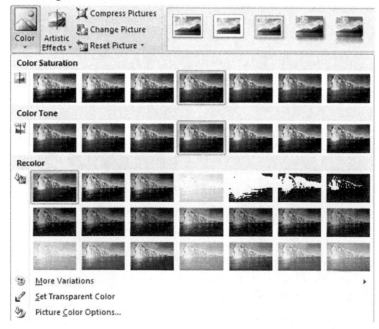

- To apply an artistic effect to the picture, under **Picture Tools**, on the **Format** tab, in the **Adjust** group, click **Artistic Effect**.

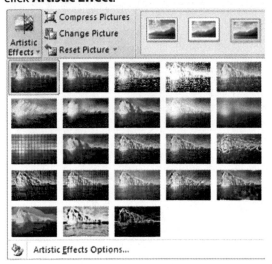

You can also activate the Format Picture dialog box to further customize the effect.

Compressing a Picture

A downside to inserting pictures into a document is how quickly the file size can grow. This is a result of the pictures being embedded into the document that then adds to the size of the initial text file. Pictures can be reduced in size by compressing them; however, be aware that when you compress a picture you are also potentially reducing the image resolution or quality, or permanently removing cropped areas of a picture.

Take note that you cannot compress pictures with the .wmf file type, but can compress pictures with the .gif, .jpg, .bmp, .png, or .tif file formats.

To compress a picture, select the picture and then under **Picture Tools**, on the **Format** tab, in the **Adjust** group, click **Compress Pictures**.

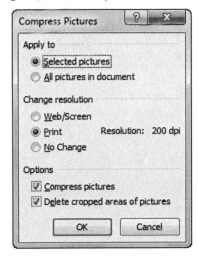

Apply to	Select whether to compress this one picture or all pictures in the document.
Change resolution	Different resolutions will affect the quality of the picture but also make the picture smaller, thereby reducing the overall size of the document.
Options	Select which option you want to include with the compression. If you cropped any portion of the picture, you can also reduce the size of the picture by permanently deleting these areas.

Learn the Skill

In this exercise, you will add some effects to a picture in the Experiencing Antarctica – Student report.

1   With the picture at the bottom of the document selected, under **Picture Tools**, click the **Format** tab and then in the **Picture Styles** group, click **More** to display the style gallery.

2   Point at different styles to preview how these will affect the picture. Then click **Reflected Rounded Rectangle** as the final choice.

This is a nice effect on the picture but, if you would like a softer effect so the white area won't contain as much glare when printed:

3   In the **Adjust** group, click **Corrections** and then **Soften: 25%**.

Suppose you now want to apply some color on the horizon.

4   In the **Adjust** group, click **Color** and then in the **Saturation** area, click **300%.**

5   In the **Adjust** group, click **Color** and then in the **Color Tone** area, click **Temperature: 7200K**.

6   Click the **Home** tab, and in the **Paragraph** group, click **Center**.

7   Save and close the document.

Working with Shape Objects

4.1
4.2

In addition to inserting graphics into your document, you can enhance your documents by creating your own drawings using the Shapes feature located on the **Insert** tab, in the **Illustrations** group. Click **Shapes** to see all the options available:

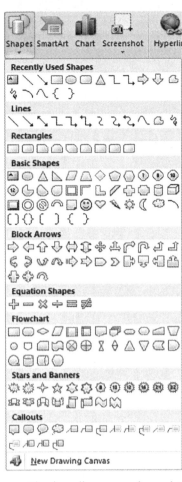

Shapes have been organized so you can see all the available shapes in one location as well as how each type of shape might be used.

When creating a number of shapes that are related to each other, consider using a drawing canvas to keep the shapes together in that canvas. By default, Word does not display a drawing canvas when you activate a shape. However, you can change this using one of the following options:

To create a drawing canvas only when you need one, on the **Insert** tab, in the **Illustrations** group, click **Shape** and then click **New Drawing Canvas**.

To set up a drawing canvas to appear every time you create a shape, click the **File** tab and then click **Options**. Click the **Advanced** category and under **Editing options**, click **Automatically create drawing canvas when inserting AutoShapes**.

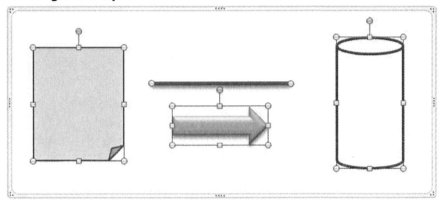

The handles around an object are similar to those for a picture. When an object is selected, the **Drawing Tools** ribbon displays with options to format the object. The options often provide a preview of the effect, and may become active for the selected object, as seen in the second Ribbon.

Note the following when working with objects:

- After clicking the shape to be drawn, the mouse cursor changes to show a ╋ (cross hair).

- Most objects are created by clicking in the document where you want the top left corner of the object to start, and then dragging the mouse until the object is the required size.

- Once an object has been drawn, the selected tool deselects. If you want to draw another object of the same type, you must click the appropriate tool and then draw the new object.

- Click an object to select it.

- To select multiple objects, click the first object, press (Shift) or (Ctrl) and click other required objects.

- You can also select items using the **Home** tab. In the **Editing** group, click **Select** and click **Select Objects**. You can then draw a marquee around the objects to select all of them at the same time.

- Once you select an object, circular handles appear around the object until you click somewhere else in the document window. You can then apply or remove as many options to the object as desired.

- The number of handles that appears depends on the drawing object, e.g. a straight line or arrow will only have two handles whereas a square or oval will show eight handles.

- To size an object, click the object to display the handles. Point to one of the handles until the cursor appears as a double-headed arrow, then click and drag the handle until the object is the desired size.

- To move an object, click the object to select it. Point anywhere on the object (but not on one of the handles), until the cursor appears as a four-headed arrow, then drag it to its new location. Word also displays a ghost image of the object being moved.

- To delete an object, click the object to select it, then press Delete.

- When drawing objects where precise placement is required, on the **View** tab, in the **Show/Hide** group, click **Gridlines** to display a grid. These appear on screen only and provide a reference for aligning objects.

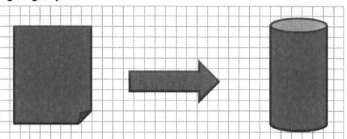

- You can also display gridlines from the **Drawing Tools** ribbon. Click the **Format** tab, and in the **Arrange** group, click **Align** and then click **View Guidelines**.

- To draw a straight line or a perfectly proportioned object such as a square, circle or triangle, click and drag to begin drawing the object, press Shift as you draw the object to the required size.

- To draw an object that is an equal distance in height or width from its center point, press Ctrl as you draw the object to the required size.

  You can combine the Shift and Ctrl keys together to draw a proportionally-sized object starting from its center point.

- When you want objects to share a side or point, draw the first object. Increase the zoom factor so you can see more of the drawing area. Then draw the second object and then move this object so the shared side or point is above the side or point of the first object. When the side or point is shared, the border on the second object does not appear. In some cases, as with the following line sample, the crosshair changes the color of the shared line area.

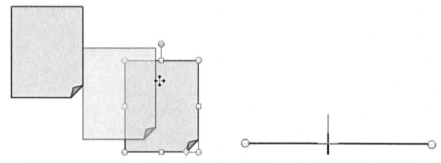

4.4

- To insert text into an object, select the object and begin typing. Alternatively, click **Draw Text Box** to create an object for the text, or right-click the object and then click **Add Text**.

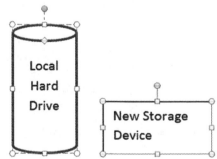

- A shape can be manipulated in a similar way to text such as cutting, copying, pasting, and formatting. When you paste a shape, it appears close to the location of the original shape.

Customizing Shapes

Customizing an object can refer to anything that changes the text in a text box such as adding, changing, or removing a fill or color applied on an object, or grouping several objects together. The number and type of options available to you within each enhancement tool depend on the object selected, e.g. line versus rectangle shape.

When a shape is selected, handles appear around the perimeter:

- Use the blue handles to resize the selected shape.
- Use the green handle to rotate the selected shape.
- Use the yellow diamond to change the width or depth of the selected shape.

You can also click the appropriate option in the **Format** tab of the **Drawing Tools** ribbon to enhance or change the appearance or position of the shape. Commands in the **Arrange** or **Size** group remain the same.

- Use the commands in the **Arrange** group to lay out the position of the shapes. For example, if you want to overlap two objects, you will need to send one of them to the back. If you want several objects to be affected at the same time, each time you want to apply a feature, group these objects so they are treated as one large object instead of multiple individual objects.

- Use the **Size** group to change the height or width of a shape. You can also use the **Size** tab in the Format Shape dialog box to set the height and width.

Learn the Skill

In this exercise, you will learn to insert some shapes to show a process flow.

1. Create a new blank document and save it as New Tour Process Flow – Student.

2. Type: New Tour Process as the title and then press Enter.

3. Click the **Insert** tab, and in the **Illustrations** group, click **Shapes**.

4. In the **Flowchart** area of the Shapes menu, click **Flowchart: Document**.

5. Click and drag to draw to a shape approximately **1.5"** (**3.8 cm**) wide by **1"** (**2.5cm**) high, starting at the left margin.

New Tour Process

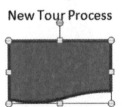

6. With the object still selected, type: Tour Proposal.

When drawing multiple objects for this type of chart, you may want to display the grid to align the objects.

7. Under **Drawing Tools**, click the **Format** tab and then in the **Arrange** group, click **Align** and then click **View Gridlines**.

8. Click the **Insert** tab, and in the **Illustrations** group, click **Shapes**. In the **Flowchart** area, click **Flowchart: Process**.

9. Draw the new object approximately ½" (1.25 cm) to the right of the first object, and about the same size.

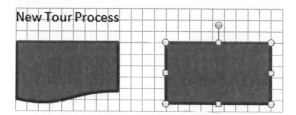

10   With the new object still selected, type: Experience Tour?

11   Click the **Insert** tab, and in the **Illustrations** group, click **Shapes**. In the **Flowchart** area, click **Flowchart: Decision**.

12   Draw the rest of the chart, as illustrated below:

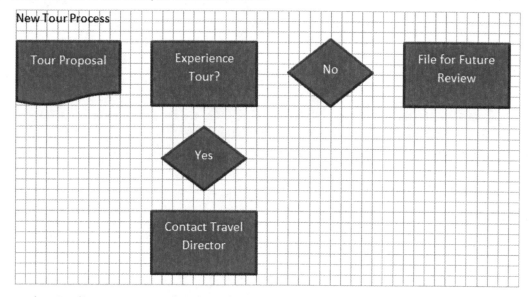

Now try drawing lines to connect the chart elements.

13   Click the **Insert** tab, and in the **Illustrations** group, click **Shapes**. In the **Lines** area, click **Arrow**. Then draw an arrow as shown below:

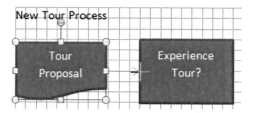

14   Repeat step 13 to draw the arrows in the rest of the diagram, as shown below:

New Tour Process

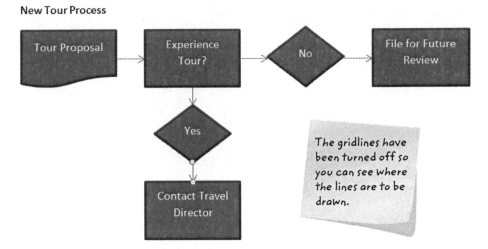

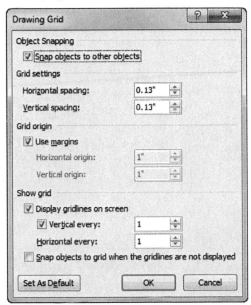

The gridlines have been turned off so you can see where the lines are to be drawn.

Don't worry if the lines do not match the gridlines or are not as seen in the diagram. You will adjust these in the following steps.

15 Save the document.

As you can see from the sample in step 14, having a gridline is helpful, but may not set up the items exactly where you want them. The format and location of items can be modified to suit your document.

16 Click one of the arrows you want to adjust. Then on the **Drawing Tools** ribbon, click **Format**. In the **Arrange** group, click **Align** and then **Grid Settings**.

17 Click **Snap objects to other objects** to turn this option off, click **Display gridlines on screen** to turn this feature off as well, and then click **OK**.

Deselecting this option enables you to use your arrow keys to nudge an object in any direction.

18 Change the zoom for the document to approximately 125% or more so you can see the objects in a larger view.

19 With the same arrow selected as in step 16, press the appropriate arrow key to nudge the arrow closer to the edge of the object. For example, press the Right arrow key to nudge the arrow closer to the right edge of the Tour Proposal shape.

Occasionally you may find the arrows or lines you draw in the diagram align but the object may not, even though you used the gridlines as a reference. Using the sample diagram here, note how the decision box is positioned slightly higher than the arrows. When manipulating diagrams, you may find you want to move the object instead of an arrow or line.

20 Select the decision shape and then using the ⬇ key, press the key enough times to align the points of the decision shape with the arrows.

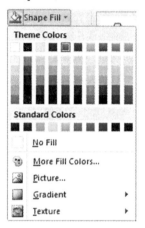

21 Adjust the position and length of the arrows and shapes in your diagram.

22 Save the document again.

Now try changing the format and colors in the diagram.

23 Click one of the objects in the diagram, press (Shift) and click each of the flowchart objects.

24 Under **Drawing Tool**s, click the **Format** tab and then in the **Shape Styles** group, click the arrow for **Shape Fill**.

25 Click any lighter color you wish.

26 With all flowchart objects still selected, in the **Shape Styles** group, click the arrow for **Shape Outline**.

27 Click one color darker than the color you chose in step 26.

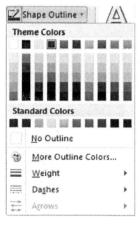

28 With all flowchart objects still selected, in the **Shape Styles** group, click the arrow for **Shape Outline**. Click **Weight** and then click **¼ pt**.

29 With all flowchart objects still selected, in the **WordArt Styles** group, click the arrow for **Text Fill** and then click a color that is darker than the color you chose in step 26.

30 Click any arrow in the diagram. Press (Shift) and then click the remaining arrows in the diagram.

31 In the **Shape Styles** group, click **Shape Outline** to use the same color chosen in step 28.

You have just changed the format of objects in your diagram. You can change one or all objects as required.

Suppose you would like the decision boxes to have different colors to ensure everyone understands a decision is made at this point in the flow process.

32 Select the No decision shape. In the **Shape Styles** group, click a fill color that is opposite to the color chosen for the other shapes. Change the outline to be one shade darker than the fill color.

33 Select the Yes decision shape. In the **Shape Styles** group, click a fill color that is complementary to the color chosen previously for the chart objects. Change the outline to be one shade darker than the fill color chosen in this step.

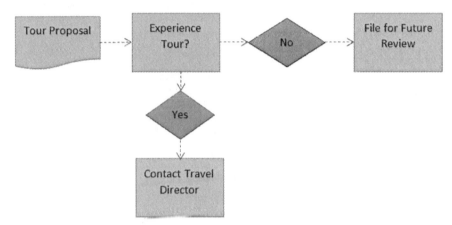

34 Save and close the document.

Using WordArt

You can create special text effects by inserting WordArt drawing objects. With WordArt, you can choose a variety of patterns and styles, select a font and size, type text up to 200 characters and insert the text into your document. After the WordArt drawing object is inserted, it can be edited using the **Drawing Tools** ribbon. You can select preset shapes, create unusual alignments, rotate the text and change the character spacing. You can also enhance the WordArt drawing object using features such as shadows, 3-D effects and fill colors.

To add WordArt into a document, on the **Insert** tab, in the **Text** group, click **WordArt**.

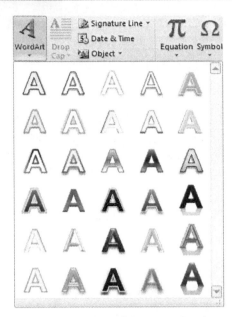

Once the WordArt object is created, you can manipulate it using the same options as with a drawn object.

 **Learn the Skill**

In this exercise you will learn how to create WordArt and then modify it.

1   Open *Heli Ski Tours Review* and save as `Heli Ski Tours Review – Student`.

2   Click the **Insert** tab, and in the **Text** group, click **WordArt**.

3   In the gallery list, click **Fill – Red, Accent 2, Warm Matte Bevel**.

4   Type: `Adventure Alert` as the text for the WordArt.

5   Drag the WordArt object to the right side of the title.

6   On the **Format** tab of the **Drawing Tools** ribbon, in the **WordArt Styles** group, click **More** to display the gallery of styles.

Many of the styles here are the same as when you first activated this feature. You can change the text to use one of these styles, or use the individual options to change specific options.

7   Point at several of these styles to preview the change to the WordArt. Then click away from the gallery to display all the options in the ribbon again.

8   Click the arrow for **Text Fill** and point at different colors to preview the change to the WordArt.

As this is a report warning of a potential issue with a tour category, you may want to leave the color in the red shades, but it may not need to be the deep red originally selected.

9   In the Text Fill list, click **Red, Accent 2, Lighter 60%.**

Quarterly Review

Heli-Skiing Tours

10 Save the document.

Using Drop Caps

4.4

Use a **drop cap** to capitalize the first letter in the body of a document and position or drop it so the tallest part of the character aligns with the tallest part of the first line of the paragraph. These are commonly used in newsletters or invitations. You can position a drop cap within the paragraph margins, or in the margin area.

To create a drop cap, select the character and then on the **Insert** tab, in the **Text** group, click **Drop Cap**.

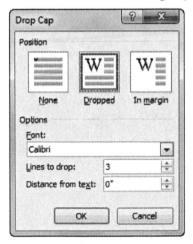

As you point at the **Dropped** or **In margin** option, Word displays the effect of applying this feature on the selected character. To change options for the drop cap character, click **Drop Cap Options**.

Using Text Boxes

4.1

In addition to adding a text box shape, you can also insert a text box that is a pre-formatted text box where you can enter the text for a specific area of the document to offset information or draw attention to a particular message. Word provides a gallery of several styles of text boxes as well as the option to create your own and position it anywhere in a document.

To use a text box, on the **Insert** tab, in the **Text** group, click **Text Box**.

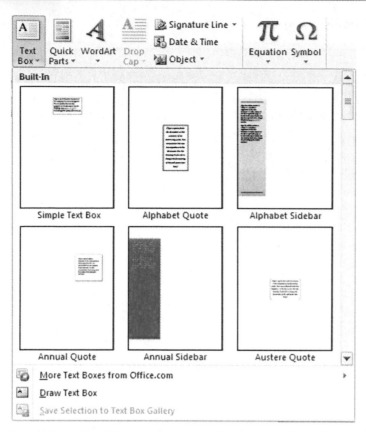

Once a text box is inserted use the Drawing Tools ribbon to format or enhance this text box as if you created a text box shape.

You can also choose to save the text box format and style in the Text Box Gallery for future use. When a text box is formatted and set the way you want it, on the **Insert** tab, in the **Text** group, click **Text Box** and then click **Save Selection to Text Box Gallery**.

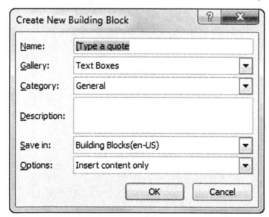

Enter information to identify this text box in the gallery for future use. You will then be able to select it for other documents as needed.

Learn the Skill

In this exercise you will learn how to create WordArt and then modify it.

1   Ensure *Heli Ski Tours Review – Student* is active on the screen.

2   Select the G at the beginning of the first paragraph.

3   Click the **Insert** tab and in the **Text** group, click **Drop Cap**.

4   Point at the two different options to see which one may be suitable for the document. Then click **Drop Cap Options**.

5   Click **Dropped** and then click the arrow for **Font**. Scroll in the list to choose **Times New Roman**. Click **OK**.

G iven the number of avalanches that have occurred in the last few months, we should review this tour and decide whether to continue offering it.

Many vendors have indicated that the number of avalanches has increased this year but, in comparison to the total number of years in business, the number of fatalities is quite low. However,

6   Click anywhere away in the document to view the overall effect.

Now try inserting a text box that draws attention to the purpose of this report.

7   Click the **Insert** tab, and in the **Text** group, click **Text Box**.

8   Scroll in the list and then click **Sticky Note**.

9   Type the following text inside the text box:

> This is the type of crisis we want to avoid. Although warnings are given by the authorities in those locales, we need to stay on top of these and alert our customers accordingly.

10   Under **Drawing Tools**, click the **Format** tab and in the **Shape Styles** group, click the arrow for **Shape Fill** and click **Olive Green, Accent 3, Darker 50%**. In the Quick Styles gallery, click **Fill – White, Drop Shadow**.

Quarterly Review

Heli-Skiing Tours

Adventure Alert

Given the number of avalanches that have occurred in the last few months, we should review this tour and decide whether to continue offering it.

Many vendors have indicated that the number of avalanches has increased this year but, in comparison to the total number of years in business, the number of fatalities is quite low. However, given the other activities offered for extreme sports enthusiasts, it may be time for Ian Hanover to visit some of these tour sites to determine the environmental impact of our tours.

Below is a list of vendors offering this type of adventure:

- Extreme Skiing Adventures
- Mountain Rush Tours
- Snow Run Tours
- Heli Travel

This is the type of crisis we want to avoid. Although warnings are given by the authorities in those locales, we need to stay on top of these and alert our customers accordingly.

11   With the text box still selected, click the **Insert** tab, and in the **Text** group, click **Text Box**. Then click **Save Selection to Text Box Gallery**.

12   Type: Tour Warnings for the name, and then type: Text box containing warning message. Click **OK**.

13   Click anywhere away from the text box and then click the **Insert** tab, in the **Text** group, click **Text Box**.

14   Scroll in the list until near the bottom and in the General area, your new saved text box is listed.

15   Save and close the document.

Using SmartArt

4.2

Use the SmartArt feature to create a diagram such as an organization chart or to show a process of tasks. A variety of types and styles of diagrams is available. You can also create diagrams manually.

To create a SmartArt object, on the **Insert** tab, in the **Illustrations** group, click **SmartArt**.

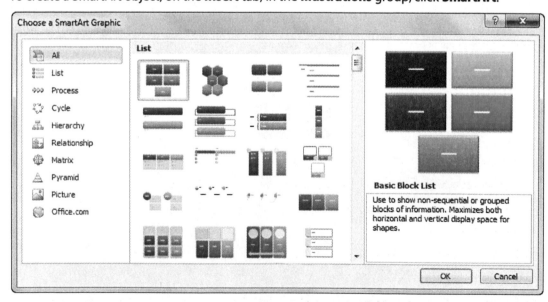

Once the object is created, the SmartArt Tools displays with two tabs for enhancing the SmartArt object:

• The **Design** tab displays options to modify the design of the SmartArt object.

- The **Format** tab displays options to modify how the text will appear in the SmartArt object.

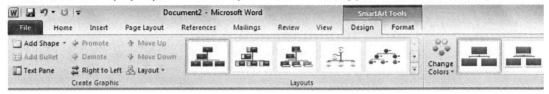

When entering text into the SmartArt object, you can choose to enter the text directly into the shapes, or use the Text Pane.

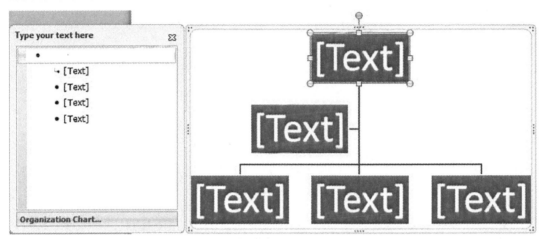

MMM
Text Cycle
SmartArt
Online
Exercise

Depending on how the system was set up, this pane may appear as a small tab at the left of the SmartArt border. Click this tab to show the Text Pane; click **Close** to hide the Text Pane. Demote text by pressing (Tab) or promote text by pressing (Shift)+(Tab). If you want more blocks in the SmartArt diagram, press (Enter) on a bulleted line. To move from one bulleted line to another, click the line you want to move to, or press the (↑) or (↓) key.

Learn the Skill

In this exercise, you will learn how to create a report to show the adventure process using a SmartArt object and then enhance it.

1   Create a new document and save as Adventure Process - Student.

2   Click the **Insert** tab, then in the **Illustrations** group, click **SmartArt**.

3   Click **Process** from the list of categories at the left, click **Staggered Process** in the dialog box, and then click **OK**.

4   Click the arrow at the left of the drawing object to enter text for the chart.

5   Type: Adventure Approved and then press (Enter).

    Notice how Word has created a new blank line in the Text pane as well as a new object in the diagram.

6   Type: Site Assessment and press the (↓) key.

7   Type: Travel Director Experience and press the (↓) key.

8 Complete the rest of the text entries as shown:

9 Save the document.

10 With the cursor in the SmartArt diagram, click the **Design** tab, and then in the **SmartArt Styles** group, click **Change Colors**.

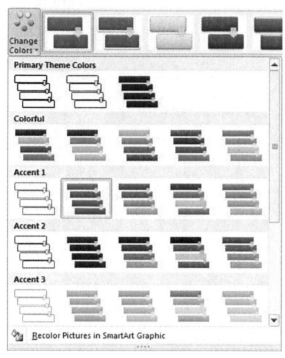

11 Click the first option in **Colorful**.

Notice how each step in the process appears in a different color, giving visual emphasis to specific information.

12 Click **Close** in the Text pane to close this pane.

13 Click the **Design** tab and, in the **SmartArt Styles** group, click **More** to display the gallery of styles.

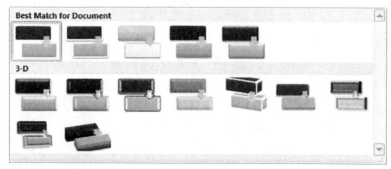

14 Point at the different styles and then click which style effect you want to apply.

15 Save the document.

Adding Captions

Occasionally you may want to put a statement or caption below a picture as a reference to text in the document or for the audience's information such as *Figure 1 - Lithograph #3 by John Smith, Table 3 – 2013 Projected Product Sales*. This can be very handy if the picture, table, or figure does not immediately follow the text reference.

To insert a caption, position the cursor on the location for the caption and then on the **References** tab, in the **Captions** group, click **Insert Caption**.

Caption	Displays the currently selected caption label with the cursor at the end of the line for further data entry, usually the description of the item being captioned.
Label	Select one of the existing labels of **Equation**, **Figure**, or **Label** as the labels for the caption. You can also create your own labels as required.
Position	Select whether the caption should display above or below the item.
Exclude label from caption	Turn this feature off if you don't want the label to be shown with the caption description, e.g., Lithograph by John Smith versus Figure 1 - Lithograph by John Smith.
New Label	Use this when you want to create a different label than those provided in Word.
Delete Label	Delete one of the labels.
Numbering	Determine the numbering style to be used with the captions.
AutoCaption	Set up which items Word will automatically mark to have a caption added, e.g., Excel worksheet, Word table, media clip, etc.

To delete a caption, select it and press Delete.

Learn the Skill

In this exercise you will add captions to pictures in the document.

1   Ensure the *Adventure Process – Student* is active and move the cursor to below the SmartArt diagram.

2   Click the **References** tab, in the **Captions** group, click **Insert Caption**.

3   After the Figure 1 text, press (Spacebar) and then type: Process for all Tolano Adventures Tours.

Figure 1 Process for all Tolano Adventures Tours

4   Select the caption text and increase the font size to **12**.

5   Save and close the document.

Using Screenshots

The Screenshot feature can be helpful when you need to capture a screen of information that may change or expire. An example could be a special deal on a Web page, a diagram you need for reference or to capture an error message on the screen.

To capture a screen, on the **Insert** tab, In the **Illustrations** group, click **Screenshot**.

Screens in the Available Windows list are any programs that are open and available to capture as a screenshot. Click the picture in this list if you want to use it as your screenshot entry. Otherwise, to take a screenshot, click **Screen Clipping**.

The cursor changes to a large crosshair and Word switches you to another program so you can take the screenshot. When the program is active, click at the top left corner of what the screenshot is to contain and drag to the bottom right corner of what will be the contents of the screenshot.

Once you release the mouse, Word will automatically insert the screenshot into the cursor location in the document.

Learn the Skill

In this exercise you will learn how to use Screenshot to capture a picture of the screen to show the status of a process on your computer.

1   Create a new blank document. Press `Ctrl`+`Alt`+`Delete` to display the Task Manager and then click the **Processes** tab.

2   Switch to Word and then click the **Insert** tab. In the **Illustrations** group, click **Screenshot** and then **Screen Clipping**.

3   Starting at the top left corner of the second item in the list, click and drag to highlight the next four lines in this list.

dwm.exe	swong	02	11,644 K	Desktop ...
EXCEL.EXE	swong	00	14,464 K	Microsoft ...
explorer.exe	swong	00	29,248 K	Windows ...
msnmsgr.exe	swong	00	18,184 K	Windows ...
MSOSYNC.EXE	swong	00	3,004 K	Microsoft ...

The list items will vary on different screens depending on which processes are running on the computer.

The focus here is on using Screenshot and not the processes being highlighted.

You should notice that Word has automatically inserted this screen into your document immediately.

4   Close the document without saving.

Lesson Summary

In this lesson, you looked at different types of illustrations such as pictures, object shapes, text boxes, and diagrams you can insert into a document, as well as what types of modifications or enhancements can be applied to these illustrations. You should now be able to:

☑ insert or modify pictures or Clip Art

☑ insert, modify and enhance text boxes

☑ insert and modify WordArt objects

☑ create, arrange and enhance shapes

☑ create drop caps

☑ insert and modify SmartArt diagrams

Review Questions

MMM
Go online for
Additional
Review and
Activities

1. Explain the difference between inserting pictures and Clip Art.

2. Explain what an inline graphic is versus a floating graphic.

3. Discuss when or why you might want to use a drawing canvas when creating shapes.

4. Give examples of when you might use WordArt instead of a text box.

5. Explain what SmartArt is and when you might use it.

Microsoft®
Word 2010
Core Certification

Lesson 9: **Creating Mass Mailing Documents**

Lesson Objectives

In this lesson, you will look at what merging means in relation to mass mailings - including documents, envelopes and labels. On successful completion, you should be able to:

☐ understand what mail merge means   ☐ use a data source

☐ create a main document or form   ☐ merge documents automatically or manually

Creating Simple Mailing Documents

What are Mailings?

The **Mailings** feature enables you to create mass mailings by combining a list of variable information with a document. This means that each person on your mailing list receives a personalized letter without you typing the same letter several times. This is referred to as a mail merge.

A mail merge uses the following files:

Main Document	The standard letter, label, envelope or list format that you can merge with the Data Source. It contains text that is identical for each personalized document, along with special *merge fields* to indicate where each type of variable from the Data Source is to be placed.
Data Source	The list of variable information to insert into the Main Document (e.g. names and addresses). Word provides *fields* where one variable ends and another variable begins.

Understanding the Main Document

As noted, the main document is the standard form you want everyone to receive when the merge process is complete. This could be an invitation letter, name badges, labels for your Christmas mailing list, etc. You set this up once with the appropriate merge fields. Word then finds matching information from the data source and inserts it in the merge field location.

You can insert the merge fields individually yourself, or use one of the preset merge fields provided. For example, if you were setting up a letter as the main document and in a specific location, you want to insert the customer's name and address, you could use the Address Block merge field that includes all this information. This is much faster than inserting the merge fields for the first name, last name, address, city, province/state, and postal/zip code individually along with any punctuation.

Having the flexibility to insert individual merge fields is useful when you need to include a merge field in a non-standard style. For example, you have to create name labels for everyone who is attending a trade show your company is sponsoring. The trade show consists of several seminars that are full- or half-day sessions. By placing a field that identifies the seminar type, you can insert this merge field on each label and Word then merges the information into this location. This helps coordinators quickly identify which session the individual is attending.

Merge fields appear with « and » around the merge code, similar to «AddressBlock». When you click on a merge field, it also appears as «AddressBlock» to show it is a special code that performs a pre-defined task. To delete a merge field, you must select the code, including the chevrons on either side of the code.

You can also activate the Step-by-Step Wizard to guide you through this process by selecting options from a task pane at the right of the screen. This is similar to using the Mailings tab, but provides more explanation at each step. Activate this feature from the **Start Mail Merge** command.

Understanding Data Sources

The data source contains all the variable information to insert into the main document. The variables change from each record and have field names assigned to them. Word refers to data sources as Recipient Lists.

Data sources can come from several different sources including a merge list, table, plain text file, XML file, or even a different program. Irrespective of source, there are several things in common for all data sources. When working with a data source, keep in mind the following:

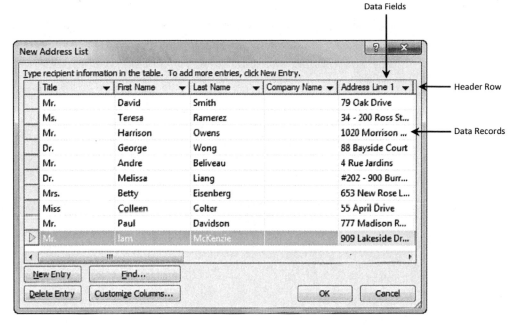

- The entire group of information relating to one person is called a data record (e.g. all the information for one customer). Each record must be consistent and have the same number of data fields, in the same order, as the rest. If a data record does not include a particular item of information, leave that field blank.

- The separate items in the data record (the variables) are called data fields (e.g. full name, address, salutation). It is important to note that each field in the data file must have a unique name.

- The field names that identify the data fields you are using are listed in the first record of the data source, called the header row. This can also be referred to as the column headings for the table or database.

- If you create a data source from scratch for the first time during the Mail Merge process, Word will save the data source file in a folder called Data Sources (usually located in the Documents folder). You can, however, save the file to any location.

- When you create a new data source, Word provides a table using a number of standard fields for data entry.

- To change the order, delete, or add new fields to the standard data source form, use **Customize Columns** in the Edit Data Source dialog box.

- Note that the file is saved with an *.mdb* extension type, or the default file type for Access database files. You do not need to have Access to use this file in the mail merge process. However, if you want to open it as with a regular document in Word, you will need to convert it before being able to see the contents of the file.

- If using a data source file created in a previous version of Word or another program, it can be in the form of a table, or as a plain text list of information separated by commas or tabs. You can also create a data source file using a Word format or a specific format saved from a Word document type, if preferred.

First Name	Last Name	Address	City	State/Prov	Zip/Postal	Country	E-mail
James	Wong	#101 – 55 Mainland Drive	Vancouver	WA	98661	USA	jwong44@gmail.com
Patricia	Johnson	342 125th Avenue	Surrey	BC	V2H 4Y1	CA	patrice_j@hotmail.com
Adam	Johnson	342 125th Avenue	Surrey	BC	V2H 4Y1	CA	afj25@gmail.com
Balbinder	Sandhu	3200 Valley Street	Vancouver	BC	V6M 2H3	CA	balbi@hotmail.com
Marianne	Lewis	12 Applegate Court	Seattle	WA	98105	USA	mlewis8765@western.com
John	Wately	12 Applegate Court	Seattle	WA	98105	USA	jwately@msd.edu
Madison	James	800 Buena Vista Drive	Orlando	FL	32807	USA	madison_j@release.org
Andrew	Tomison	56 Maine Road	Winnipeg	MN	M3H H5J	CA	andy-tom@yahoo.com

Data Source file using table format in Word

```
Title,First Name,Last Name,Address,City,State,ZIP Code,Country,Home Phone,E-mail Address
Mr.,David,Smith,79 Oak Drive,Vancouver,WA,98176,USA,206 555 1122,dsmith33@gmail.com
Ms.,Teresa,Ramierez,34 - 200 Ross Street,Seattle,WA,98101,USA,206 663 2323,teresa_r@sprint.com
Mr.,Harrison,Owens,1020 Morrison Road,Portland,OR,97212,USA,503 333 6676,harry_owens@sprint.com
Dr.,Andrew,Wong,88 Bayside Court,San Francisco,CA,94134,USA,415 888 0088,dr-a-wong@gmail.com
```

Data Source file saved in txt (Text) format

- To view the information in a data source at any time, on the **Mailings** tab in the **Start Mail Merge** group, click **Edit Recipient List**.

- Consider very carefully how you enter the information in the data source. For instance, to personalize a letter using a client's first name, you need to have a separate field for the first name. By default, Word sets this up automatically if you create a new data source or recipient list during the merge process. However, information you merge from an existing data source may all be contained in one field and consist of several lines. You will need to separate this information into different fields.

- By default, a new data source created during the mail merge process is created as an address list as most mail merge tasks use address lists to set up a template that addresses the mailing to others. Word provides the option of creating different fields or customizing the default fields during the data source creation. Alternatively, you can create the data source such as a list of products in your inventory in another format (e.g. text format, Word table, etc.) and select it during the merge process.

- To change the order of the fields in the data source, drag the column heading to the new location where you want the data to appear.

How Do I Merge?

The Mailings tab displays a number of features to set up a merge for mass mailings. This tab also contains commands for creating envelopes or labels individually.

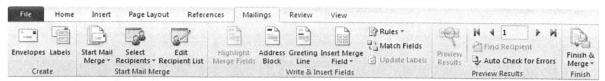

Use the Mailings tab to start the merge process as the commands activate as you progress through each step. Word guides you through the process of creating or opening the main document, then creating or opening a data source, and lets you preview the merge results for any modifications that may be needed prior to completing the final merge task.

Each step of the mail merge process provides options on how to handle the document type or the recipient (e.g. address book) list. You can also move to the next step or move back to a previous step to change or add items.

When you are ready to perform the merge, you can use the **Auto check for Errors** feature to check for any errors that might exist in the merge documents prior to printing or saving the file.

Learn the Skill

In this exercise, you will create labels for all the Travel Directors who will be arriving at Head Office in New York next week for a meeting about existing tours.

1   Create a new blank document and then click the **Mailings** tab. In the **Start Mail Merge** group, click **Start Mail Merge**.

2   Click **Labels**.

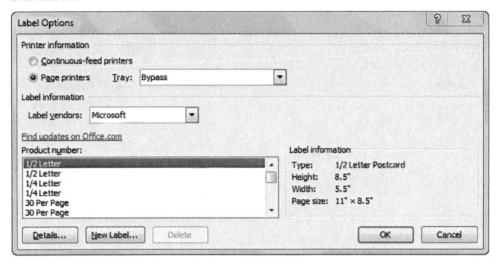

3   In the Label information area, click the arrow to the right of Label vendors and change this to **Avery US Letter**.

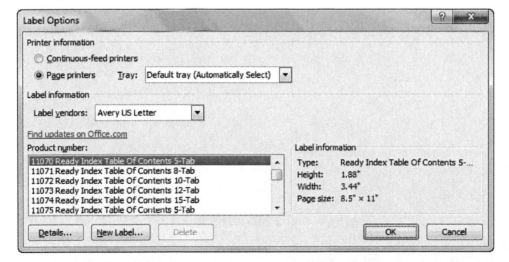

4   In the Product number list, scroll and then click **5390 Name Badges Insert Refills**. Click **OK**.

Press the key for the letter or number of the label size you want. Word will then quickly move to the first name in the list that matches, thereby reducing the amount of time to scroll to find the label option you want to use.

5   On the **Mailings** tab, in the **Start Mail Merge** group, click **Select Recipients** and then click **Type New List**.

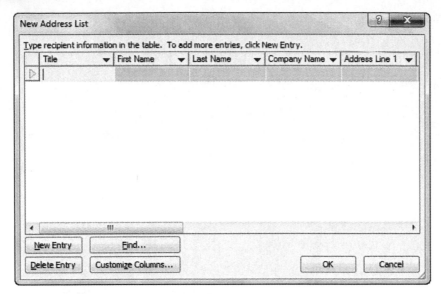

A new blank address list is available for you to enter the contacts. As this is a list of our Travel Advisors, we can change the number and type of columns for text entry.

6   Click **Customize Columns**.

7   Click Title in the list and then click **Delete**.

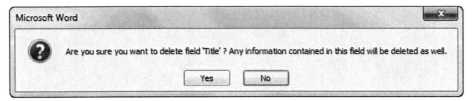

8   Click **Yes** to delete this field.

You are only deleting the field from this list and not all future or existing lists.

9   Repeat steps 7 and 8 for the Company Name field.

You could choose to continue deleting fields but, for the purpose of this exercise, you will only delete these two.

10   Click **OK.**

You can now enter all the Travel Directors.

11   Click in the first cell and type: Nick. Press (Tab) to move to the next cell and type: Klassen. Click in the blank cell for City and type: New York.

12   Click **New Entry**.

13   Repeat steps 11 and 12 for the remaining names and cities:

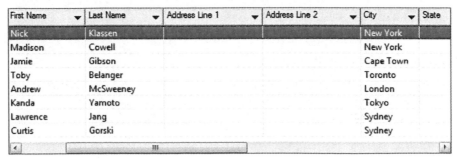

First Name	Last Name	Address Line 1	Address Line 2	City	State
Nick	Klassen			New York	
Madison	Cowell			New York	
Jamie	Gibson			Cape Town	
Toby	Belanger			Toronto	
Andrew	McSweeney			London	
Kanda	Yamoto			Tokyo	
Lawrence	Jang			Sydney	
Curtis	Gorski			Sydney	

14 Click **OK** after entering Curtis' information.

15 Navigate to where the student data files location is and then save this as Travel Directors –
Student.

The label document now appears as:

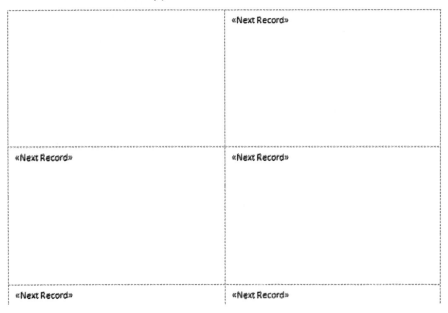

This is the structure Word needs to recognize and include the information you want to appear on
each label. You can now set up the labels to show information from the three fields you used in the
list.

16 With the cursor in the first cell, on the **Mailings** tab and in the **Write & Insert Fields** group, click
Address Block.

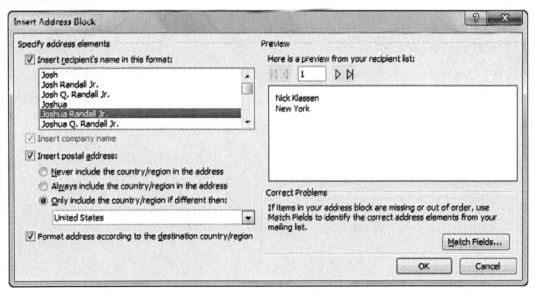

17 Click **OK** to accept all the defaults here.

The labels are not yet complete. So far you have entered the information only for the first label. In order for
Word to continue adding names using the same document, it needs to propagate or update all the labels
on the sheet to display the same information.

18 On the **Mailings** tab and in the **Write & Insert Fields** group, click **Update Labels**.

Your label form should appear similar to the following:

«AddressBlock»	«Next Record»«AddressBlock»
«Next Record»«AddressBlock»	«Next Record»«AddressBlock»

19 On the **Mailings** tab, in the **Preview Results** group, click **Preview Results**.

Nick Klassen New York	Madison Cowell New York
Jamie Gibson Cape Town	Toby Belanger Toronto

Now that you see that the information is correct, format the text so the names appear bigger and centered on the label.

20 On the **Mailings** tab, in the **Preview Results** group, click **Preview Results**.

21 Select the code in the first cell of your labels and center the text, change the size to 20, and apply a text color of your choice.

22 On the **Mailings** tab and in the **Write & Insert Fields** group, click **Update Labels** to make all the labels have the same format.

23 Select the entire table and under **Table Tools**, on the **Layout** tab, in the **Alignment** group, click **Align Center**.

24 Preview the results again and then, on the **Mailings** tab, in the **Preview Results** group, click **Auto Check for Errors**.

Word takes a few minutes to check your documents to ensure there are no errors.

25 On the **Mailings** tab, in the **Finish** group, click **Finish & Merge**.

Notice you have three options for handling the merged document. If you are sharing a printer, you will need to let others know that you will be printing with special paper or for a long time, depending on the number of names in your list that were merged. Alternatively, you may choose to print at a later time when the printer is not busy. For the purpose of this exercise, you will merge to individual documents so you can see the final results.

25 Click **Edit Individual Documents**.

You can choose to print all the merged documents or specific ones.

26 Ensure **All** is selected and then click **OK**

27 Save the merged document as Travel Director Name Badges – Student and then close it.

28 Save the label merge form as Name Badges Form – Student and then close it.

Using Existing Documents

In addition to creating new merge recipient lists or forms, you can use existing files created in Word or other programs such as an Excel worksheet, an Access database, Outlook contacts, text files, XML files, etc.

You can make changes or selections in the files as if you had created the files yourself. Individual fields can be included in a file, as well as selecting specific items in the data source.

Learn the Skill

In this exercise, you will personalize an announcement flyer by merging the flyer with information from an Excel worksheet.

1 Open *New Location Plans* and save this as New Location Plans – Student.

2 Position the cursor at the beginning of the first paragraph after the title. Click the **Mailings** tab, and in the **Start Mail Merge** group, click **Select Recipients** and then click **Use Existing List**.

3 Navigate to the student data files location and then select *Tour Customers* (this is an Excel file).

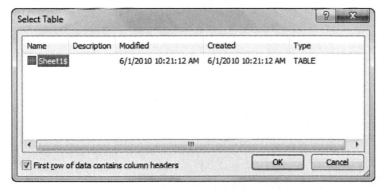

4 Click **OK** to indicate the information is in this sheet of the Excel file.

5 On the **Mailings** tab, in the **Write & Insert Fields** group, click **Address Block** and then click **OK**. Press ⟮Enter⟯.

New Location Plans

«AddressBlock»

Tolano Adventures is very pleased to announce its intention to set up a new location to better serve our customers on the Pacific coastline. We need your help to decide on the best location ...

6   Scroll to the last paragraph in the document and position the cursor between the two commas near the beginning of the paragraph.

7   In the **Write & Insert Fields** group, click **Insert Merge Field**.

This is a list of all the fields you can now use to insert information into the document. You are not restricted to setting up address fields only; you can use any field in the form document.

First_Name
Last_Name
Address
City
StateProv
ZipPostal
Country
Email
Home_
Mobile_
Ice_Climb
Rock_Climb
Whale_Watch
Heli_Ski
Hot_Air
Cycle

8   Click **First Name** to set this field in this location. Then click **Preview Results** to view how the data will appear in the document.

Your document should now appear similar to the following, with a personal reference in the last paragraph:

New Location Plans

James Wong

#101 – 55 Mainland Drive

Vancouver

Tolano Adventures is very pleased to announce its intention to set up a new location to better serve our customers on the Pacific coastline. We need your help to decide on the best location ...

- Vancouver, BC, Canada   • San Francisco, CA, USA

- Seattle, WA, USA   • Hong Kong, Macao, China

Each site offers unique opportunities to provide a wider variety of adventures.

That's why we need you, James , to help us determine the new location. Go to our web site at www.tolanoadventures.com for details on each site and then cast your vote! Thank you for helping us decide on our fabulous new location!

You should also notice that the address at the top of the document has too much spacing between the lines of the address.

9   Using the Selection Bar, select the first two lines of the address block. Click the **Page Layout** tab, and in the **Paragraph** group, change the spacing **After** to be **0**.

> James Wong
> #101 – 55 Mainland Drive
> Vancouver
>
> Tolano Adventures is very plea
> customers on the Pacific coast

10   In the **Finish** group, click **Finish & Merge** and then **Edit Individual Documents**. Ensure **All** is selected and then click **OK**.

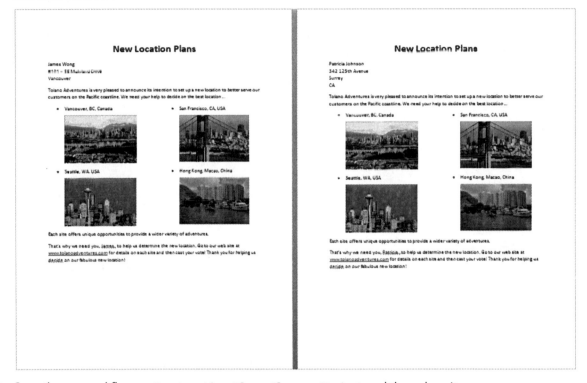

11   Save the merged flyer as New Location Plans Flyer - Student and then close it.

12   Save the changes to the New Location Plans form and then close it.

Using the Mail Merge Wizard

7.2

An alternative to using the commands in the Mailings tab to merge information for mass mailings is to use a wizard that Word provides. This option enables you to work through the process of merging one step at a time and also displays options in a task pane on the screen.

To activate the Mail Merge Wizard, on the **Mailings** tab, in the **Start Mail Merge** group, click **Start Mail Merge** and then click **Step by Step Mail Merge Wizard**.

> MMM
> Invitation to
> Annual
> Meeting Online
> Exercise

Learn the Skill

In this exercise, you will use the wizard to create a quick list of customer names.

1   Create a new blank document and save it as Customer List - Student.

2   Change the line spacing to be 1 and remove any spacing after the paragraph.

3   Click the **Mailings** tab and then in the **Start Mail Merge** group, click **Start Mail Merge** and **Step by Step Mail Merge Wizard**.

You should now see the following task pane on the screen:

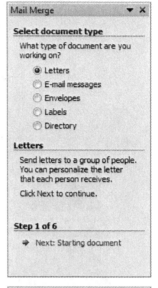

4   Click **Directory** as the document type and then click **Next: Starting document**.

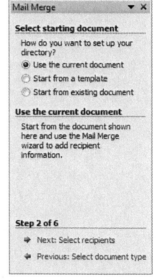

5   Ensure **Use the current document** is selected and then click **Next: Select Recipients**.

6   Ensure **Use an existing list** is selected and then click **Browse**. Navigate to where the student data files are located, select *Tour Customers* and then click **OK**.

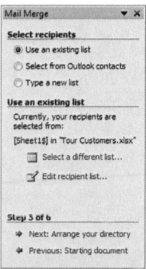

7   Click **OK** to accept the Tour Customers list. Then click **Next: Arrange your directory**.

8   Click **Address block**. Click **Always include the country/region in the address** and then click **OK**.

9   Press ⟨Enter⟩ twice and then click **Next: Preview your directory**.

James Wong
#101 – 55 Mainland Drive
Vancouver

Notice how you only have one name listed on this page. By default, Word will merge the data source information onto different pages unless it sees the Next Record code as was seen with the labels in an earlier exercise. To set up the page to show as many addresses as it can, you will need to insert this code.

10   In the Mail Merge task pane, click **Previous: Arrange your directory**. Click in the blank line below the <<AddressBlock>> field. Then in the **Write & Insert Fields** group, click **Rules** and click **Next Record**.

Your codes should appear similar to:

«AddressBlock»
«Next Record»

11   Click **Next: Preview your directory**.

Notice how you have the option to exclude this person in the report; alternatively, if you want to exclude several people, click Edit recipient list and deselect the names from the list. For the purpose of this exercise, you will include everyone.

12   Click **Next: Complete the merge**.

13 Click **To New Document**. Click **All** and then click **OK**.

James Wong
#101 – 55 Mainland Drive
Vancouver
USA

Adam Johnson
342 125th Avenue
Surrey
CA

Marianne Lewis
12 Applegate Court
Seattle
USA

Madison James
800 Buena Vista Drive
Orlando
USA

Masoud Jasmali
1 Emaar Boulevard
Downtown Dubai UAE

14 Save the merged document as Customer List Report - Student and then close it.

15 Save and close the Customer List document.

Lesson Summary

In this lesson, you looked at what merging means in relation to mass mailings, including documents, envelopes and labels. You should now be able to:

☑ understand what mail merge means

☑ use a data source

☑ create a main document or forms

☑ merge documents automatically or manually

Review Questions

MMM
Go online for
Additional
Review and
Activities

1. What is a mail merge?

2. Describe the purpose of a Main Document and the Data Source.

3. Explain the following terms and how you would use each in a data source:

4. What is the benefit of using <<Address Block>> instead of inserting individual fields such as <<First Name>>, <<Last Name>>, <<Address>>, <<City>>?

5. If you wanted a guide to take you through the merge process one step at a time, which option would you use?

Microsoft®
Word 2010
Core Certification

Lesson 10: Sharing Documents

Lesson Objectives

In this lesson, you will be introduced to different ways of sharing documents with others, including building content for use in other documents, handling different versions of a document, and protecting documents. On successful completion of this lesson, you will be able to:

☐ use building blocks

☐ create and edit building blocks

☐ insert Quick Parts items or fields

☐ navigate documents

☐ manage document versions

☐ protect your documents with a password

Understanding Building Blocks

Building blocks save time for items you use frequently and ensure consistency in your documents, similar to using AutoCorrect. Building block content includes headers and footers, cover pages, text boxes, bibliographies, citations, placeholders, equations, themes, and content controls (fields). A number of these have been created like templates, but you can create and modify your own.

Building blocks can be selected from Quick Parts, or you can create and design your own and add them to the Quick Parts Gallery.

Using Quick Parts

Quick Parts are building blocks that you might use often - headers, footers, tables, cover pages, or signatures. You can also use Quick Parts to build or set up a new template for standard documents.

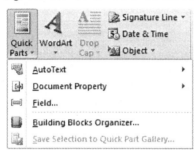

AutoText	Insert information from your document into the building block. This can be text, graphics, or a combination of both, and can be any size. AutoText items created in earlier versions of Word can also be used with Word 2010, provided they were saved in a template document.
Document Property	Insert information into the building block using one of the listed fields, usually set up in the properties for a document or within **Options** in Backstage.
Field	Display all the different fields to insert into the document.
Building Blocks Organizer	List all the building blocks available. Word provides you with a number of common types of data.
Save Selection to Quick Part Gallery	Save the selection as a building block in the Quick Parts Gallery for use in other documents.

The most common building blocks are headers and footers as these can be set up with specific fields. This is similar to setting up a template, but you can also add, modify, or remove items quickly using Quick Parts. You may not have this ability with templates if the template is shared with others.

You can create all kinds of information and save it as a building block e.g. a table, text box, sidebar, or cover page.

Inserting Fields

Fields are placeholders for information that can be inserted into a document and saved as a Quick Part for future use. Fields include information such as author name, company name, file name and location, bar code, hyperlink, total page count, or an automatic sequence number.

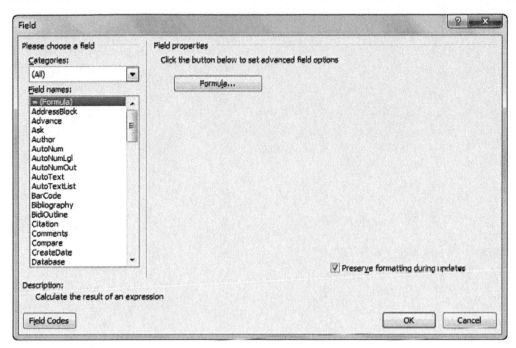

Categories	Lists categories for the different fields that can be inserted.
Field names	Lists the different types of fields you can insert using names that are very similar to the command function.
Field properties	Displays different options for the field chosen.
Field Codes	Displays how the field code appears when inserted into the document.

When you make a change to a building block by editing its properties or recreating it, Word prompts you to replace the previous entry. Make sure you are replacing the correct building block as, once it's replaced, you will need to recreate the building block if you inadvertently replaced the wrong one.

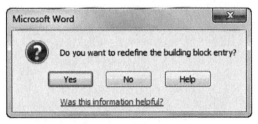

As you insert building blocks, these are saved in the Building Blocks Organizer as well as the different galleries used for each block. When you exit Word you will be prompted to save all the new entries into the *Building Blocks.dotx* template. This is the only way you can have these blocks available to all documents.

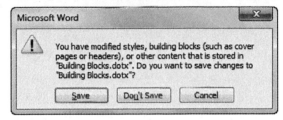

Learn the Skill

In this exercise you will create some AutoText entries for text you may use frequently as well as set up specific building blocks for other types of tasks.

1   Create a new blank document and then type the following:

Nick Klassen↵
Vice President↵
Tolano Adventures¶

Press SHIFT+ENTER to insert the text wrapping code for the first two lines of Nick's information.

2   Select the three lines of text. Click the **Insert** tab, in the **Text** group, click **Quick Parts**, click **AutoTex**t and then click **Save Selection to AutoText Gallery**.

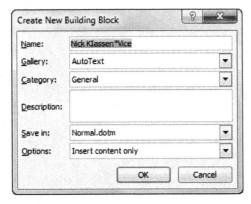

3   Type: NK for the name and then type the following for the description and then click **OK**:

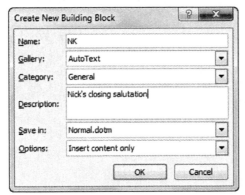

4   Create another blank document, press Enter several times, type: NK and then press F3.

Nick's information should appear in this new document.

Now create another AutoText entry to automatically show in a document where the file is saved.

5   Switch to the document where you inserted the AutoText for Nick Klassen.

6   Press Enter to move the cursor past Nick's information and then, on the **Insert** tab, in the **Text** group, click **Quick Part** and click **Field**.

7   In the Field names list, scroll and select **FileName**:

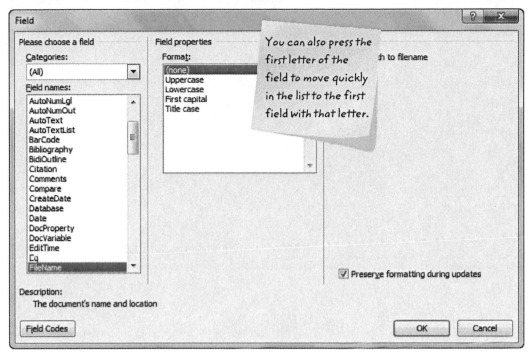

8   In the Format list, click **Lowercase**. Also click **Add path to filename** and click **OK**.

9   Select the text only (do not include the paragraph mark at the end of the line). Change the font to **Times New Roman** and size 9.

10   With the text still selected, click the **Insert** tab, in the **Text** group, click **AutoText** and then click **Save Selection to AutoText gallery**.

11   Type the following for this building block and click **OK** when done:

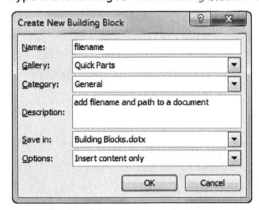

This AutoText can now be used anywhere in a document where you want to show the file name and the path to where the file was saved.

12   Switch to the blank document where you inserted the first AutoText.

13   On the **Insert** tab, in the **Header & Footer** group, click **Footer** and then click **Blank**.

14   Ensure the **Type Text** field is selected and then on the **Insert** tab, In the **Text** group, click **Quick Part**, click **AutoText**.

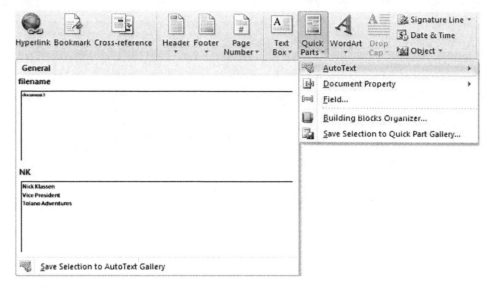

15 Click **filename**.

Note how the footer now shows the path for your document. In this case, the name of the blank document appears as you have not saved this file. To test that your new building block works on any document, you can open one of your existing documents.

16 Open a file from the student data files location. Then repeat steps 13 to 15 to insert the AutoText.

17 Close all documents without saving.

18 Exit Word.

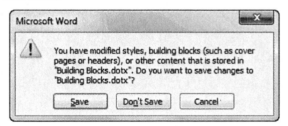

19 Click **Save** to ensure all your new entries are saved.

20 Restart Word.

Navigating with References

6.1

Word provides a number of ways to navigate or move to different parts of a document without scrolling page by page in the document. A common method is to use hyperlinks which can direct you to another part of the same document, a different document, a Web page or site on the Internet, or open a new blank e-mail.

In many cases, when you type text similar to an e-mail or a Web site address, Word will automatically convert this to a hyperlink.

To change text to a hyperlink, on the **Insert** tab, in the **Links** group, click **Hyperlink**.

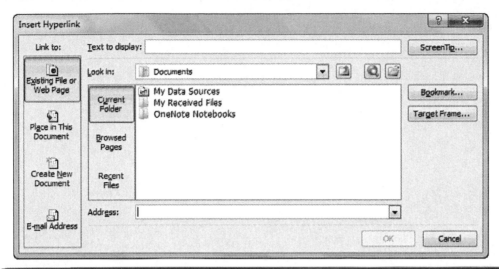

Learn the Skill

In this exercise, you will insert some hyperlinks into a document.

1 Open *Memo on Live Meeting* and save as Memo on Live Meeting with links - Student.

2 Move to the end of the document and type the following:

> If you want more information on what Live Meeting is, go to or send a message to David at dsingh@tolano.com.

3 Press (Enter) to have Word automatically change the email address to a hyperlink.

4 Position the cursor before the word "or" in the last sentence and type: www.microsoft.com/livemeeting. Press (Spacebar) to insert a space between this link and the existing text.

> If you want more information on what Live Meeting is, go to www.microsft.com/livemeeting or send a message to David at dsingh@tolano.com.

Now try setting up a hyperlink on existing text.

5 Select Nick Klassen near the front of the document. Click **Insert**, and in the **Links** group, click **Hyperlink**.

6 In the Link to area, click **E-mail Address** and then type the following as shown in the following:

7   Click **OK** when done.

Nick's name is now set up as a hyperlink.

8   Press (Ctrl) and then click his name to send him an e-mail.

9   Close the message without saving.

10   Save the document and then close it.

Using the Navigation Pane

2.2

You can navigate quickly to different areas of a document by using the Navigation Pane. This pane appears at the left and is similar to having a table of contents for your headings.

To display the Navigation Pane, on the **View** tab, in the **Show** group, click **Navigation Pane**. Then click the heading for the text you want to view.

This pane can be turned off using the same method as to activate it or by clicking the ⊠ in the task pane.

Learn the Skill

In this exercise, you will display the Navigation Pane to move around in the document.

1   Open *Tolano Employee Handbook* and save as `Tolano Employee Handbook - Student`.

2   Click the **View** tab and, in the **Show** group, click **Navigation Pane**.

3   Click **Tolano Organization Chart** to move to that page.

4   Scroll in the pane and then click **Dental**.

Creating a Table of Contents

6.3

Word has a feature that creates a table of contents, complete with the corresponding page numbers and selected formatting. One advantage of using this feature is that, when you edit the document, you can easily update the table of contents. Another advantage is having Word automatically generate a table of contents for any title that has a heading style applied to it.

To create a table of contents, you must work through three basic steps:

1. Specify the heading text you want to include.
2. Select the format.
3. Compile the table of contents.

Consider the following regarding the table of contents feature:

- The fastest and simplest way to create a table of contents is to use Word's standard heading styles (Headings 1 through 9).

- You can choose your own custom styles; however, it is more time consuming and you must provide details for the table of contents about these styles.

- If you want the table of contents to use a different page numbering format, add a section break after the table of contents page and then start the page numbering at 1 for the first page where the document content begins. Otherwise, the table of contents affects the page numbering for the rest of the document.

- When including an index in a document, create it (and apply a standard Word heading style to the title) before you compile the table of contents to include the index in the table of contents.

- The table of contents entries behave similar to hyperlinks. Click any entry in the table of contents to move to that item's location. This can be turned off if you don't want the links for the table of contents.

Once you have applied styles to the document headings and specified the text for the table of contents, you are ready to compile and format the table of contents. To generate or compile a table of contents, on the **References** tab, in the **Table of Contents** group, click **Table of Contents**.

Word provides different styles you can apply to the table of contents. To customize this, on the **References** tab, in the **Table of Contents** group, click **Table of Contents** and then click **Insert Table of Contents**.

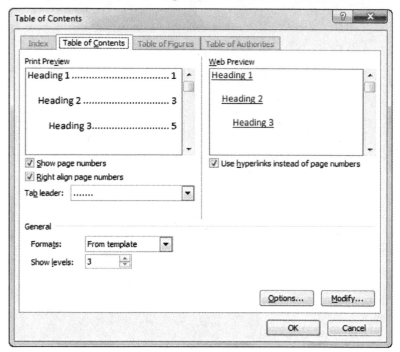

Print Preview	Displays a preview of the table of contents with the selected options.
Web Preview	How the table of contents appears if you save this document as a Web page.
Show page numbers	Use if you want page numbers for the table of contents entries.
Right align page numbers	Use if you want the page numbers to be aligned at the right margin.
Tab leader	Select the leader option from the table of contents entry to the page number.
Use hyperlinks instead of page numbers	Use if you want the table of contents entries to appear as hyperlinks instead of page numbers. This is useful for sharing documents where the users can move to the heading instead of looking for the page number.
General	Select the format or layout style to use for the table of contents. You can also set which heading levels you want to include in the table of contents.
Options	Select the styles to use as table of contents entries. For instance, if you create your own styles for headings, select these instead of the default Heading styles provided in Word.
Modify	Change the formatting attributes set for the styles to use in the table of contents.

If you make changes to your document, you must also change the table of contents. Changes that affect pagination, headings or text placement, also affect the table of contents entries. Word does not automatically reflect the changes; the table of contents must be refreshed.

To edit an entry in the table of contents, edit its corresponding heading in the document, or use the **Add Text** command appropriately. To update a table of contents, click anywhere in the existing table of contents and then use one of the following methods:

- On the **References** tab, in the **Table of Contents** group, click **Add Text** or **Update Table**, or

- in the tab above the table of contents, click **Update Table**.

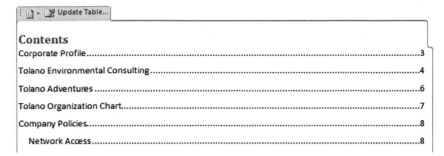

Contents

Corporate Profile...3

Tolano Environmental Consulting...4

Tolano Adventures 6

Tolano Organization Chart...7

Company Policies..8

    Network Access...8

The first button in the tab for this feature displays the built-in styles for the table of contents and includes the option to remove the table of contents.

Learn the Skill

In this exercise, you will insert a table of contents into an employee handbook and then update the table after editing the report.

1 Ensure *Tolano Employee Handbook – Student* is active on the screen. Go to page 2 and position the cursor in the first blank line on the page.

2 Click the **References** tab, in the **Table of Contents** group, click **Table of Contents** and then **Automatic Table 1** in the Built-in list.

Contents

Corporate Profile...3

Tolano Environmental Consulting...4

Tolano Adventures 6

Tolano Organization Chart...7

Company Policies..8

    Network Access...8

    Business Expenses 8

    IT Requirements...8

    Vacation Days...8

        Year 1 8

        Years 2 to 5 8

        Years 6+...8

    Time-Off Days..9

    Sick Days 9

    Bereavement Leave 9

Health Benefits...10

    Medical..10

    Dental..10

    Long Term Disability...10

    Life Insurance 10

Note that Word has automatically created the table of contents for you based on the heading styles. Word has also set up hyperlinks for each item in the table of contents, enabling the reader to quickly navigate to another part of the document.

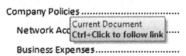

As you now browse through the report, you notice that the Vacation Days topic splits between two pages. You have also been informed that this document will be placed on the intranet so it would be helpful if the contents had links for employees to navigate quickly to specific topics.

3 Use the Navigation Pane to go to page 8 and then insert a page break before the Vacation Days title.

4 Repeat step 3 for the Bereavement Leave title.

5 Move to the Contents page and click anywhere in the table of contents. Then click **Update Table**.

6 Click **OK** to update the page numbers only, since you did not add or edit any headings in the document.

The page numbers are now correct, but there are no links for the online version of this document.

7 With the cursor inside the table of contents, click the **References** tab and, in the **Table of Contents** group, click **Table of Contents**. Then click **Insert Table of Contents**.

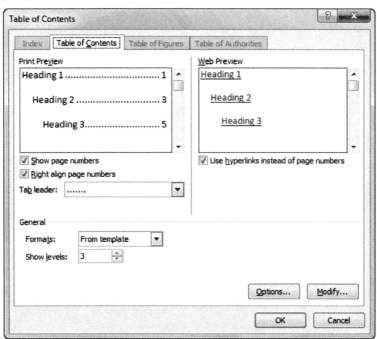

8 Deselect **Use hyperlinks instead of page numbers** and then click **OK**.

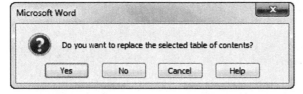

9 Click **Yes** to replace the existing table of contents.

10 Point the cursor at one of the title headings to view the prompt to move to that text.

Notice there is no prompt enabling you to navigate to that title.

11 Save and close the document.

Using Footnotes or Endnotes

6.2

Footnotes are references that usually appear at the bottom of the page, but may also be placed directly below the text. Each footnote has a numbered note reference mark, which often restarts on each page. The footnote reference mark is generally placed after the text you are referencing.

To create a footnote, on the **References** tab, in the **Footnotes** group, click **Insert Footnote**. The footnote will appear at the bottom of the screen, similar to:

[1]|

You can then enter the text for the footnote. The footnote number changes to match the number and placement of the footnotes in the document.

Endnotes usually appear at the end of the document or section to cite reference material. To create an endnote, on the **References** tab, in the **Footnotes** group, click the **Footnotes & Endnote Dialog box launcher**. Then click **Endnotes**.

To customize the footnote or endnote, on the **References** tab, in the **Footnotes** group, click the **Footnotes & Endnote Dialog box launcher**.

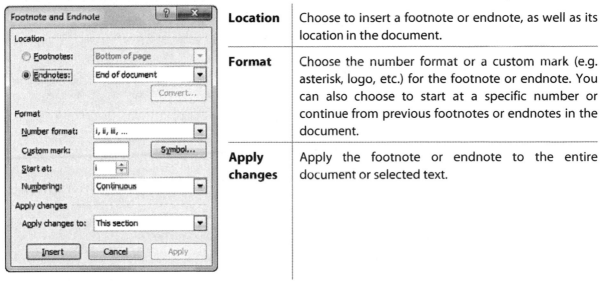

Location	Choose to insert a footnote or endnote, as well as its location in the document.
Format	Choose the number format or a custom mark (e.g. asterisk, logo, etc.) for the footnote or endnote. You can also choose to start at a specific number or continue from previous footnotes or endnotes in the document.
Apply changes	Apply the footnote or endnote to the entire document or selected text.

To view the text for a footnote or an endnote, hover on the note reference mark in the document.

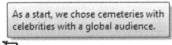

ere:

To move a footnote or endnote to another location in the document, cut the footnote or endnote reference in its current location in the document and paste it into the new location.

To delete a footnote or endnote, delete the footnote or endnote reference mark.

To convert a footnote to an endnote or vice versa, select the reference and then on the **References** tab, in the **Footnotes & Endnotes** group, click the **Footnotes & Endnotes Dialog box launcher**. Then click the **Convert** button.

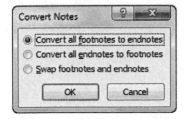

Learn the Skill

In this exercise, you will insert a footnote and endnote into a document.

1 Open *Haunted Sites Proposal* and save as Haunted Sites Proposal – Student.

2 Position the cursor at the end of the paragraph after the Haunted Sites title.

3 Click the **References** tab and, in the **Footnotes & Endnotes** group, click **Insert Footnote**.

4 At the bottom of the page after the reference mark, type the following:

> We have not included penitentiaries in the list due to the controversial nature of these buildings. We may want to start slowly with the buildings first.

- Dracula Halloween Tours, Bucharest

[1] We have not included penitentiaries in the list due to the controversial nature of these buildings. We may want to start slowly with the buildings first.

5 Move the picture away from the footnote.

6 Position the cursor at the end of the paragraph after the Celebrity Burial Sites. Repeat steps 3 and 4 to enter the following:

As a start, we chose cemeteries where international celebrities are buried.

Notice how, as you add more footnotes on a page, Word reduces the amount of text on the page to accommodate the space used by the footnotes.

7 Press (Ctrl)+(Home) to move quickly to the beginning of the document and position the cursor at the end of the main title.

8 On the **References** tab, in the **Footnotes & Endnotes** group, click the **Insert Endnote**.

9 Type the following:

> All lists were compiled from research done via the Internet and chosen from lists of the most well-known examples.

10 Change the document view to show two pages.

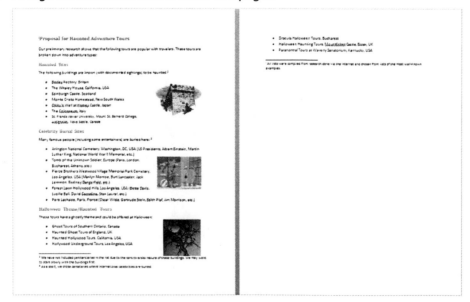

11 Save the document.

Protecting Documents

1.2

When you have a document that is sensitive or confidential, you can protect it from changes by adding a password using Backstage, marking the document as final, or restricting access from editing or formatting.

Using Passwords

A password can contain any combination of letters, numbers, spaces, and symbols. Passwords are case-sensitive so, if you use capitalization when you assign the password, you must use the same capitalization when you enter the password.

Give consideration to the type of password you should use on the document. Most people have a small list of passwords they use for online information and alternate between these when picking a password. Below are some guidelines to follow when choosing a secure password:

- Do not use your name or the name of your spouse/companion, children, or pets. Any unauthorized user who can obtain information about you will try these names first.

- Do not use any nicknames for yourself or others close to you. Again, any unauthorized user who can obtain information about you will try these names first. A mix of text and numbers is a good strategy, but refrain from using passwords such as Jan01, Feb02, or Sep2012.

- Passwords are case sensitive so use a mix of upper and lower case characters.

- The longer the password, the less chance someone will be able to guess which characters make up the password. Most network administrators recommend a minimum of 8 characters for a password.

If you need to share the password for a sensitive document, change the password as soon as the need to share the document has passed.

When you create a password, write it down and keep it in a safe place. If you lose the password, you cannot open or access the password-protected document. Consider keeping a password protected list of passwords, or providing this list to the network administrator for safekeeping.

To add a password to a document, click the **File** tab, click **Save As**, click **Tools** in the Save dialog box, and then click **General Options**.

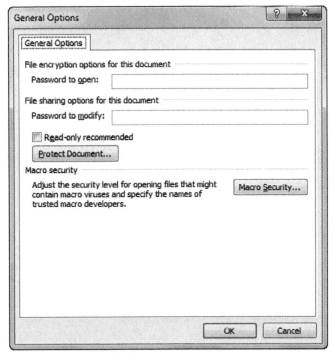

MMM
Annual Report
Online
Exercise

Password to Open	User must enter the correct password to open this document.
Password to modify	User must enter the correct password to open this document as well as another password to edit the document.
Read-only recommended	User can open and modify the document, but must save it with a different name, leaving the original document intact.

To remove or change a password you must know the existing password. You then simply change or delete the password at the time of saving the document.

Learn the Skill

In this exercise, you will set different types of passwords on a proposal until you are ready to present it.

1   Ensure the *Haunted Sites Proposal – Student* is active on the screen.

2   Click the **File** tab and then click **Save As**.

3   Click **Tools** and then click **General Options**.

4   In the **Password to open** field, type: haunted and press (Enter).

5   Retype the password and then click **OK**.

It may appear as if nothing has changed in the file, but you have just added a password to this file.

6   Close the document and then try opening it.

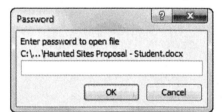

7   Type: haunted as the password and click **OK** (or press (Enter)).

The document appears on your screen.

Now try making the file read-only access.

8   Click the **File** tab, click **Save As**, click **Tools** and then click **General Options**.

9   Delete all the characters in the **Password to open** field and click **Read-only recommended**.

10   Click **OK**, save the document and then close it.

11   Open the document.

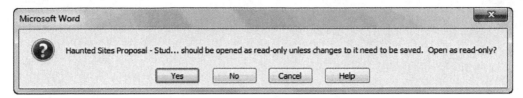

12 Click **Yes**.

13 On the Quick Access toolbar, click **Save**. Click **Save** in the Save As dialog box.

Note that you cannot save this file with the same name, even though you made no changes to it.

14 Click **OK** and close this document.

15 Open the document again, but this time click **No** to read-only access.

16 Click **File**, click **Save As**, click **Tools**, and then click **General Options**.

17 Uncheck the **Read only access**.

18 Type: haunted for the password to open and then type: sites as the password to modify the document.

19 Re-enter the passwords as needed.

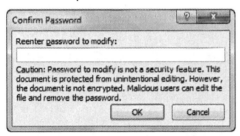

20 Click **OK** and then save and close the document.

21 Open the document by entering the correct password to open it.

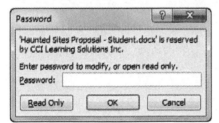

22 Type the password to modify the document.

Now remove all passwords from this document.

23 Click the **File** tab, click **Save As**, click **Tools** and then click **General Options**.

24 Delete the passwords from both fields and then click **OK**. Save the file and then close it.

25 Open the file once more to test if you have any passwords still assigned to the document.

 ## Marking a Document as Final

1.2

Another option to protecting a document is to mark it as final. By doing this, you can send it out to others and prevent them from accidentally making changes. When the final status is turned on, all typing, editing, and proofing commands are turned off and the file is set to read-only.

To mark a document as final, click **File**. With the Info category selected, click **Protect Document**, and then click **Mark as Final**,

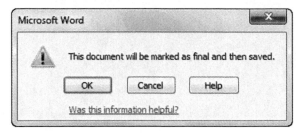

Note that this is not meant as a security feature by preventing all changes to the document as the final status can be turned off. To reverse this status, select **Mark as Final** again.

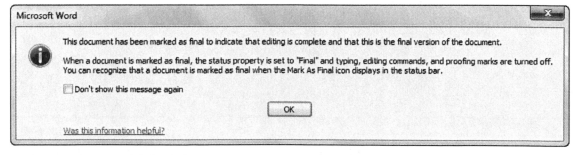

Learn the Skill

In this exercise, you will protect a document using the Mark as Final option to prevent others from changing it.

1   Ensure the *Haunted Sites Proposal – Student* document is active on the screen.

2   Click **File** and ensure the Info category is selected. Click **Protect Document** and then click **Mark as Final**.

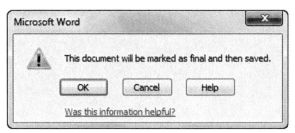

3   Click **OK**.

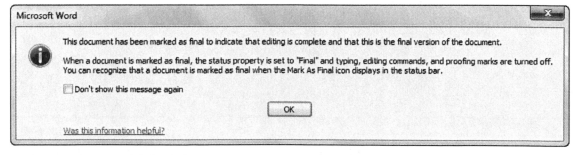

4   Read the message and then click **OK**.

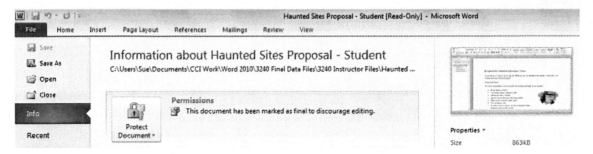

Notice what information Word now shows you about this file, both for protection and in the title bar.

5 Click **File** to go back to the document.

Word has protected this document and displays a message to others accordingly.

6 Close the document.

Restricting Access to Documents

Instead of adding a password is to restrict specific formatting or editing of the document. The document cannot be changed without entering the correct password. This is beneficial when you want people to review the document, provide comments, fill in forms, etc. but not modify the contents of the document.

To restrict a document, on the **Review** tab, in the **Protect** group, click **Protect Document**, and then click **Restrict Formatting and Editing**. The Restrict Formatting and Editing pane appears for further options. You can then set up restrictions based on your needs.

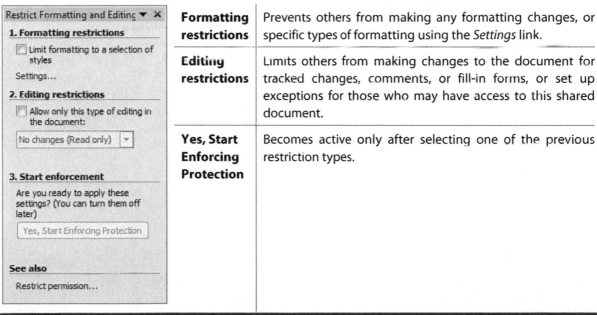

Formatting restrictions	Prevents others from making any formatting changes, or specific types of formatting using the *Settings* link.
Editing restrictions	Limits others from making changes to the document for tracked changes, comments, or fill-in forms, or set up exceptions for those who may have access to this shared document.
Yes, Start Enforcing Protection	Becomes active only after selecting one of the previous restriction types.

Learn the Skill

In this exercise you will set different types of restriction access to a document.

1 Open *Corporate Profile* and save it as Corporate Profile for intranet – Student.

2 Click the **Review** tab and in the **Protect** group, click **Restrict Editing**.

3   In the Restrict Formatting and Editing task pane, click **Allow only this type of editing in the document**.

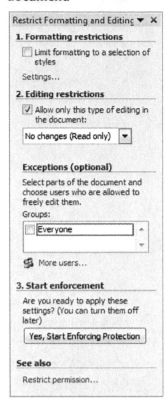

4   As this contains the restrictions options you want for this document, click **Yes, Start Enforcing Protection**.

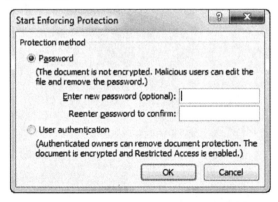

5   Type: tolano as the password for both fields.

Hint: To ensure others cannot edit your document, use a secure password that cannot be easily guessed. For the purpose of this demonstration, we have chosen to use a simple one.

6   Click **OK**.

7   Save and close the document.

8   Open the document again and try to delete a word in the document.

    You should not be able to make any changes to the document. Look at the task pane to see what options are available for editing.

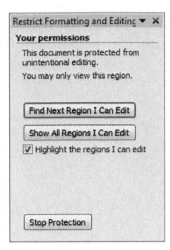

If you scroll through the document, you will notice there are no areas you can edit. This is a result of choosing no changes can be made and the file was saved with Read-only access.

9   Click **Stop Protection**.

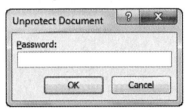

10   Type: tolano for the password and click **OK**.

Word now displays the Restrict Formatting and Editing task pane again so you can make changes as needed.

11   Close the document without saving.

Recovering Document Versions

As you work on documents, you do not need to save the file after each change and in fact, may not save the file for a length of time. However, you may want to take advantage of a tool Word provides a tool to automatically save your files so they can be recovered should you experience a system failure such as a power outage.

You can also set Word to automatically save a copy of the file at a set interval. You then do not need to save the file each time a change is made. It also enables documents to be recovered when Word stops responding. It is recommended that you activate this feature if you use Word for the majority of your daily work, or if working with large documents with multiple pictures.

To set the time to automatically save versions for AutoRecovery, click the **File** tab and click **Options**. Then click **Save** and make the appropriate choices in the Save documents area:

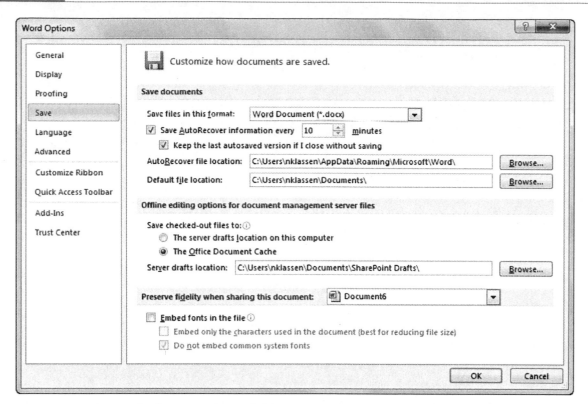

Note you can change the location where all documents recovered are stored. You can also view the files in this location using Windows Explorer. This location will vary if you use a notebook connected to a network, as seen in this example.

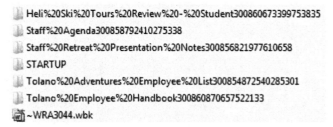

Heli%20Ski%20Tours%20Review%20-%20Student300860673399753835
Staff%20Agenda300858792410275338
Staff%20Retreat%20Presentation%20Notes300856821977610658
STARTUP
Tolano%20Adventures%20Employee%20List300854872540285301
Tolano%20Employee%20Handbook300860870657522133
~WRA3044.wbk

The list here will also show all the backups that were made for a particular document in addition to the AutoSaved files.

Alternatively, use Backstage to manage any versions that you may not have saved. These could be drafts of a document that you may not have saved yet, or been saved by the AutoSave option.

You can view all the versions of the document that have been saved by using one of the following:

- Click **File** and, with **Info** selected, click **Manage Versions**. Then click **Recover Unsaved Documents**, or

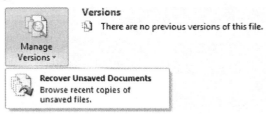

Versions

There are no previous versions of this file.

Recover Unsaved Documents
Browse recent copies of unsaved files.

- Click **File**, click **Recent** at the left, and then click **Recover Unsaved Documents**.

Doc2((Unsaved-300856482392892192)).asd
Doc3((Unsaved-300856533681815712)).asd
Doc3((Unsaved-300860142384841856)).asd
Doc4((Unsaved-300854324134818128)).asd
Doc4((Unsaved-300858182689191872)).asd
Doc5((Unsaved-300858253276700800)).asd
Doc6((Unsaved-300854370093951648)).asd
New Tour Process((Unsaved-300858602878545440)).asd
Nick Klassen((Unsaved-300860164239797264)).asd
Popular Bicycling Tours((Unsaved-300854563398233024)).asd
Staff List((Unsaved-300858520786563808)).asd

Select the file from the list. If this is the unsaved file you want, click the **File** tab and, with **Info** selected, click **Manage Versions**.

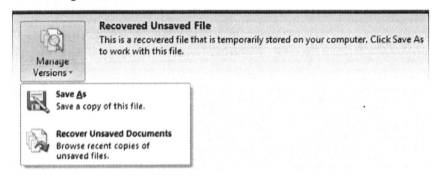

You are notified immediately that this file has not been saved as yet with the option now to save it.

When Word stops responding, it may restart itself or you may need to shut it down. However, once you start Word again, the Recovery pane appears containing the documents last active on the screen prior to the conflict. You can then click the document you want to recover from the list. It is strongly recommended that you save the document at that time before resuming work on it in case another failure occurs.

Alternatively, if you want to clear all documents in the AutoRecovery area, you can choose to delete these:

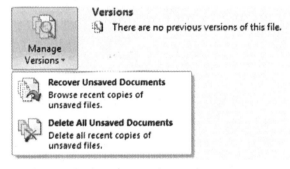

Lesson Summary

In this lesson, you were introduced to building content for use in other documents, including Quick Parts and organizing these building blocks. You should now be able to:

☑ understand what building blocks are

☑ create and edit building blocks

☑ insert Quick Parts items or fields

☑ navigate documents

☑ manage versions for documents

☑ protect your documents with a password

Review Questions

MMM
Go online for
Additional
Review and
Activities

1. Explain what a Quick Part is.

2. Provide two examples of ways you can move around quickly in a document.

3. What is the difference between a footnote and an endnote?

4. What are some general guidelines in regards to picking a password for a document?

5. How can you reduce the amount of work you would need to do on documents in the case of a power failure?

Microsoft®
Word 2010
Core Certification

Appendices

Appendix A
Courseware Mapping

Appendix B
Glossary of Terms

Appendix C
Index

Appendix A: Courseware Mapping

Skills Required for the Microsoft® Office Specialist Word 2010 Core Exam 77-881:

	Objective Domain	Lesson
1	**Sharing and Maintaining Documents**	
	1.1 Apply different views to a document	2
	1.2 Apply protection to a document	10
	1.3 Manage document versions	10
	1.4 Share documents	1
	1.5 Save a Document	1
	1.6 Apply a template to a document	1
2	**Formatting Content**	
	2.1 Apply font and paragraph attributes	3
	2.2 Navigate and search through a document	2, 10
	2.3 Apply indentation and tab settings to paragraphs	3, 4
	2.4 Apply spacing settings to text and paragraphs	3
	2.5 Create tables	7
	2.6 Manipulate tables in a document	7
	2.7 Apply bullets to a document	4
3	**Applying Page Layout and Reusable Content**	
	3.1 Apply and manipulate page setup settings	5
	3.2 Apply themes	5
	3.3 Construct content in a document by using the Quick Parts tool	10
	3.4 Create and manipulate page backgrounds	5
	3.5 Create and modify headers and footers	5
4	**Including Illustrations and Graphics in a Document**	
	4.1 Insert and format Pictures in a document	8
	4.2 Insert and format shapes, WordArt, and SmartArt	8
	4.3 Insert and format Clip Art	8
	4.4 Apply and manipulate text boxes	8
5	**Proofreading documents**	
	5.1 Validate content by using spelling and grammar checking options	6
	5.2 Configure AutoCorrect settings	6
	5.3 Insert and modify comments in a document	6
6	**Applying References and Hyperlinks**	
	6.1 Apply a hyperlink	10
	6.2 Create Endnotes and Footnotes in a document	10
	6.3 Create a Table of Contents in a document	10
7	**Performing Mail Merge Operations**	
	7.1 Setup mail merge	9
	7.2 Execute mail merge	9

Appendix B: Glossary of Terms

Alignment – The position of text in relation to the margins (such as center, left, right, or justify), tab settings, or a specific location.

AutoCorrect – A feature that automatically corrects many common spelling, punctuation and capitalization errors as you type. This feature can also be used to expand abbreviated words.

Backgrounds – Set a color or picture to apply as the background behind text.

Baseline – The "base" where the bottom of most characters are aligned. The baseline is used as the base from which to measure line spacing.

Bookmark – A feature for marking text or a place in the document to find a marked place quickly and easily.

Building Blocks – Building block content includes headers and footers, cover pages, text boxes, bibliographies, citations, placeholders, equations, themes, and content controls (fields). See Quick Parts.

Building Blocks Organizer – A feature that stores all Quick Parts created by you or Microsoft for items that are used frequently in documents such as company header, standard footer text that contains the file name and its location, etc.

Bullets – The feature that enables you to apply bullets to text.

Caption – A piece of text that identifies the table or figure shown in the document. Can be placed above or below the table or figure.

Change Case – The feature that enables you to switch the casing of text from all lowercase to all uppercase or to Title Case.

Clip Art – Images created by Microsoft or other third party vendors and made available for use in Word documents.

Column – A vertical arrangement of text that is separated from other columns by white space or a ruling line.

Comments – A feature that allows initialed comments to be added by different people who are reviewing a document. These comments can either be deleted or pasted into the document.

Copy – An editing function used to duplicate designated text, objects or files using the Office Clipboard.

Cross-Reference – A reference in a document that has been linked to another item in the document, e.g., page number, heading, etc.

Cut – An editing function used to move designated text, objects or files to the Office Clipboard.

Document Inspector – A tool to assist in removing any personal or hidden information you don't want others to see when they open this file.

Drawing Canvas – A placeholder where you can insert objects, including text, and keep the items within that canvas as a single entity.

Drawing Objects/Shapes – Objects that can be selected from the Insert tab or the Drawing Tools tab to be drawn in a document. See Shapes.

Edit – The process of manipulating (adding, removing, formatting) text.

Extension – The last part of the name given to a file. An extension may be up to three characters and usually describes the type of file (e.g., .DOCX for Word documents).

Fields – A code that Word inserts to represent a specific type of information, such as file name, date, page number, etc.

File name – The first part of the name given to a file. The file name may be up to 255 characters and usually describes the contents of the file.

Find – A feature that enables you to find specified text within a document.

Font – A specific typeface design.

Font Size – The vertical measurement to identify the height of proportionally printed characters (72 points equals 1 inch).

Footer – Text or graphics that repeat at the bottom of every page. A footer may include automatic page numbers.

Format – Word processing instructions as to how the text is to be printed (e.g., margins, tabs, bold text, underline, etc.).

Gutter – The extra space provided at the inside margin to accommodate punch holes or binding.

Header – Text or graphics that repeat at the top of every page. A header may include automatic page numbers.

Hyperlink – A feature that allows you to link one item to another to move quickly to another location. Hyperlinks can be set up in a Word document or a web page.

Indent – A temporary left and/or right margin, usually in effect for one paragraph at a time.

Main Document – The form that contains the consistent information for a mass mailing and will receive data matching the merge codes from the source data, e.g., letter, envelope, labels, etc.

Margin – The white space or area from the edge of the paper to the text.

Merge – The process of combining two documents to create a third, usually a list of names and addresses with a letter or envelope.

Merge Codes – A code identifying the type of data to be inserted into the main document during the merge process, e.g., date, first name, address, invoice #, etc.

Monospacing – The type of consistent spacing used between characters, measured in CPI (characters per inch) or pitch. Each character uses the same amount of space.

Multilevel List – The feature that enables you to apply numbering or bullets to multiple levels of text.

Non-printing Characters – Codes provided by Microsoft to help identify certain features or actions in the document, e.g., ¶ displays when the Enter key is pressed, → displays when the Tab key is pressed, etc.

Normal.dotx – The default template provided by Word whenever you create a blank document. Macros, AutoText, or customization of toolbars or menus will be saved with this template unless otherwise indicated.

Numbering – The feature that enables you to apply numbering to text.

Office Clipboard – A place to store data temporarily pending retrieval.

Orientation – The direction of the paper for text flow; Portrait takes advantage of the length of the paper vertically whereas Landscape uses the length of the paper horizontally.

Page – The number of lines designated to create a page of data. Word automatically divides the document into pages based on the margin settings, the line spacing and the size of text.

Page Break – The division between two pages. Word automatically creates Soft Page Breaks that are adjusted accordingly when you add or remove text. You can create Hard Page Breaks which are always in effect.

Page Numbering – The feature that enables you to have Word display the current page number in the document.

Page Setup – The process that determines how Word displays or prints the document, e.g., margins, paper size, etc.

Passwords – A feature you can apply to a document to make it more secure from access by other users unless authorized. You can choose from read only, modify only, or both. See Encryption for another method to secure documents.

Paste – The editing function of placing cut or copied data into a new location.

Paste Special – The editing function of pasting a specific type of information in this location.

Picture – A graphic file that can be inserted into a Word document. This can be in a large variety of file formats, including Windows Metafile (*.wmf), JPEG File Interchangeable format (*.jpg, *jpeg), Portable Network Graphics (*.png), Windows Bitmap (*.bmp), or Graphics Interchange format (*.gif).

Properties – A feature you can use to access or enter information about a file such as the author's name, the department responsible for updates to this document, etc.

Proportional Spacing – The space used for individual characters and is measured in point size. With proportional spacing five WWWWW's take up more space than five IIIII's. Proportionally spaced text is easier to read than monospaced text and allows approximately 25% more text per page.

Quick Access Toolbar – By default, located next to the Office Button and contains popular commands such as Save, Undo, and Redo. This toolbar can be customized for those commands you use frequently.

Quick Part – A feature that enables you to store text or graphics for repetitive use. These can be stored as a Quick Part or in the Building Blocks Organizer. See Building Blocks.

Replace – A feature that enables you to find and then replace specified text throughout the document.

Ribbon – A collection of tabs located directly below the title bar, providing quick access to commands required to complete a task.

Ribbon Tabs – Relates to a type of activity, organizing command buttons into logical groups. The group name appears on the Ribbon tab below the group of command buttons.

Ruler – Located below the Ribbon. The ruler displays icons that allow you to perform functions such as changing margins, tabs and indents quickly.

Save – The process of storing or copying the information in the memory to a disk. If you turn the computer off without saving to a disk, you lose all the information you have entered in the memory.

Section Break – The division between two different sections or areas of text, indicating a change that affects only that section or area, e.g., portrait versus landscape orientation, different headers and footers, etc.

Shapes – Objects that can be selected from the Insert tab or the Drawing Tools tab to be drawn in a document.

SmartArt – An illustration type for common types of diagrams, containing a text pane for easy text entry.

Source Document – A file containing the data to be used in the merge process; can contain any type of data, e.g., inventory, names and addresses, product/catalog items, etc.

Spacing – Refers to the amount of white space between individual characters, words, or lines of text or objects.

Symbol – A character that can be inserted into a document, either as a text character or for a bullet or numbering style.

Tab – A character that causes the text to move to an exact predefined location (tab stop). Could also refer to a divider indicator within a dialog box.

Table – A grid design that allows you to enter columnar information that can then be formatted. Often considered to be easier to set up for columns of information instead of setting up tab positions.

Table of Contents – A feature that uses the headings in the document to outline the contents.

Template – A pre-designed form created either by Microsoft or a user that can be used to create a specific type of document. Setting up a template enables documents of that type to have a consistent look.

Themes – A set of integrated document design elements that make your online documents appealing and effective.

View Options – Different ways of being able to view the document, usually to assist in working with the text, page layout, web layout, an outline, or reading.

Watermark – Text, graphics, AutoShapes, drawing objects, or pictures that usually appear behind text.

Appendix C: Index

Developing Visual Memory

Materials:

Cuisenaire rods for each child
Centimetre graph paper for each child
Unlined paper for each child

Settings:

Two children working together
A small group, children working in pairs
A whole class, children working in pairs

Learning Experience:

Ask the first child in each pair to build a design on centimetre graph paper, using no more than six rods. The second child watches.

When the design has been built, the second child studies it while the first child counts slowly to ten.

Now the first child hides the rod design under a sheet of plain paper. The second child tries to build the same design from memory on the sheet of centimetre graph paper.

This activity requires the child to deal abstractly with the specific length or color characteristics of the rods. It also calls upon the skill of visual memory. Visual memory or the lack of it has specific ramifications on success in many mathematical topics. Hence this type of activity should be repeated throughout the year.

A more difficult version of this experience is to provide the child with a picture of a colored rod design which must be built from memory. The pictures from previous activities or the one provided on page 46 may be used.

Once color and length are established firmly, uncolored rod designs and free form designs could be used as even greater challenges.

Underlying Mathematics:

Visual memory of shapes
One-to-one correspondence
Association of 3-dimensional rods with 2-dimensional representations
Association of colors with lengths

Picturing Rod Staircases

"Photographing" a Staircase

Materials:
Cuisenaire rods for each child

Settings:
A small group led by the teacher
A whole class led by the teacher

Learning Experience:

Ask each child to make a staircase as a reminder of the order of the rods.

Tell the children to concentrate on the staircase and to "photograph" it in their minds.

With eyes closed, the children chant the colors in order from smallest to largest:

White, red, green, purple, yellow
Dark green, black, brown, blue, orange.

It is helpful to concentrate on the five smallest rods and then on the five largest rods before all ten rods.

Now ask the children to name the rods from largest to smallest, first with eyes opened and then closed.

The children may wish to continue building their staircase down from orange to white. As a challenge, name the rods from white to orange going up the staircase, and then from orange to white going down the staircase. Have the children try this in unison five times, with their eyes closed as much of the time as possible.

For fun, children may want to name the sequence in another way; for example using flavors:

Vanilla, strawberry, lime, grape, lemon
Spearmint, licorice, root beer, blueberry, orange.

Underlying Mathematics:

Ordering of lengths
Recognition of rod lengths
Visual memory of shapes

Music for "Oh When the Saints Come Marching In"

Marching with the Rods

Materials:

Cuisenaire rods for the teacher
A Cuisenaire Rod Rack or box lid for the teacher

Settings:

Ten or more children led by the teacher

Learning Experience:

Make a staircase on the Cuisenaire Rod Rack (or box lid) to remind the children of the order of the rod colors.

Give each child a Cuisenaire rod so that all ten colors are used. There will be repeats if there are more than ten children.

Lead the children in singing this adaptation of the song, "Oh When the Saints Come Marching In." When a particular color is mentioned, the children holding the corresponding rod stand up and march around, holding the rods in front of them.

Chorus: Oh when the rods come marching through,
                Oh when the rods come marching through,
                We can see all ten colors,
                When the rods come marching through.

Verse 1:   Oh, there'll be white, and there'll be red,
                And there'll be green and purple too.
                We can see all those colors,
                When the rods come marching through. (Repeat Chorus.)

Verse 2:   Then there'll be yellow and dark green,
                And there'll be black and brown and blue.
                We can see all those colors,
                When the rods come marching through. (Repeat Chorus.)

Verse 3:   The longest rod is yet to come.
                We know that orange follows blue.
                We can see all ten colors,
                When the rods come marching through. (Repeat Chorus.)

Underlying Mathematics:

Association of colors with rods
Recognition of rod lengths
Ordering of lengths

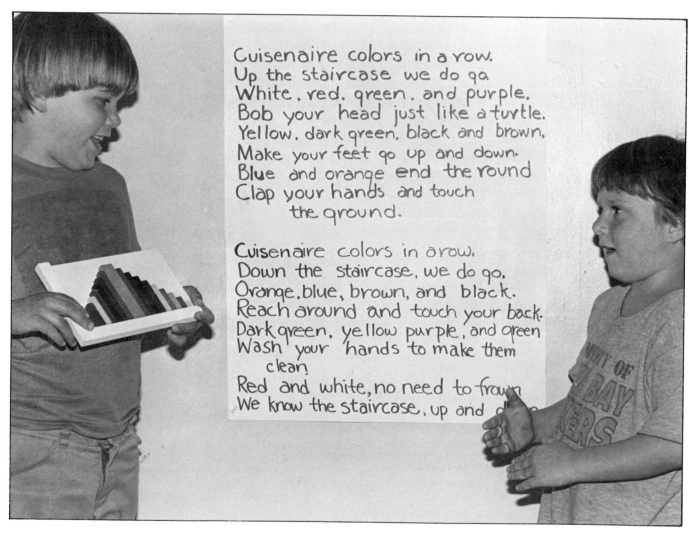

Cuisenaire colors in a row.
Up the staircase we do go
White, red, green, and purple,
Bob your head just like a turtle.
Yellow, dark green, black and brown,
Make your feet go up and down.
Blue and orange end the round
Clap your hands and touch
          the ground.

Cuisenaire colors in a row.
Down the staircase, we do go.
Orange, blue, brown, and black.
Reach around and touch your back.
Dark green, yellow purple, and green
Wash your hands to make them
    clean.
Red and white, no need to frown
We know the staircase, up and down.

Learning the Rod Colors through Rhymes

Acting Out Rhymes

Materials:

Cuisenaire rods for each child

Settings:

A small group led by the teacher
A whole class led by the teacher

Learning Experience:

Ask each child to build two staircases, one from smallest to largest and one from largest to smallest.

Lead the children in saying and acting out this rhyme. Children can either stand or sit. They can look at their staircases for help in remembering the colors.

Cuisenaire colors in a row
Up the staircase, we do go,
White, red, green, and purple,
Bob your head just like a turtle.
Yellow, dark green, black, and brown,
Blue and orange end the round.
Clap your hands and touch the ground.

Cuisenaire colors in a row,
Down the staircase, we do go,
Orange, blue, brown, and black.
Reach around and touch your back.
Dark green, yellow, purple, and green
Wash your hands to make them clean.
Red and white, no need to frown
We know the staircase, up and down.

Underlying Mathematics:

Association of colors with rods
Recognition of rod lengths
Ordering of lengths

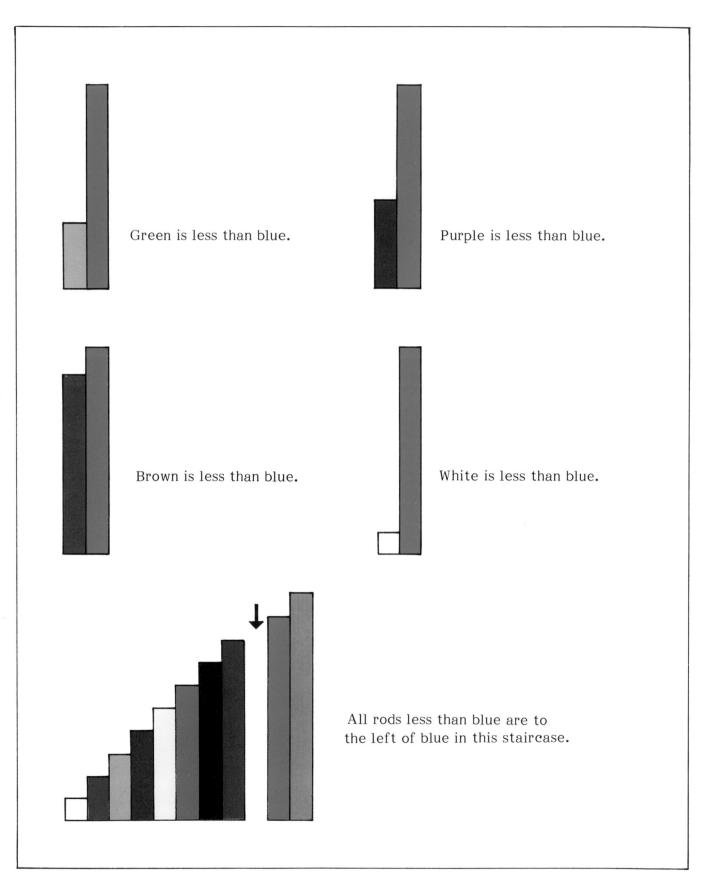

Green is less than blue.

Purple is less than blue.

Brown is less than blue.

White is less than blue.

All rods less than blue are to the left of blue in this staircase.

Finding Rods Less Than the Blue Rod

Finding Rods Less Than . . .

Materials:

Cuisenaire rods for each child
Cuisenaire rods for the teacher

Settings:

A small group led by the teacher
A whole class led by the teacher

Learning Experience:

Choose a yellow rod and a blue rod and place them side by side ...

like this ...   or like this.

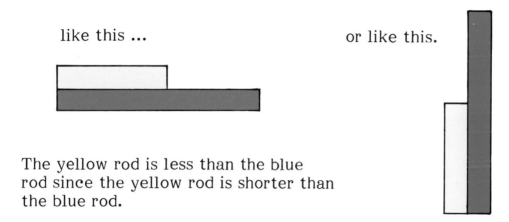

The yellow rod is less than the blue
rod since the yellow rod is shorter than
the blue rod.

Ask the children to find other rods less than the blue rod. (All
possible answers include white, red, green, purple, yellow, dark
green, black, and brown.)

Choose another rod and ask the children to find all the rods less
than it. Children should be able to prove the inequality by placing
the rods side by side.

In finding all rods less than a given rod, some children will discover
that it is possible to select an appropriate portion of a staircase.

Some interesting questions include:

Is there any rod which has no rods less than it? (White)
Is there any rod less than all other rods? (White)
All of these rods (random handful) are less than what rod?
Is there more than one correct answer?

Underlying Mathematics:

Inequalities (less than)
Comparisons of lengths
Ordering of lengths

Finding Any Rod Greater Than a Purple Rod

Finding Rods Greater Than . . .

Materials:
Cuisenaire rods for each child
Cuisenaire rods for the teacher

Settings:
A small group led by the teacher
A whole class led by the teacher

Learning Experience:

Choose a black rod and a purple rod and place them side by side.

The children will find that:

>The black rod is greater than the purple rod since the black rod is longer than the purple rod.

Ask the children to find other rods greater than the purple rod. (All possible answers include yellow, dark green, black, brown, blue, and orange.)

Hold up another rod and have the children respond by holding up any rod greater than it. Have the children prove each inequality by placing the rods side by side.

In finding all rods greater than a given rod, some children will discover that it is possible to select an appropriate portion of a staircase.

Some interesting questions include:

>Is there any rod which has no single rod greater than it? (Orange)
>Is there any rod greater than all other rods? (Orange)
>All of these rods (random handful) are greater than what rod?
>Is there more than one correct answer?

Children should be encouraged to ask each other questions so that they have the opportunity to use the vocabulary of greater than and less than.

Underlying Mathematics:

Inequalities (greater than)
Comparisons of lengths
Ordering of lengths

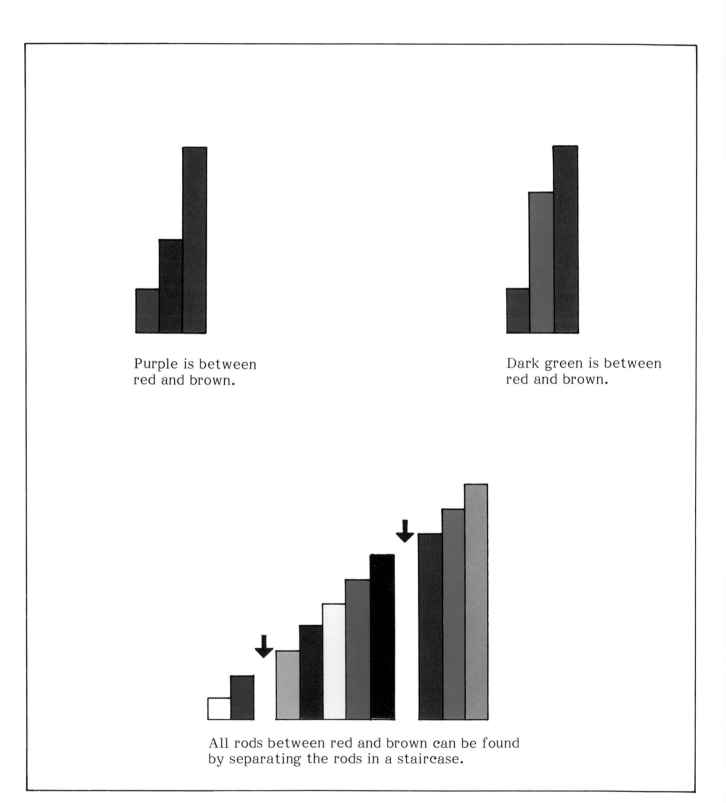

Purple is between
red and brown.

Dark green is between
red and brown.

All rods between red and brown can be found
by separating the rods in a staircase.

Finding Rods Between Red and Brown

Finding Rods Between . . .

Materials:

Cuisenaire rods for each child
Cuisenaire rods for the teacher

Settings:

A small group led by the teacher
A whole class led by the teacher

Learning Experience:

Choose a red, a yellow, and a brown rod and place them in order
as shown:

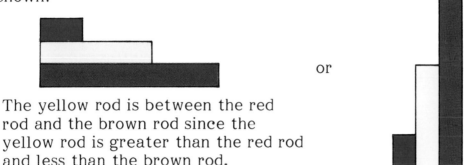

or

The yellow rod is between the red
rod and the brown rod since the
yellow rod is greater than the red rod
and less than the brown rod.

Ask the children to find other rods between red and brown. (All
possible answers include green, purple, yellow, dark green, and
black.)

Choose two different rods and ask the children to find all the rods
whose lengths lie between the lengths of those two. Children should
be able to prove their answers by placing the rods in order.

In finding all rods between two given rods, some children will discover that it is possible to select an appropriate portion of a staircase.

Some interesting questions include:

Name all of the rods between purple and yellow. (There are
none.)
Name two other rods for which no rods lie between them.
What two rods have the most rods between them? (White and
orange.)

Underlying Mathematics:

Inequalities (between)
Comparisons of lengths
Ordering of lengths

Two Ways of Measuring a Dark Green Rod with White Rods

Measuring with White Rods

Materials:
Cuisenaire rods for each child
A Cuisenaire Rod Rack or ruler for each child

Settings:
A small group led by the teacher
A whole class led by the teacher

Learning Experience:

Ask each child to take one rod at a time and to match it with white
rods. A Rod Rack or ruler can be used to help children line up
the rods. The children count how many white rods are needed to
match each rod.

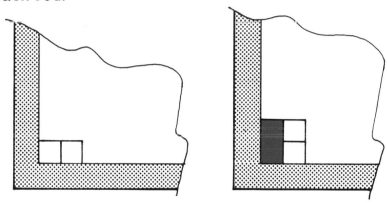

This experience provides counting experience for young children.
It also gives the children the opportunity to establish equivalences:
for example, 1 red = 2 whites; 1 green = 3 whites; 1 yellow = 5
whites; 1 orange ⁻ 10 whites.

Some interesting questions include:

Which rod matches the smallest number of whites? (White.)
Which rod matches the most whites? (Orange.)
Which rods match more than 5 whites? (Dark green, black,
brown, blue, and orange.)
Which rods match less than 4 whites? (White, red, and green.)
How many more white rods does black match than purple? (3)
Which rod is one white more than a dark green rod? (Black)
If there were a rod one white more than the orange rod, how
many whites would it take to match it? (11)

Underlying Mathematics:
Recognition of equivalences of lengths
Representation of lengths in terms of white rods
Counting from 1 to 10
Association of numbers with rods

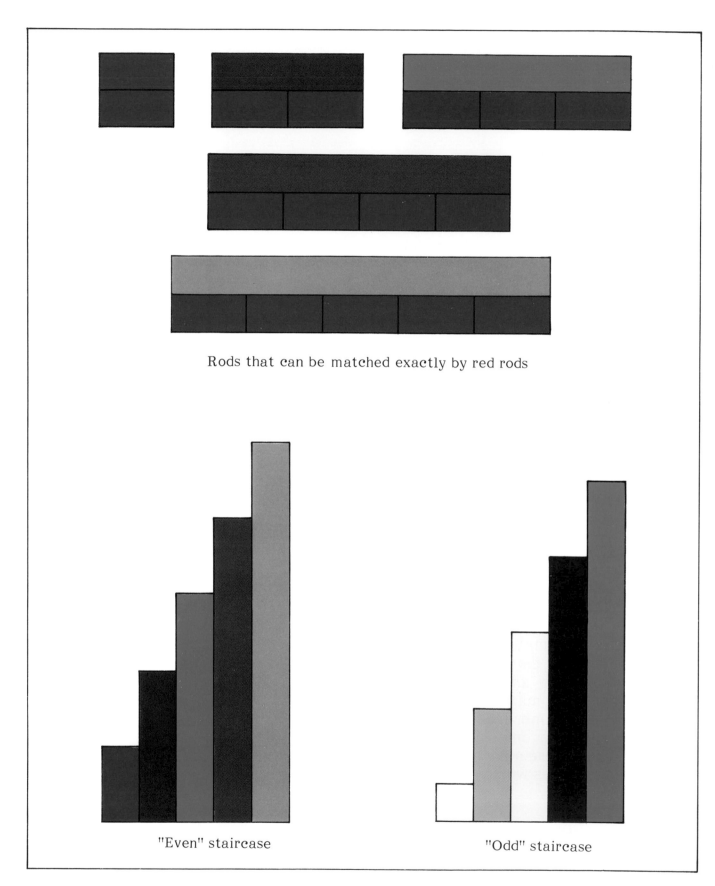

Rods that can be matched exactly by red rods

"Even" staircase

"Odd" staircase

Measuring with Red Rods

Measuring with Red Rods

Materials:

Cuisenaire rods for each child
A Cuisenaire Rod Rack or ruler for each child

Settings:

One child working individually
A small group, children working individually

Learning Experience:

Ask each child to take one rod at a time and to match it with red rods.
A Rod Rack or ruler can be used to help children line up the rods.

The children should note that some rods cannot be matched exactly
by red rods.

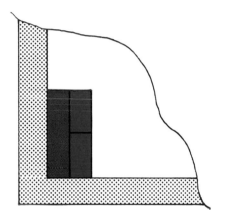

Purple can be matched
with 2 red rods.

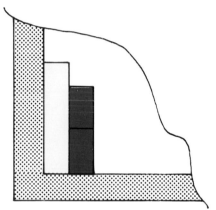

Yellow cannot be matched
with red rods.

Ask the children to select those rods which can be measured by red
rods and to make a staircase:

Red, purple, dark green, brown, orange.

This staircase starts with a red rod, and each step increases by a red
rod. This staircase is often called an "even" staircase. Any rod that
can be measured by red rods is an even rod. The rods that are not
even (white, green, yellow, black, and blue) are called "odd".

Underlying Mathematics:

Recognition of equivalences of lengths
Representation of lengths in terms of red rods
Counting from 1 to 10
Association of numbers with rods

Measuring a Blue Rod with Green Rods

Measuring with Green Rods

Materials:

Cuisenaire rods for each child
A Cuisenaire Rod Rack or ruler for each child

Settings:

One child working individually
A small group, children working individually

Learning Experience:

Ask each child to take one rod at a time and to match its length with green rods. A Rod Rack or ruler can be used to help children line up the rods. The children should note that only a green rod, a dark green rod, and a blue rod can be matched exactly with green rods.

Ask the children to make a staircase with these three rods and to describe it. As a challenge, ask the children to continue the pattern beyond the blue rod by using more than one rod to form each step.

Further questions include:

How many greens does it take to match a dark green rod? (2)
How many greens does it take to match a blue rod? (3)
Which rods can be matched with purple rods? (Purple and brown.)
Which rods can be matched with yellow rods? (Yellow and orange.)

Underlying Mathematics:

Recognition of equivalences of lengths
Representation of lengths in terms of green rods
Counting from 1 to 10
Association of numbers with rods

Oh When the Rods Come Marching Through

Chorus:	Oh when the rods come marching through, Oh when the rods come marching through, We can measure all the colors, When the rods come marching through.
Verse 1:	First there is white. Let it be one. First there is white, and it is one. It's the first rod to march in. Here is white, and it is one.
Verse 2:	Then there is red, and it is two. Then there is red, and it is two. It's the next rod to march in. Here is red, and it is two.
Verse 3:	Then there is green, and it is three. Then there is green, and it is three. It's the next rod to march in. Here is green, and it is three.
Verse 4:	Then there is purple, and it is four. etc.
Verse 5:	Then there is yellow, and it is five. etc.
Verse 6:	Then there is dark green, and it is six. etc.
Verse 7:	Then there is black, and it is seven. etc.
Verse 8:	Then there is brown, and it is eight. etc.
Verse 9:	Then there is blue, and it is nine. etc.
Verse 10:	Then there is orange, and it is ten. Then there is orange, and it is ten. It's the longest rod to march in. Here's the orange; it is ten.

Words to Song about Rods and Numbers

Singing about Rods and Numbers

Materials:

Cuisenaire rods for the teacher

Settings:

Ten or more children led by the teacher

Learning Experience:

Give each child a Cuisenaire rod so that all ten colors are used. There will be repeats if there are more than ten children.

Review with the children the number of white rods needed to match each rod:

1 red = 2 whites; 1 green = 3 whites; 1 purple = 4 whites, etc.

Lead the children in singing the adaptation of the song, "Oh When the Saints Come Marching In", given on page 66. The tune is given on page 50.

When a particular color is mentioned, the children holding the corresponding rod stand up and march around, holding the rods in front of them.

As soon as all of the verses for the ten colors have been sung, end with verse 11.

Verse 11: Now we are here. All rods are here.
The Cuisenaire rods are all here.
We have measured all ten colors.
Numbers 1 through 10 are here.

Children enjoy performing this song for other classes and for parents.

Underlying Mathematics:

Representation of lengths in terms of white rods
Counting from 1 to 10
Association of numbers with rods

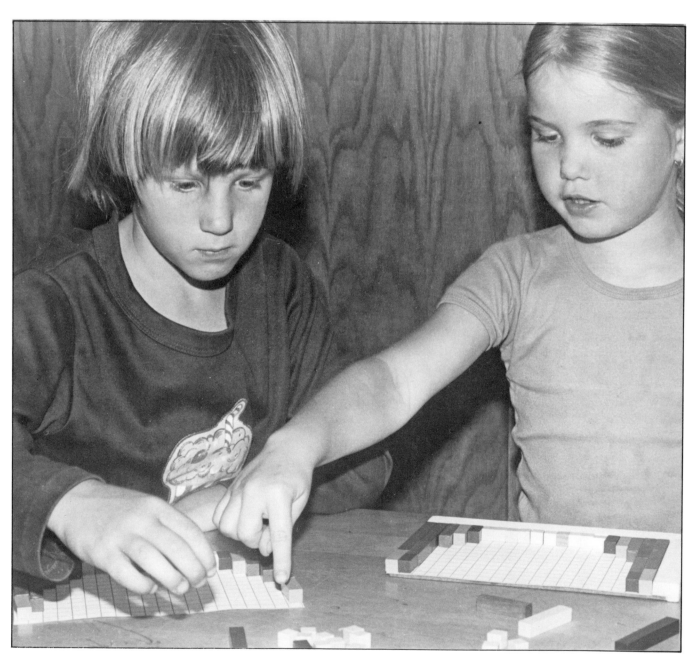

Transferring a Design from a Rod Rack to Graph Paper

Building Designs on Graph Paper

Materials:

Cuisenaire rods for each child
Centimetre graph paper for each child

Settings:

Two children working together
A small group, children working in pairs
A whole class, children working in pairs

Learning Experience:

Ask the first child to build a flat design with rods on centimetre graph paper. Each rod must be placed so that it is horizontal or vertical and exactly covers whole squares.

Now ask the second child to copy the design in exactly the same position on another sheet of graph paper.

At this stage in the development, children usually use counting to find where the rods are placed. The length of each rod is associated with the number of whites which match it, as the child notices the number of squares each rod covers.

The partners check each other to be sure that the second design is exactly the same as the first.

Now the partners switch roles. The second child makes the original design, which the first child then copies.

Underlying Mathematics:

Association of 3-dimensional rods with 2-dimensional representations
One-to-one correspondence
Congruence of shapes
Visual memory of shapes

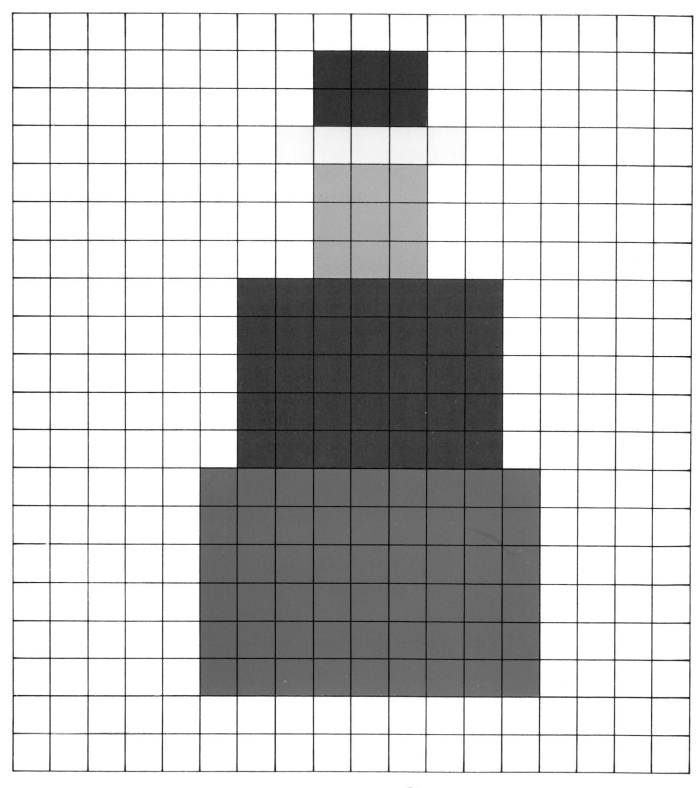

Child's Design Colored on Graph Paper

Making Pictures of Designs

Materials:

Cuisenaire rods for each child
Centimetre graph paper for each child
Crayons matching the rod colors

Settings:

Two children working together
A small group, children working in pairs
A whole class, children working in pairs

Learning Experience:

Ask the first child to build a flat design with rods on centimetre graph paper. Each rod must be placed so that it is horizontal or vertical and exactly covers whole squares.

Now ask the second child to draw and color the same design in exactly the same position on another sheet of graph paper.

At this stage in the development, the children should count to find where the rods are placed and should use the number relationships in terms of white rods to determine how many squares to color.

The partners check each other to be sure that the design and the picture of the design match. Then the partners switch roles.

Some rod discoveries which the children make include:

Only one length is associated with each color.
Only one color is associated with each length.
The color can be determined by counting the number of squares on the centimetre graph paper and finding the rod equivalent to that number of whites.

Underlying Mathematics:

One-to-one correspondence
Association of 2-dimensional representations with 3-dimensional rods
Representation of lengths in terms of white rods
Visual memory of shapes

Building a Classmate's Graph Paper Design with Rods

Drawing and Building

Materials:

Cuisenaire rods for each child
Centimetre graph paper for each child
Crayons matching the rod colors

Settings:

Two children working together
A small group, children working in pairs
A whole class, children working in pairs

Learning Experience:

Ask the first child to draw a rod design on centimetre graph paper and to color it according to the Cuisenaire colors.

Now ask the second child to build this design in exactly the same position on another sheet of graph paper.

The partners check each other to be sure that the picture and the rod design are exactly the same.

The partners switch roles. The second child draws and colors the original design. The first child builds it.

The various designs should be saved and exchanged many times among classmates.

A more difficult version of this experience is for the original design to remain uncolored, while the other partner tries to build it.

Underlying Mathematics:

One-to-one correspondence
Representation of lengths in terms of white rods
Association of 3-dimensional rods with 2-dimensional representations
Visual memory of shapes

What comes next?

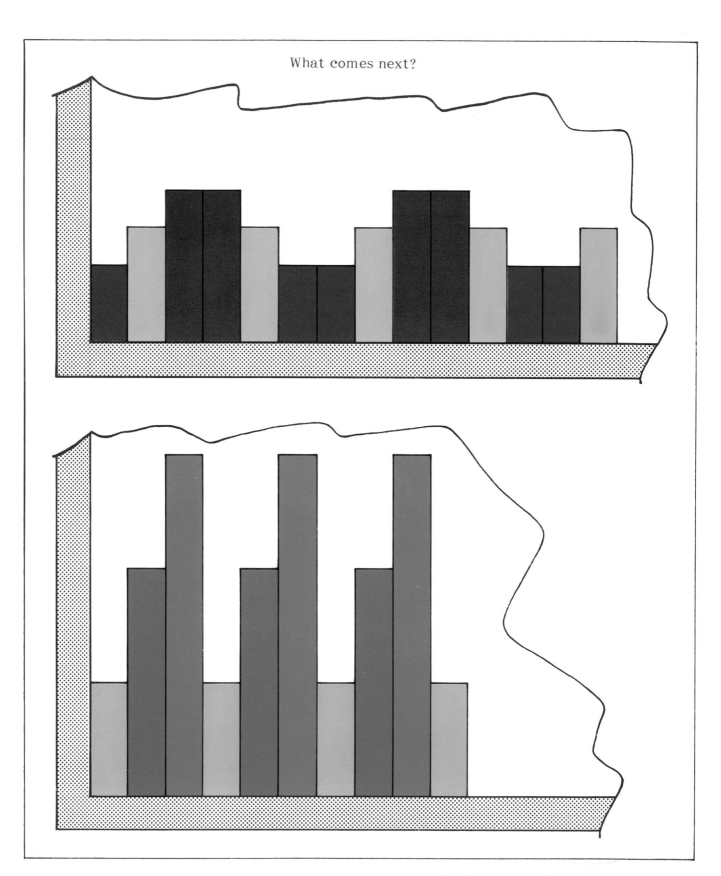

Rod Patterns Shown on a Rod Rack

Placing Rods in a Pattern

Materials:
Cuisenaire rods for each child
Cuisenaire rods for the teacher
A Cuisenaire Rod Rack or box lid for the teacher

Settings:
A small group led by the teacher
A whole class led by the teacher

Learning Experience:

As the children watch, place the following rods on a Rod Rack (or box lid) to form a pattern.

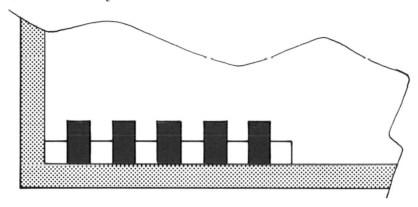

Ask the children to say the colors in order and to place their own rods in the same order.

White, red, white, red, white, red,...

Continuing the chant, the children extend the pattern by adding rods to their sequences.

More advanced patterns should be used when the children seem ready, for example:

Red, dark green, orange, red, dark green, orange, red,...
Purple, white, white, purple, white, white, purple,...
Green, yellow, green, orange, green, yellow,...

Children enjoy making patterns and sharing them with their classmates to extend.

Underlying Mathematics :

Association of colors with rods
Sequences of rod patterns
Logical thinking

Various Rod Patterns and Sequences

More Patterning with Rods

Materials:

Cuisenaire rods for each child

Settings:

A small group led by the teacher
A whole class led by the teacher

Learning Experience:

As the children watch, stand some rods on end on the table to form a pattern, such as black, orange, black, orange, black, ...

Direct the children to observe the pattern, but not to verbalize it. The children show their awareness of the pattern by coming up and placing the next rod in the sequence. As more and more rods are placed, more and more children become aware of the pattern being used. Then ask for a volunteer to describe the pattern. Ask everyone to say the colors in the rhythm of the pattern. For example:

White, green/white, green/white, green/...

Brown, purple, purple/brown, purple, purple/...

Ask the children to lead the activity. A child thinks of a pattern and whispers it to the teacher. The child places the first five rods in the sequence. The other children try to continue the pattern.

The rods can also be placed flat on the table, end-to-end like the cars of a train.

More mature children may color rod patterns on graph paper. Later the pictures can be used without rods to give children a more abstract experience of continuing a pattern.

Underlying Mathematics:

Association of colors with rods
Sequences of rod patterns
Logical thinking

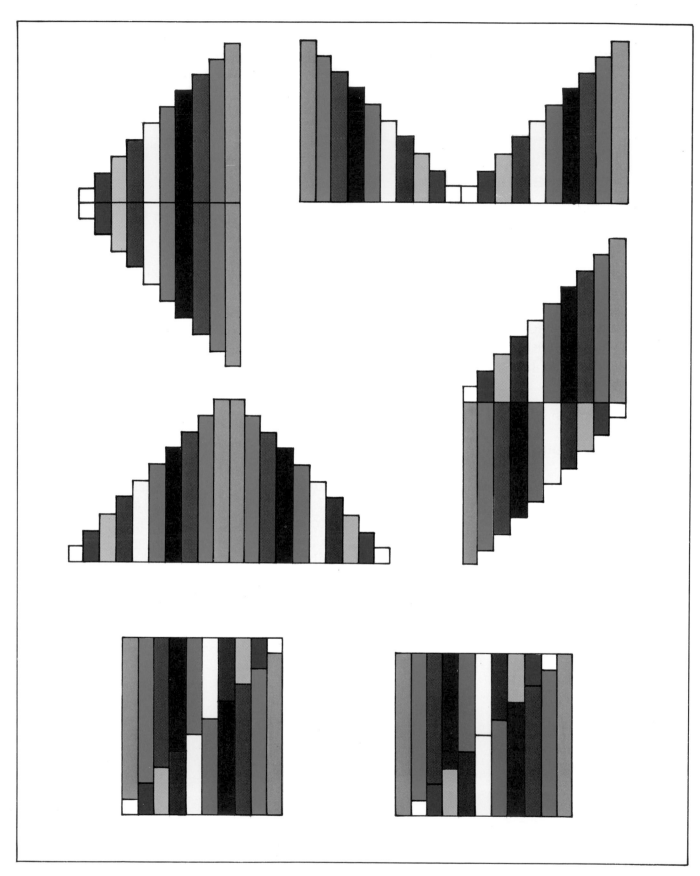

Some Ways to Combine Two Staircases

Combining Two Staircases

Materials:

Cuisenaire rods for each child
Unlined paper for each child

Settings:

Two children working together
A small group, children working in pairs
A whole class, children working in pairs

Learning Experience:

Each child should have a plain sheet of paper with a horizontal
line drawn in the center of the page.

Ask the children to build two identical staircases so that they fit
together in some way. The staircases can be built on the paper
so that the line on the paper can serve as a base line for the rods.

Two staircases may be combined in many creative ways. Share
the various ways that children do it.

Ask the children to try making one of the other children's design
or a still different one.

See how many different ways your class can combine two staircases.

Some children may wish to look at the drawings on page 78 and
replicate each of these with their rods.

Underlying Mathematics:

Ordering of lengths
Logical thinking
Symmetry

Two Staircases Back-to-Back

Combining Staircases on a Rod Rack

Materials:
Cuisenaire rods for each pair of children
A Cuisenaire Rod Rack for each pair of children

Settings:
Two children working together
A small group, children working in pairs
A whole class, children working in pairs

Learning Experience:

Ask the first child to build a flat staircase on the Rod Rack.

Ask the second child to build a flat staircase on the table and then to combine this staircase with the one already made.

Although the two staircases can be combined in several ways, the focus for this experience will be on the arrangements that form a rectangular configuration.

This exercise builds readiness for the idea of equivalence. Various combinations of two rods produce the same length. For example:

Orange is matched by blue and white.
Orange is matched by brown and red.
Black and green produce the same length as green and black.
Orange and white are matched by blue and red.
Orange and white are matched by black and purple.

Children enjoy discussing these equivalences in informal language.

Underlying Mathematics:

Ordering of lengths
Recognition of equivalences of lengths
Commutative property of addition

Top: **A Group Project — Filling a Defined Space with Rods**
Bottom: **Individuals Exploring the Boundaries of a Rod Rack**

Filling Spaces with Rods

Materials:
Cuisenaire rods for each child
A Cuisenaire Rod Rack for each child

Settings:
One child working individually
A small group, children working individually

Learning Experience:

Ask each child to make a design with rods on a Rod Rack so that the entire space is filled.

Some children will make a small design and fill the space around it with one color for background. Other children will make a design that utilizes the entire space.

Some children may explore further staircase patterns and equivalences for a given length.

Some interesting questions, include:

If you were to fill the entire space of a Cuisenaire Rod Rack with orange rods, how many would it take?
How many white rods would it take?
How many red rods would it take?
Take all of the rods that you used and line them up end-to-end on the floor. Have your classmate line up the rods from his design next to yours. Whose line is longer? (They should be the same length.)

Many rod discoveries will be made if this experience is repeated several times.

Underlying Mathematics:

Awareness of rod attributes (length, color, and shape)
Area
Logical thinking
Symmetry

Coloring Mosaic Patterns on Graph Paper

Coloring Mosaics

Materials:

Cuisenaire rods for each child
Rod Rack graph paper for each child
A Cuisenaire Rod Rack for each child
Crayons matching the rod colors

Settings:

Two children working together
A small group, children working in pairs
A whole class, children working in pairs

Learning Experience:

Ask each child to make a design with rods on a Rod Rack so that the entire space is filled.

Ask the first child to color the second child's design on a sheet of Rod Rack graph paper while the second child colors the first child's design. It may take the children more than one session to complete this activity.

Save the colored designs for another activity. Give each child a colored design to be made with rods on a Rod Rack. Younger children may find it easier to build directly on top of the picture.

To extend this activity, make a "mosaic quilt" by joining several designs together.

Underlying Mathematics:

Area
Association of 2-dimensional representations with 3-dimensional rods
Association of 3-dimensional rods with 2-dimensional representations
Visual memory of shapes

A train with three cars.

Dark green,   Red,   Red

A train with an orange rod.

Orange,   White

A train with three cars all
the same color.

Green,   Green,   Green

A short train that has lots of cars.

A long train that has
only a few cars.

Two trains which have
the same length.

Two trains that have the same
cars, but in a different order.

Sample Trains Made by Children

Making Trains

Materials:

Cuisenaire rods for each child
Cuisenaire rods for the teacher
A Cuisenaire Rod Rack or box lid for the teacher

Settings:

A small group led by the teacher
A whole class led by the teacher

Learning Experience :

Demonstrate a train by placing two rods end-to-end on a Rod
Rack or box lid.

This is a train with two cars.

Now show some other trains and describe them, as on page 86.

Ask the children to make trains that fulfill certain conditions,
such as:

> A train with three cars all the same color.
> A four-car train with a black engine and a red caboose.
> A short train that has lots of cars.
> A long train that has only a few cars.

The children should describe their trains by naming the colors left
to right.

Underlying Mathematics:

Meaning of addition
Commutative property of addition
Multiplication as repeated addition

Various Ways to Arrange Three Different Rods

Building Different Trains

Materials:
Cuisenaire rods for each child

Settings:
A small group led by the teacher
A whole class led by the teacher

Learning Experience:

Ask the children to choose a red rod, a white rod, and a yellow rod, and to make a train with these three rods.

Remind the students the way in which a train is named, by naming each rod from left to right. For example:

If the rods chosen were red, white, and yellow, there are six possible trains that can be made:

Red, white, yellow	White, yellow, red
Red, yellow, white	Yellow, red, white
White, red, yellow	Yellow, white, red

Ask the children to build all the possible trains using these three colors and to describe them orally by naming the rods.

Now try three other colors, such as green, purple, and orange, and have the children build and name the six different arrangements of colors.

Let the children choose three other colors. Are there still six different trains?

Some children may want to try four colors such as white, red, green, and purple to see how many of the 24 possible trains they can make. The design that the rods make is pretty, especially if the rearrangements are done systematically.

Underlying Mathematics :

Meaning of addition
Permutations (rearrangements of rod patterns)
Logical thinking

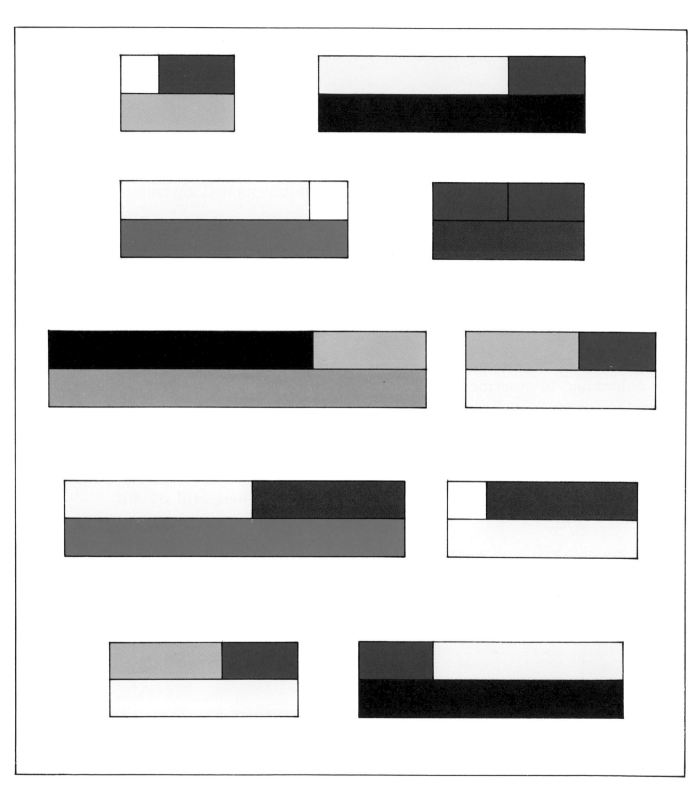

Rod Triplets for Lengths of Two-Car Trains

Finding Lengths of Trains

Materials:
Cuisenaire rods for each child

Settings:
A small group led by the teacher
A whole class led by the teacher

Learning Experience:

Ask the children to place a yellow rod and a red rod end-to-end.

Then ask the children to find a one-car train that matches this two-car train. Some children may try several rods beside the two-car train before they find the one that matches exactly.

The final result should look like this, and can be stated:

Yellow plus red equals black.

Ask the children to do several like this. Choose the two-car trains from among the five smallest rods, so that the result is always a one-car train. Some examples are given on page 90.

Students enjoy making the problems for the class to solve.

Underlying Mathematics:

Meaning of addition
Recognition of equivalences of lengths
Association of sums with addends

Finding Sums as Orange Plus . . .

Matching Longer Trains

Materials:
Cuisenaire rods for each child

Settings:
A small group led by the teacher
A whole class led by the teacher

Learning Experience:

Ask the children to place a yellow rod and a blue rod end-to-end. Help the children see that there is no one-car train that matches this two-car train.

Ask the children to find a two-car train that will match the train:

Yellow plus blue

There are many correct answers:

Black plus black
Brown plus dark green
Dark green plus brown
Purple plus orange
Orange plus purple

Explain to the children that when a two-car train is longer than orange, it is customary to state its length as "Orange plus..."

Ask the children to find the "Orange plus" two-car trains that match each of these:

Red plus blue
Black plus yellow
Brown plus purple
Yellow plus dark green

Underlying Mathematics:

Recognition of equivalences of lengths
Meaning of addition
Association of sums with addends
Readiness for tens and ones

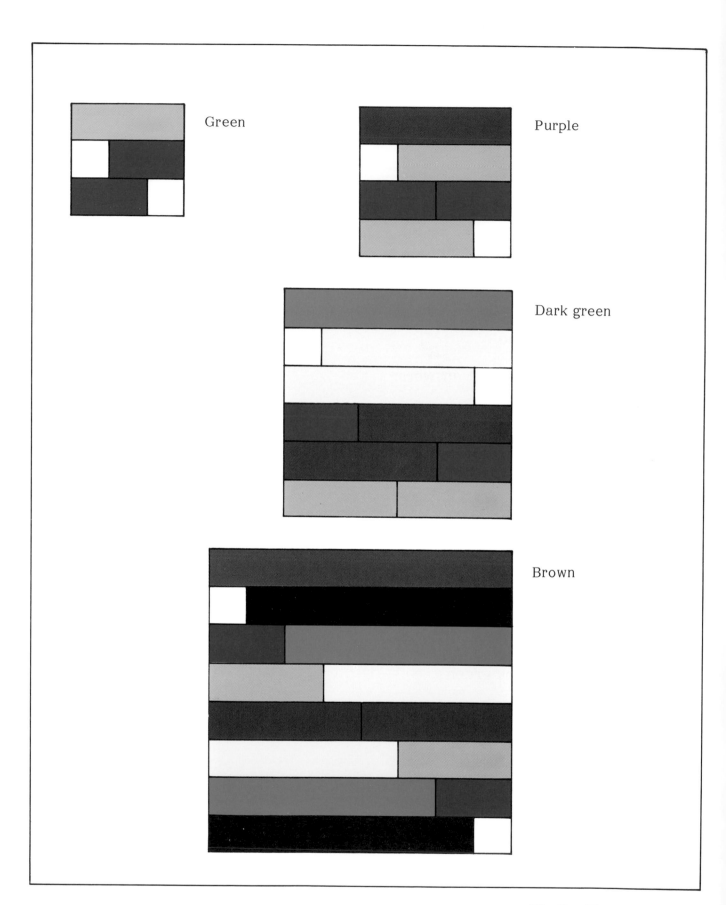

Green

Purple

Dark green

Brown

Finding Two-Car Trains

Finding All Two-Car Trains

Materials:

Cuisenaire rods for each child
Centimetre graph paper for each child
A Cuisenaire Rod Rack or ruler for each child

Settings:

A small group led by the teacher
A whole class led by the teacher

Learning Experience:

Ask the children to build all the two-car trains that match an orange rod. A Rod Rack or ruler can be used to help the children line up the rods.

In order to be sure that all trains have been found, children need a systematic approach. Two systems are:

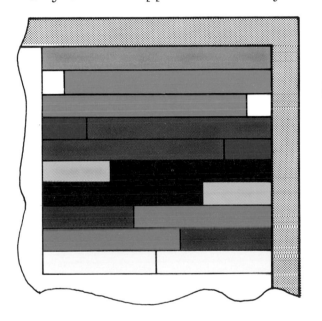

Building pairs of trains
by means of the Commutative
Property (change the order).

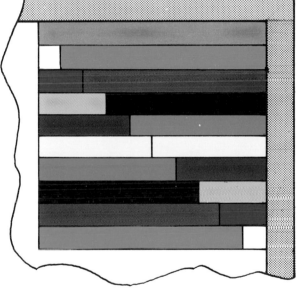

Building by means of
Staircase Patterns

Children do not usually discover these systems on their own. The children should be encouraged to rearrange the trains that they have found according to one of the systems to ensure that they have found all possible two-car trains.

Underlying Mathematics:

Recognition of equivalences of lengths
Association of various addends for a sum
Commutative property of addition

Approaching the End of a Challenge Match Game for Addends

Playing Challenge Match for Addends

Materials:
Cuisenaire rods for each pair of children

Settings:
Two children working together
A small group, children working in pairs
A whole class, children working in pairs

Learning Experience:

About 40 - 50 assorted rods should be placed in the center of the table for each pair of children.

The first player chooses a rod (other than white) and challenges the second player to make a two-car train that matches it. The second player keeps the triple of rods once the match has been made.

Then the second player chooses a rod and challenges the first player to make a two-car train that matches it. The white rod can never be used as the challenge. The first player keeps the triple of rods once the match has been made.

The players reverse roles again. The pile of rods in the center of the table gets smaller each time. The object of the game is to "stump your partner" by choosing a single rod for which no two-car train can be made from the rods in the center of the table.

The player who makes the challenge that cannot be matched is the winner of the game and scores 1 point for each rod left in the center of the table. Score may be accumulated from game to game.

Children should play this game several times, since it helps them build readiness for work with addends.

Underlying Mathematics :

Recognition of equivalences of lengths
Association of various addends for a sum

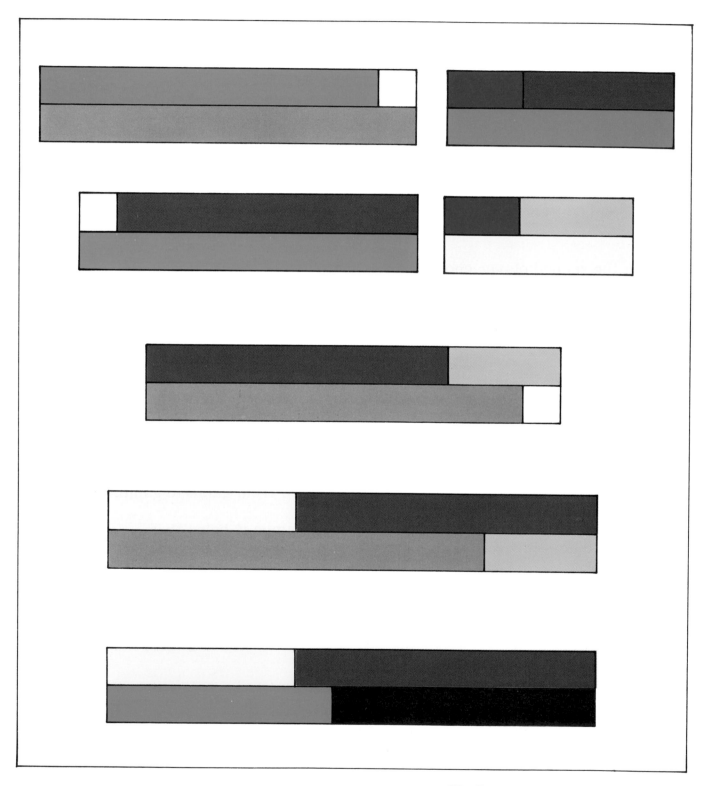

Challenge Match Game for Sums

Playing Challenge Match for Sums

Materials:
Cuisenaire rods for each child

Settings:
Two children working together
A small group, children working in pairs
A whole class, children working in pairs

Learning Experience :

About 40 - 50 assorted rods should be placed in the center of the table for each pair of children.

The first player chooses two rods and places them end-to-end in a train. The second player must find a one-car or two-car train that matches the first player's train. The second player keeps the rods involved in the match.

Then the second player chooses two rods and challenges the first player to make a one-car or two-car train that matches. The first player keeps all the rods once the match has been made.

The players reverse roles again. The pile of rods in the center of the table gets smaller each time. The object of the game is to make a challenge that cannot be matched with the remaining rods. The player to do this first wins the game and scores 1 point for each rod left in the center of the table. Score may be accumulated from game to game.

Children should play this game several times. They enjoy alternating this game with the Challenge Match for Addends Game on page 97.

Underlying Mathematics :

Recognition of equivalences of lengths
Association of sums with addends

Starting a Challenge Match Game for Many Addends

Playing Challenge Match for Many Addends

Materials:

Cuisenaire rods for each child

Settings:

Two children working together
A small group, children working in pairs
A whole class, children working in pairs

Learning Experience:

About 40 - 50 assorted rods should be placed in the center of the table for each pair of children.

The first player chooses a rod and places it in front of the second player as a challenge. The second player must match the given rod with a train that can contain any number of cars. Even a one-car train equivalent to the given rod is allowed. The second player keeps all the rods involved in the match.

The players reverse roles. The second player challenges the first player to match a rod with a train.

The player who is first to pose a challenge for which the other player cannot make any train wins. The player scores 1 point for each rod left in the center of the table.

As a variation, partners enjoy taking on a challenge together rather than challenging each other. The goal is to use every rod in the pile so that it is matched with a train. One-car trains are allowed, and as the game comes to a close, children can shift rods around to try to complete the task. With good thinking, this can almost always be done starting with any random collection of rods.

Underlying Mathematics:

Recognition of equivalences of lengths
Association of various addends for a sum

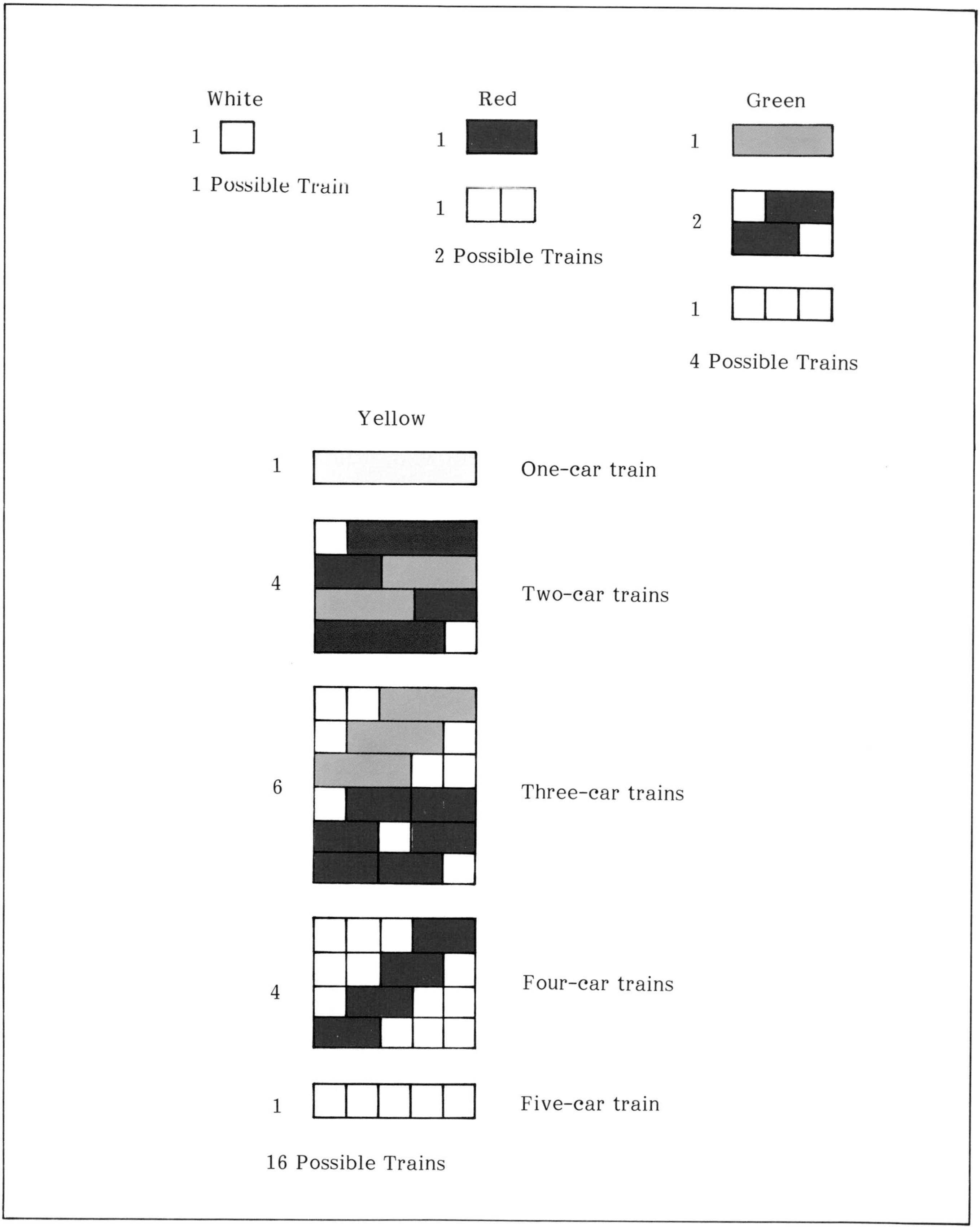

White

1 □

1 Possible Train

Red

1 ▬

1 □□

2 Possible Trains

Green

1 ▬

2

1 □□□

4 Possible Trains

Yellow

1 — One-car train

4 — Two-car trains

6 — Three-car trains

4 — Four-car trains

1 — Five-car train

16 Possible Trains

All Possible Trains for a Given Rod

Finding All the Trains

Materials:
Cuisenaire rods for each child

Settings:
A small group, children working individually
A whole class, children working individually

Learning Experience:

Ask the children to take a purple rod and to make all the possible matching trains. Sort and count the trains according to whether they are one-car trains, two-car trains, three-car trains, or four-car trains. For example, there are 8 possible trains for purple, sorted into the following piles:

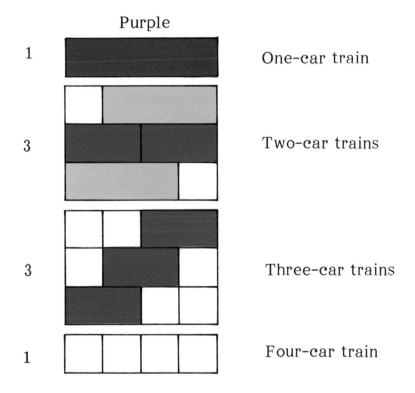

Purple

1 — One-car train

3 — Two-car trains

3 — Three-car trains

1 — Four-car train

Now have the students find all the possible trains for white, for red, for green, and for yellow.

As a group activity, some children may want to find the 32 possible trains for dark green.

Underlying Mathematics :

Association of various addends for a sum
Permutations (rearrangements of rod patterns)
Recognition of patterns in Pascal's Triangle
Logical thinking

Finding and Recording Trains for the Yellow Rod

Coloring All the Trains

Materials:

Cuisenaire rods for each child
Centimetre graph paper for each child
Crayons matching the rod colors

Settings:

One child working individually
A small group, children working individually
A whole class, children working individually

Learning Experience:

Ask the children to make all of the possible trains for a purple rod, as was done in the previous Learning Experience on page 103.

Ask the children to record the patterns by coloring on centimetre graph paper.

The children should then make and color all of the possible trains for white, for red, for green, and for yellow. Check to see that they have them all:

Color	Number of Possible Trains
White	1
Red	2
Green	4
Purple	8
Yellow	16
Dark green	32
Black	64

Some children may want to share the work in a group to go beyond yellow. For certain children, this is an exciting exercise because of the doubling pattern (powers of two) in the chart. Other children enjoy the artistic aspects of this activity since the colored designs look like Navaho rugs.

Underlying Mathematics:

Association of various addends for a sum
Permutations (rearrangements of rod patterns)
Recognition of patterns in a Pascal's Triangle
Logical thinking

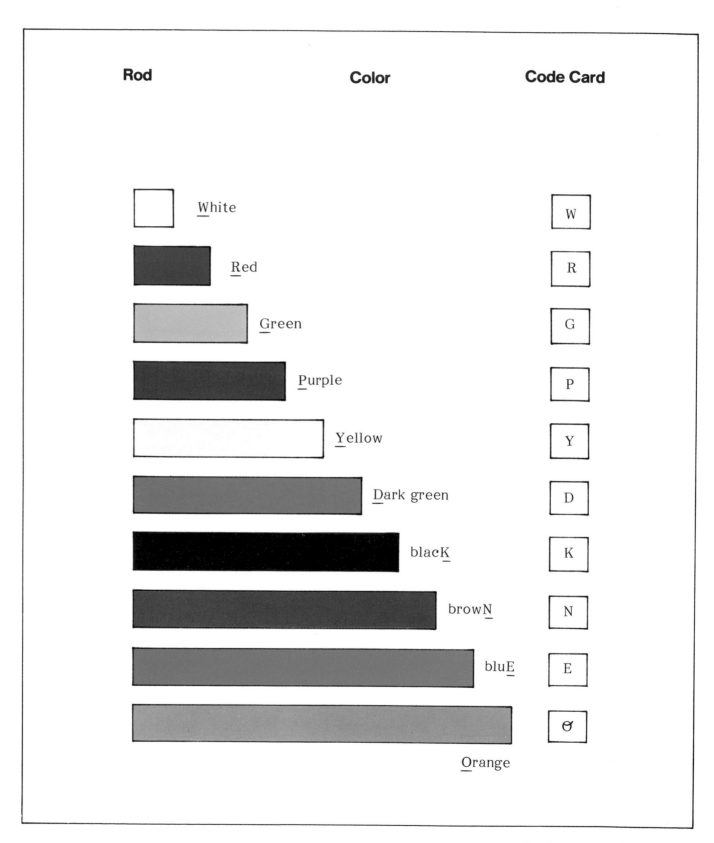

Rod	Color	Code Card
	White	W
	Red	R
	Green	G
	Purple	P
	Yellow	Y
	Dark green	D
	blacK	K
	browN	N
	bluE	E
	Orange	O

Rods and Code Names

Coding the Colors

Materials:
Cuisenaire rods for each child
Ten index cards for the teacher

Settings:
A small group led by the teacher
A whole class led by the teacher

Learning Experience:

Discuss with the children the idea of a nickname. Use examples from the children in the class. Then discuss the need for a quick way to name each rod.

Since one major characteristic of the rods is color, the color names are used to devise a code for the rods. For the first six rods, the first letters of the color names are used:

W for White   P for Purple
R for Red   Y for Yellow
G for Green   D for Dark green

The black, brown, and blue all begin with the same first letter; hence their last letters are used for the code.

K for blacK
N for browN
E for bluE

Notice that the Ø for ORANGE has a tail on it to distinguish it from the symbol for zero.

Make a deck of cards with the code letters on them. Hold up a card. The children must hold the appropriate rod over their heads.

Underlying Mathematics:

Association of colors with rods
Association of codes with rods
Association of rods with codes

Playing the Coding Game

Playing the Coding Game

Materials:
Cuisenaire rods for each group
Thirty index cards for each group

Settings:
A small group working together
A whole class working in small groups

Learning Experience:

Make a deck of 30 cards consisting of 3 cards for each of the ten rod codes: W, R, G, P, Y, D, K, N, E, Θ.

One player in each group acts as dealer and does not play. The dealer shuffles the deck of 30 code cards and places it face down in the center of the table. The dealer gives each player one rod of each of the ten colors.

On each round, the dealer turns one card face up. The first player to put the correct rod on top of this code card wins the card and recovers the rod.

The game ends when the deck runs out. The player who has accumulated the most cards wins. Children may wish to score 1 point for each card and accumulate scores for several games.

Some interesting questions include:

Did anyone get 3 codes alike?
Did anyone get 2 codes alike?
Who has a W card? Is it possible to go in order around the table to name all 10 colors in order from W to Θ?
Does the sum of all of the players' scores for each game add to 30?

Underlying Mathematics:

Association of colors with rods
Association of codes with rods
Association of rods with codes

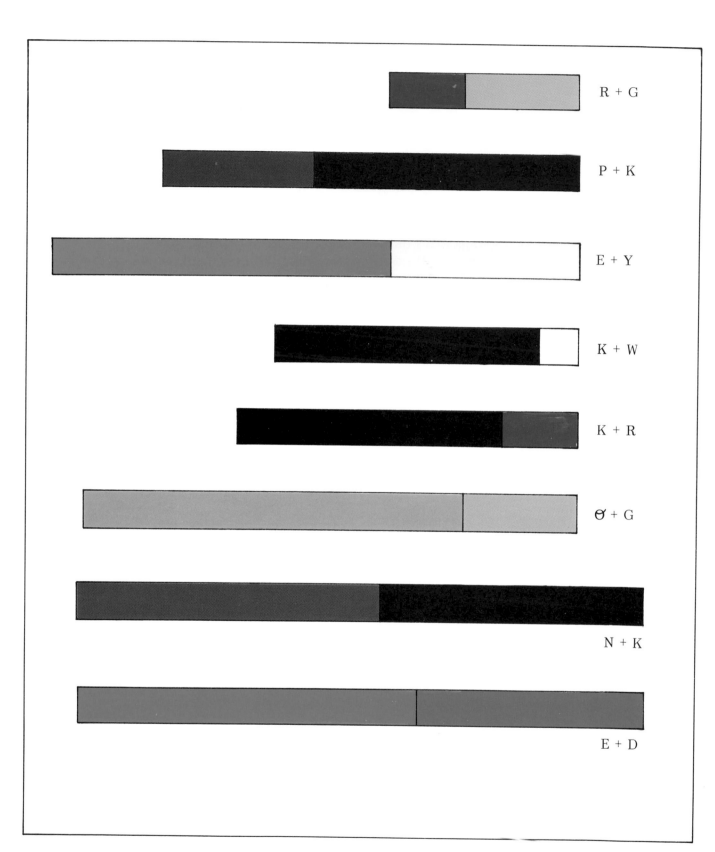

R + G

P + K

E + Y

K + W

K + R

ᴕ + G

N + K

E + D

Recording Train Stories

Materials:

Cuisenaire rods for each child
Paper and pencil for each child

Settings:

A small group led by the teacher
A whole class led by the teacher

Learning Experience:

Ask the children to place a red rod and a yellow rod end-to-end:

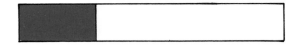

Introduce the symbol "+" for "plus", and record the train with coding:

R + Y (read as "Red plus Yellow")

Ask the children to build another train and to record with coding.

For example:

P + E (read as "Purple plus bluE")

To develop skill with coding, ask the children to build 10 trains and to record each with coding on a sheet of paper.

Then have the students exchange record sheets and build the 10 trains described.

Underlying Mathematics :

Association of codes with rods
Association of rods with codes
Use of plus sign

Top: **Recording Train Stories with Codes**
Bottom: **Recording Train Stories for the Dark Green Rod**

Recording Rod Patterns

Materials:

Cuisenaire rods for each child
Paper and pencil for each child

Settings:

Two children working together
A small group, children working in pairs
A whole class, children working in pairs

Learning Experience:

Ask the children to work together to build all the two-car trains that match a dark green rod.

One child should then record the rod patterns using codes, while the other child reads the rod story.

For example:

D = W + Y is read:
> "Dark green equals White plus Yellow."

D = R + P is read:
> "Dark green equals Red plus Purple."

D = G + G is read:
> "Dark green equals Green plus Green."

D = P + R is read:
> "Dark green equals Purple plus Red."

D = Y + W is read:
> "Dark green equals Yellow plus White."

The children should build all the two-car trains for other rods. One child should record the rod patterns using codes, while the other reads the rod story.

Underlying Mathematics:

Association of various addends for a sum
Association of codes with rods
Use of plus sign
Use of equals sign

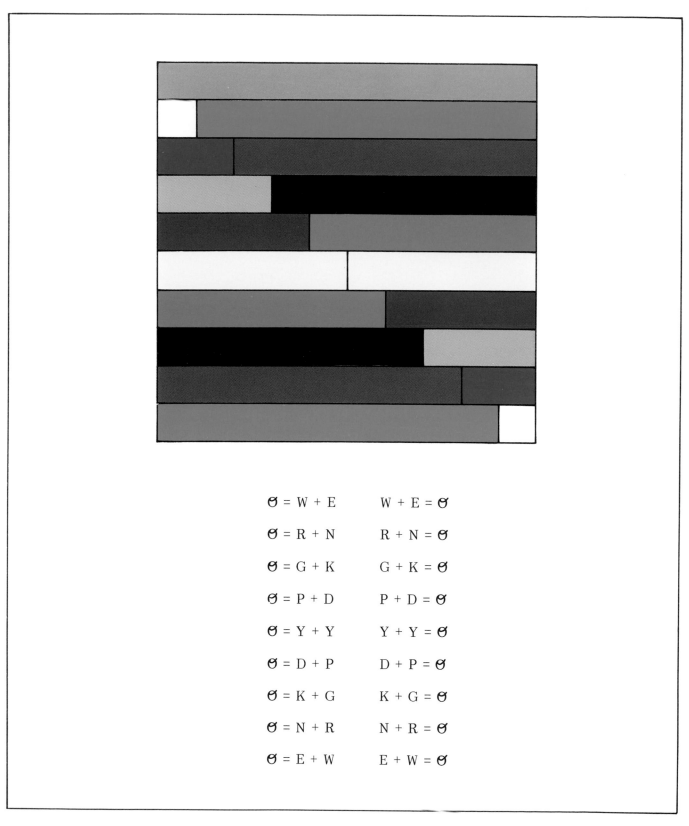

$\mathbf{O} = W + E$ $W + E = \mathbf{O}$

$\mathbf{O} = R + N$ $R + N = \mathbf{O}$

$\mathbf{O} = G + K$ $G + K = \mathbf{O}$

$\mathbf{O} = P + D$ $P + D = \mathbf{O}$

$\mathbf{O} = Y + Y$ $Y + Y = \mathbf{O}$

$\mathbf{O} = D + P$ $D + P = \mathbf{O}$

$\mathbf{O} = K + G$ $K + G = \mathbf{O}$

$\mathbf{O} = N + R$ $N + R = \mathbf{O}$

$\mathbf{O} = E + W$ $E + W = \mathbf{O}$

All the Two-Car Trains for Orange

Matching the Orange Rod

Materials:

Cuisenaire rods for each child
Paper and pencil for each child

Settings:

Two children working together
A small group, children working in pairs
A whole class, children working in pairs

Learning Experience:

Ask the partners to build all the two-car trains that match the orange rod. Children in Grades 1 and 2 should then record the rod stories using codes.

Ask one of the partners to close her eyes. The other partner removes one rod from the rod patterns for orange. On a signal, the first child opens her eyes and tries to guess the missing rod.

For example:

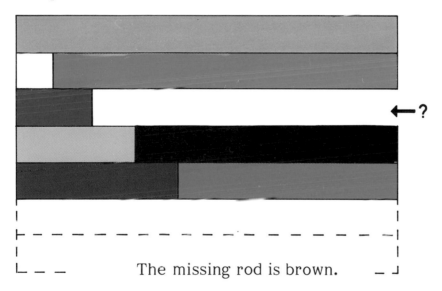

The missing rod is brown.

The children enjoy telling their clues. Some children use staircase patterns, while others use the reversed train (N + R = O) to tell what rod is missing.

Underlying Mathematics:

Association of various addends for a sum
Association of codes with rods
Missing addends
Meaning of subtraction

Finding the Missing Rod in Patterns for Orange

Finding the Missing Rod

Materials:
Cuisenaire rods for each pair of children

Settings:
Two children working together
A small group, children working in pairs
A whole class, children working in pairs

Learning Experience:

Ask the partners to build all the two-car trains for the dark green rod, the black rod, the brown rod, the blue rod, and the orange rod.

Ask one of the partners to close his eyes. The other partner removes one rod from the rod pattern for dark green. On a signal, the first partner opens his eyes and tries to guess the missing rod. Then the partners switch roles.

Next, the partners each have a turn at guessing a missing rod from the black pattern. Then they move on to the brown, blue, and orange patterns.

This activity is the beginning of a sequence of concrete experiences with the concept of missing addends. Missing addends warrant a lot of attention and continued practice at the concrete level, because they help children with arithmetic computation.

This game of finding the missing rod lays foundations at the concrete level for later computational work.

Underlying Mathematics:
Association of various addends for a sum
Association of codes with rods
Missing addends
Meaning of subtraction

117

Typical Challenges for Missing Addends

Playing Challenge Match for Missing Addends

Materials:
Cuisenaire rods for each pair of children

Settings:
Two children working together
A small group, children working in pairs
A whole class, children working in pairs

Learning Experience:

About 40 - 50 assorted rods should be placed in the center of the table for each pair of children.

The first player chooses two rods of different colors and places them side-by-side. For example:

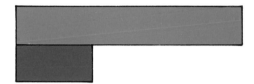

The second player must find the missing addend, the rod which will combine with the shorter rod to match the longer rod. The second player keeps the three rods involved in the match.

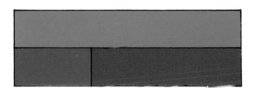

The partners reverse roles. As the game continues, the pile of rods in the center of the table gets smaller and smaller. The object of the game is to make a challenge that cannot be matched with the remaining rods. The player to do this first wins the game and scores 1 point for each rod left in the center of the table. Score may be accumulated from game to game.

Underlying Mathematics

Recognition of equivalences of lengths
Missing addends
Meaning of subtraction

Top: **The Wishing Game for Missing Addends**
Bottom: **Getting Ready for the Next Wish**

Making a Wish

Materials:

Cuisenaire rods for each child
Cuisenaire rods for the teacher

Settings:

A small group led by the teacher
A whole class led by the teacher

Learning Experience:

Take a red rod in your hand. Tell the children:

> I have a red rod.
> I WISH I HAD a yellow rod.
> Find the rod I need.

Some children will need to try several rods before finding the correct answer. By trial and error, children can see that some rods are too long; some are too short; but one is "just right," namely the green rod.

Play "I WISH I HAD" for other rods.

The fantasy of wishing is very motivating for children. It is also possible to decorate a box or can with crepe paper to make a wishing well. One child acts as leader and tosses a rod into the well, while making a wish for a longer rod. Another child tells the missing addend and checks the results by completing the rod train.

Underlying Mathematics:

Recognition of equivalences of lengths
Missing addends
Meaning of subtraction

The Cuisenaire Hopscotch Mat

Playing Cuisenaire Hopscotch

Materials:

One sheet each of dark green, black, brown
blue, and orange construction paper
Masking tape
Cuisenaire rods for each group
An empty container for each group

Settings:

A small group working together
A whole class working in small groups

Learning Experience:

Tape the construction paper to the floor or pavement to form a
HOPSCOTCH MAT, as shown on page 122.

Place the corresponding rod in the upper left corner of the piece
of paper of the same color.

The children take turns reaching into the bag and choosing a rod.

On a turn, the player tosses the rod onto one of the squares on
the HOPSCOTCH MAT. The player hops through the path. (The
children may hop on one foot or two feet.)

When the player lands on the square with the two rods, the player
must tell what rod should be combined with the smaller rod to
make a train the same length as the longer rod.

The player may actually match the rods to find the correct missing
addend.

If the player is correct, he finishes hopping through the path in
both directions. The children may play as many rounds as they
wish.

Underlying Mathematics:

Recognition of equivalences of lengths
Missing addends
Meaning of subtraction

Playing Cuisenaire Hopscotch for Missing Addends

Varying Cuisenaire Hopscotch

Materials:
One sheet each of dark green, black, brown
blue, and orange construction paper
Masking tape
Cuisenaire rods for each group
An empty container for each group

Settings:
A small group working together
A whole class working in small groups

Learning Experience :

Tape the construction paper to the floor or pavement to form a
HOPSCOTCH MAT, as shown on page 122.

Place the corresponding rod in the upper left corner of the piece
of paper of the same color.

The children take turns reaching into the bag and choosing a rod.

On a turn, the player holds this rod and hops from square to square
on the HOPSCOTCH MAT. (The children may hop on one foot
or two feet.)

When landing on each square, the child must name the rod which
would combine with the rod in his hand to make a train the length
of the rod on the square.

For the first few games, children may need to match the rods to
find the correct missing addends.

The goal is to be able to hop in both directions of the mat without
a mistake. Note that the return trip provides the same missing
addend problems and should act as reinforcement of the learning.
The children may play as many rounds as they wish.

Underlying Mathematics :

Recognition of equivalences of lengths
Missing addends
Meaning of subtraction

Subtracting by Finding How Much More One Rod is Than Another

Subtracting by Finding How Much More

Materials:

Cuisenaire rods for each child
Cuisenaire rods for the teacher

Settings:

A small group led by the teacher
A whole class led by the teacher

Learning Experience:

Ask the children to choose a yellow and a green rod. Direct their attention to the difference in the lengths of the two rods.

How much more is the yellow rod than the green rod?

The children must find a rod which will combine with the green rod to make the length of the yellow rod.

Any of these arrangements can be used to show that the red rod exactly fits. Just as addition is shown by placing rods end-to-end, subtraction is shown by placing rods side-by-side.

Most children will sense that this way of viewing subtraction is similar to a missing addend situation.

Do several more examples using the rods:

How much more is a brown rod than a red rod?
How much more is an orange rod than a brown rod?
How much more is a blue rod than a yellow rod?
How much more is a green rod than a white rod?

Underlying Mathematics:

Missing addends
Meaning of subtraction

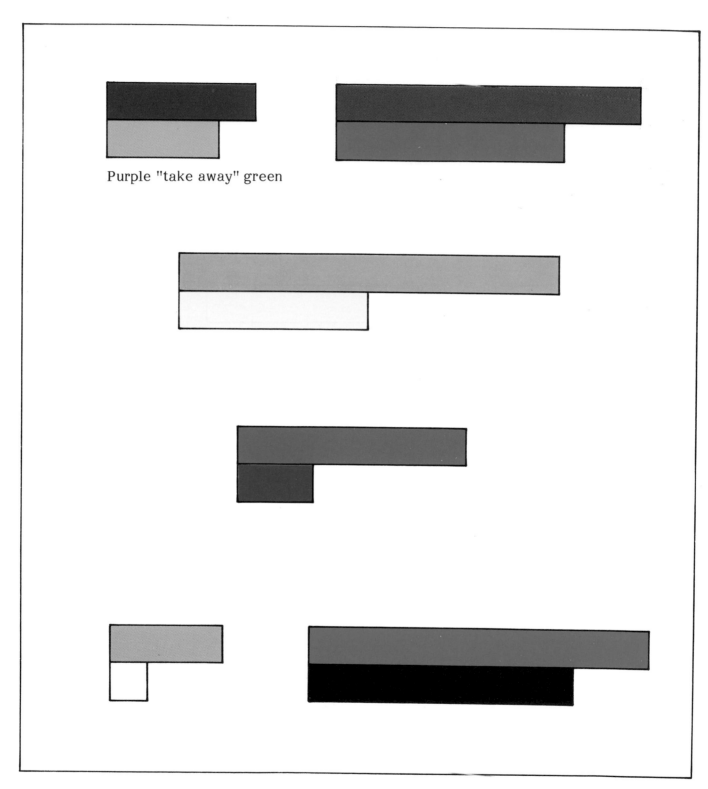

Purple "take away" green

Treating Subtraction as Take Away

Materials:

Cuisenaire rods for each child
Cuisenaire rods for the teacher

Settings:

A small group led by the teacher
A whole class led by the teacher

Learning Experience:

Choose two rods, for example a purple and a black rod. Ask the children to imagine that an amount equal to the purple rod is "taken away" or "cut off from" the black rod. This can be demonstrated by placing the purple rod in front of or on top of the black rod so that the portion of the black rod showing can be matched by a green rod.

Black "take away" purple equals green.

Solve the following "take away" problems using the rods:

Purple "take away" red.
Green "take away" white.
Orange "take away" dark green.
Dark green "take away" yellow.

Now use the illustrations on page 130 to interpret the rod situations as subtraction problems. Children should use their rods to find the solutions.

Underlying Mathematics:

Meaning of subtraction

Recording Subtraction Stories

Recording Subtraction Stories

Materials:

Cuisenaire rods for each child
Cuisenaire rods for the teacher
Paper and pencil for each child

Settings:

A small group led by the teacher
A whole class led by the teacher

Learning Experience:

Ask the children to take an orange and a purple rod and to build
a subtraction situation, either as "how much more" or "take away".
Introduce the minus sign, " - ", for subtraction.

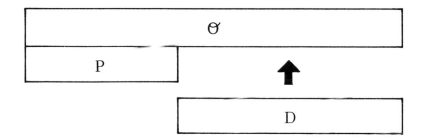

Θ - P = D is read "Orange minus Purple equals Dark green."

Ask the children to interpret and solve these subtraction sentences:

P - R = ?   E - W = ?   G - R = ?

An interesting exercise for children is to take three rods such as
green, yellow and brown and to form all the possible addition and
subtraction sentences for these three rods. They are:

$$G + Y = N \qquad N = G + Y \qquad N - G = Y \qquad Y = N - G$$
$$Y + G = N \qquad N = Y + G \qquad N - Y = G \qquad G = N - Y$$

Underlying Mathematics:

Association of codes with rods
Use of minus sign
Use of equals sign
Use of plus sign

Orange train for multiples of ten

1 2 3 4 5 6 7 8 9 ⑩ 11 12 13 14 15 16 . . .

Red train for multiples of two

1 ② 3 ④ 5 ⑥ 7 ⑧ 9 ⑩ 11 ⑫ 13 ⑭ 15 ⑯ . . .

Green train for multiples of three

1 2 ③ 4 5 ⑥ 7 8 ⑨ 10 11 ⑫ 13 14 ⑮ 16 . . .

One-Color Trains for Multiples

Generating Multiples from One-Color Trains

Materials:

Cuisenaire rods for each child
A Cuisenaire Rod Rack or ruler for each child
Extra white rods for each child
Cuisenaire rods for the teacher

Settings:

A small group led by the teacher
A whole class led by the teacher

Learning Experience:

Ask the children to make a one-color train using only yellow rods.
Add one yellow at a time, making the train longer and longer.
A metre stick, 50 cm or a 25 cm ruler will help the child line
up the train.

Once the train is quite long, five or six cars, ask the children to
match the train with white rods.

Count the white rods with the children. Emphasize the number
associated with the end of each yellow rod.

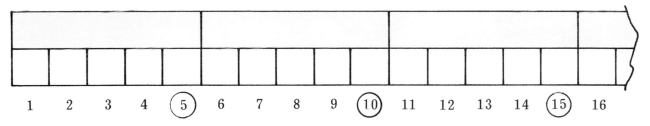

Ask the children to recount the white rods, having them say aloud
only the number associated with the end of each yellow rod. The
other number names are whispered.

Eventually the sequence of multiples of five might be remembered.
However, mastery is not expected at this stage of the development.

Repeat the same activity making a one-color orange train. The
multiples of ten are generated.

Making a one-color red train generates the multiples of two, the
even numbers. Try this when the children seem ready.

Underlying Mathematics:

Readiness for multiplication
Representation of lengths in terms of white rods

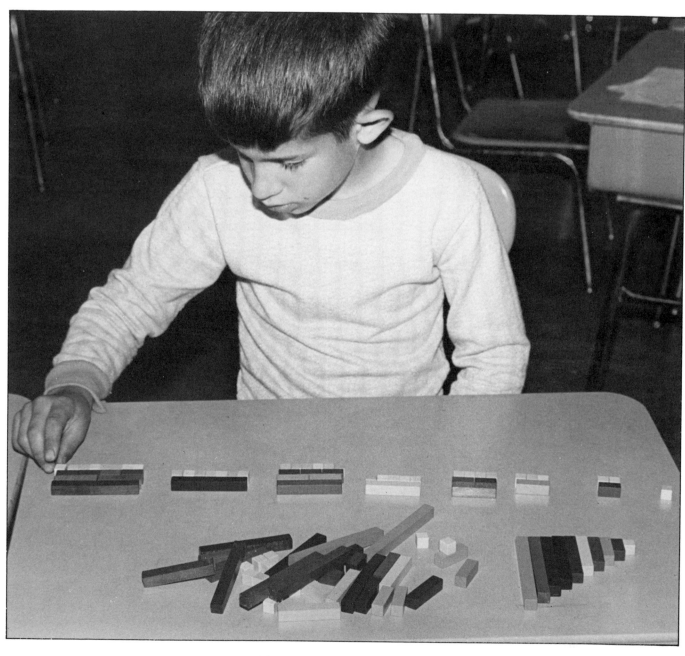

Matching Each Rod with All the Possible One-Color Trains

Finding Factors from One-Color Trains

Materials:

Cuisenaire rods for each child
Cuisenaire rods for the teacher

Settings:

A small group led by the teacher
A whole class led by the teacher

Learning Experience:

Ask the children to take a dark green rod and to match it with trains whose cars are all the same color. The one-color trains for dark green are:

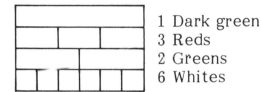

1 Dark green
3 Reds
2 Greens
6 Whites

Since a dark green rod can be matched by a one-color train of red rods, red is called a factor of dark green. The factors of dark green are white, red, green, and dark green.

Ask the children to find the one-color trains for orange:

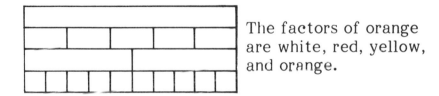

The factors of orange are white, red, yellow, and orange.

The term factor is not important for the children at this stage in the development, but the concept of one-color trains interpreted in this way lays the groundwork for division, factors, prime numbers, and fractions.

Some interesting questions are:

What one-color train matches every rod? (White)
Which rods have only 2 one-colored trains? (Red, green, yellow and black)

Underlying Mathematics:

Readiness for factors
Readiness for division
Readiness for prime numbers

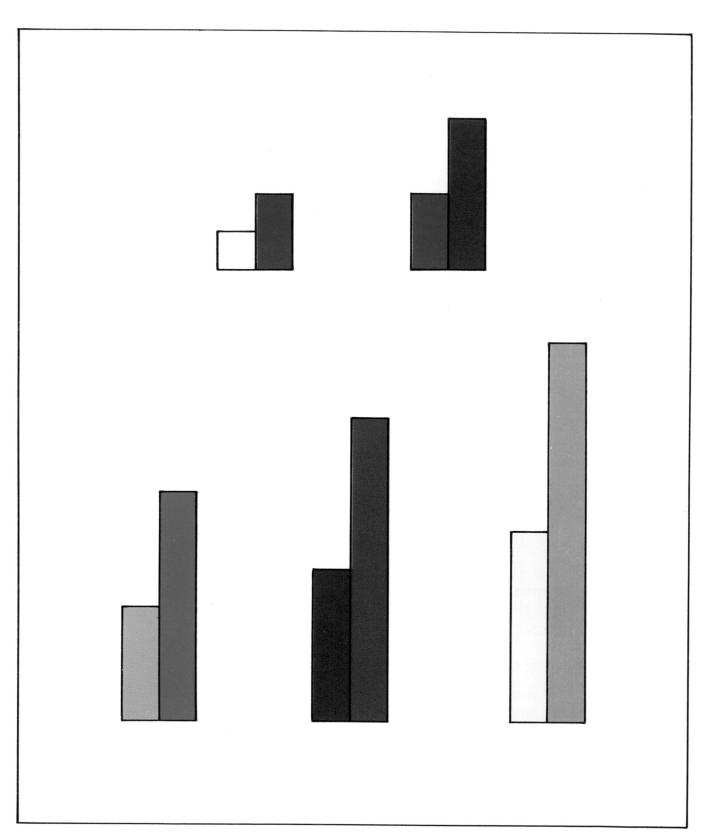

Examples of One-Half Relationships

Finding Halves

Materials:

Cuisenaire rods for each child
Cuisenaire rods for the teacher

Settings:

A small group led by the teacher
A whole class led by the teacher

Learning Experience:

Ask each child to take one rod of each of the ten colors. Check each rod to see if it can be matched with a one-color train with two cars.

Since two white rods match one red rod, a white rod can be described as one-half of a red rod.

Since two red rods match one purple rod, a red rod can be described as one-half of a purple rod.

Ask the children to describe the relationships for the other rods that can be matched with a one-color train with two cars.

A green rod is one-half of a dark green rod.
A purple rod is one-half of a brown rod.
A yellow rod is one-half of an orange rod.

This experience helps children see one-half as a relationship rather than a fixed quantity.

Underlying Mathematics:

Readiness for fractions
Association of numbers with rods

Exploring One-Color Trains with Two Cars for Halves

Interpreting One-Color Trains as Fractional Parts

Materials:

Cuisenaire rods for each child
Cuisenaire rods for the teacher

Settings:

A small group led by the teacher
A whole class led by the teacher

Learning Experience:

Ask the children to build all the one-color trains to match the purple rod.

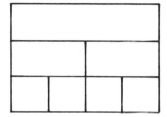

Since two red rods match the purple rod, each red rod is described as one-half of the purple rod.

Since four white rods match the purple rod, each white rod is described as one-fourth of the purple rod.

Now ask the children to build all the one-color trains to match the dark green rod. The fractional parts, halves, thirds and sixths, are generated.

Ask the children to find a rod relationship for tenths. (Since ten white rods match one orange rod, a white rod is one-tenth of an orange rod.)

The children should build all one-color trains to match the brown rod and to describe the fractional parts that emerge.

Underlying Mathematics

Readiness for fractions
Association of numbers with rods

Finding Lengths of One-Color White Trains

Finding Lengths of White Rod Trains

Materials:
Cuisenaire rods for each child
Extra white rods for each child
A Cuisenaire Rod Rack or ruler for each child

Settings:
A small group led by the teacher
A whole class led by the teacher

Learning Experience:

Ask the children to count a certain number of white rods from their collections of rods. Start with numbers between 2 and 10.

Direct the children to make a one-color white rod train, using the Rod Rack or ruler to help them line up the rods. Ask the children to match each white rod train with a single rod.

When the children seem ready, choose numbers between 11 and 20. Ask the children to match each white rod train with an orange rod plus another rod.

For example:　　17 white rods

The 17 white rods can be thought of as:

10W + 7W

= O + K

This activity builds readiness for regrouping into tens and ones and prepares for work with place value.

Underlying Mathematics :

Representation of lengths in terms of white rods
Counting from 1 to 10
Place value (tens and ones)
Readiness for tens and ones

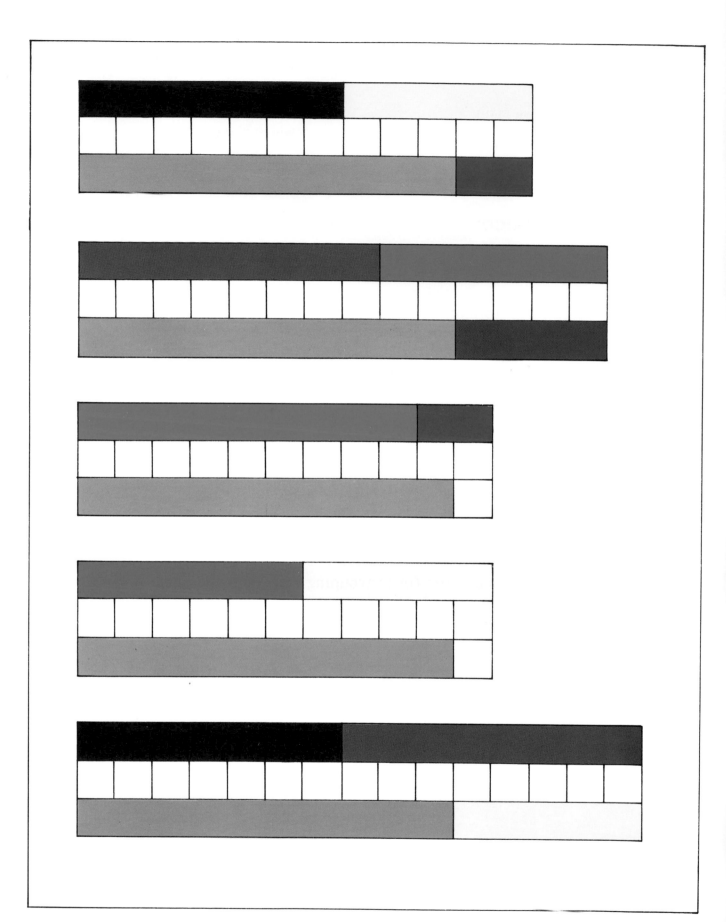

Practicing Orange Plus Stories

Materials:

Cuisenaire rods for each child
A Cuisenaire Rod Rack or ruler for each child

Settings:

A small group led by the teacher
A whole class led by the teacher

Learning Experience:

Ask the children to make a train with a blue rod and a purple rod
and to match this train with a one-color white train. The children
should then match this length with an orange rod plus another rod.
For example:

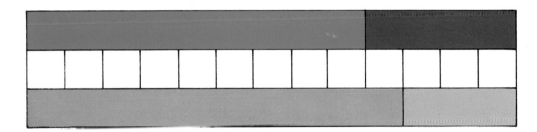

Children in Grades 1 and 2 will relate this to their number work.
In terms of white rods, E + P represents 9W + 4W which equal 13
whites. The 13 whites are equivalent to O + G.

This experience builds readiness for addition facts with sums larger
than ten, and for regrouping into tens and ones.

Some further examples of trains include:

blacK + Yellow	Yellow + blacK
browN + Dark green	Dark green + browN
bluE + Red	Red + bluE
Dark green + Yellow	Yellow + Dark green
blacK + browN	browN + blacK
bluE + blacK	blacK + bluE

Underlying Mathematics :

Representation of lengths in terms of white rods
Counting from 1 to 10
Place value (tens and ones)
Readiness for tens and ones

Playing the Trading Game

Playing the Trading Game

Materials:
Cuisenaire rods for each group
One die for each group

Settings:
A small group working together
A whole class working in small groups

Learning Experience:

Choose one child in each group to be Banker. The Banker does
not play the game, but is in charge of the rods. The Banker makes
a staircase to remind players throughout the game of each rod
length in terms of white rods.

The child on the Banker's left starts the game. The player tosses
the die and asks the Banker for that number of white rods. Then
the player trades the whites for a single rod of the same length.

On each turn (other than the first), the player combines this rod
with those already accumulated. At the end of each turn, a player
may have only one rod other than orange.

For example:

If a player has accumulated 2 orange rods and a blue rod
and then tosses a six on the die, the player would ask the
Banker for 6 whites and trade them for a dark green. The
player then combines the dark green and the blue for orange
plus yellow. The player ends the turn with 3 orange rods
plus a yellow rod.

The first player to accumulate 4 orange rods wins the game. Children enjoy playing this game many times throughout the year.

Underlying Mathematics :

Representation of lengths in terms of white rods
Recognition of equivalences of lengths
Association of sums with addends
Place value (tens and ones)

145

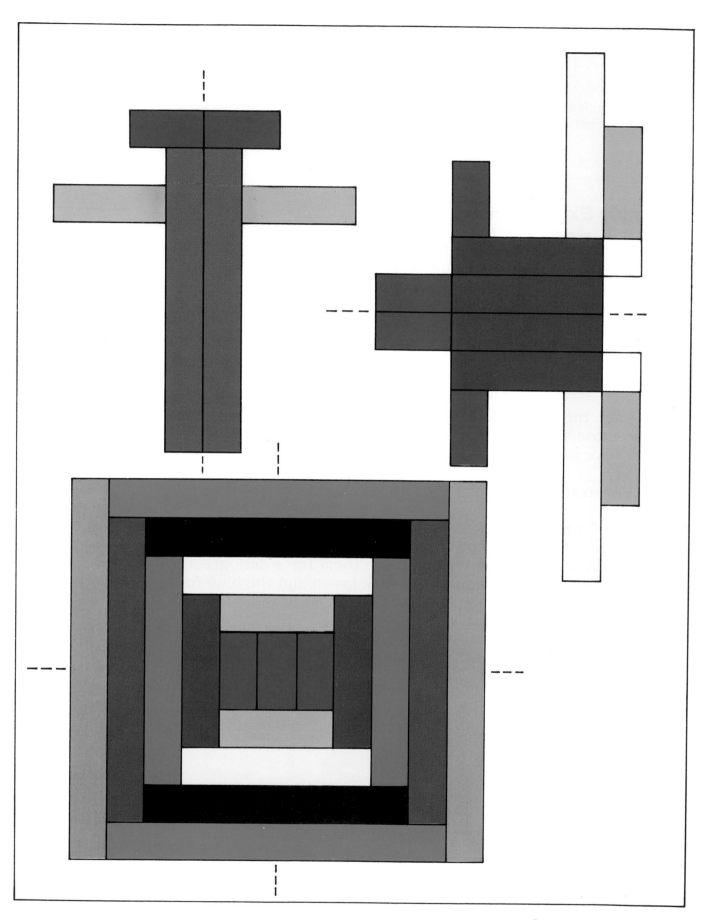

Symmetrical Designs

Exploring Symmetry

Materials:

Cuisenaire rods for each child
A mirror for each child (optional)

Settings:

One child working individually
A small group, children working individually
A whole class, children working individually

Learning Experience:

Explain to the children the meaning of a line of symmetry by having
them make some symmetric designs. The portions of the design
on both sides of a line of symmetry match. For example:

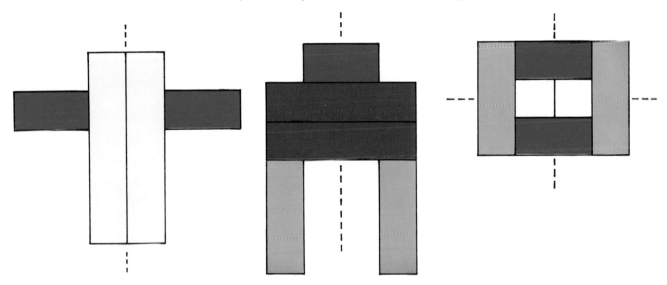

The dotted lines show the lines of symmetry for these designs.

Some children will enjoy placing a mirror along the line of symmetrical
so as to view the other half of the design in the mirror.

In their free exploration with rods, children naturally create designs with lines of symmetry. Symmetry is so prevalent in nature,
architecture, paintings, and interior decorating that children are
exposed to many examples daily. Share a list on the bulletin board,
with the name of the child who thought of each example.

Underlying Mathematics :

Symmetry
Congruence of shapes

Changing One Rod in a Symmetrical Design

Completing a Symmetrical Design

Materials:

Cuisenaire rods for each child

Settings:

Two children working together
A small group, children working in pairs
A whole class, children working in pairs

Learning Experience:

Together the pair of children build a design with one line of symmetry.

Then one of the children closes his eyes. The other child "spoils" the symmetry by making one change. For example:

Moving a rod to another position
Interchanging two rods in the design
Removing a rod
Replacing a rod with another color

The first child opens his eyes and looks at the design to see what was changed. This child verbalizes what is wrong with the design and then corrects it so that the symmetrical design is complete once again.

The children switch roles. The first child makes a change in the design, while the second child closes his eyes.

Children may want to extend this experience to allow two changes to be made in the design.

Underlying Mathematics :

Symmetry
Congruence of shapes
Visual memory of shapes

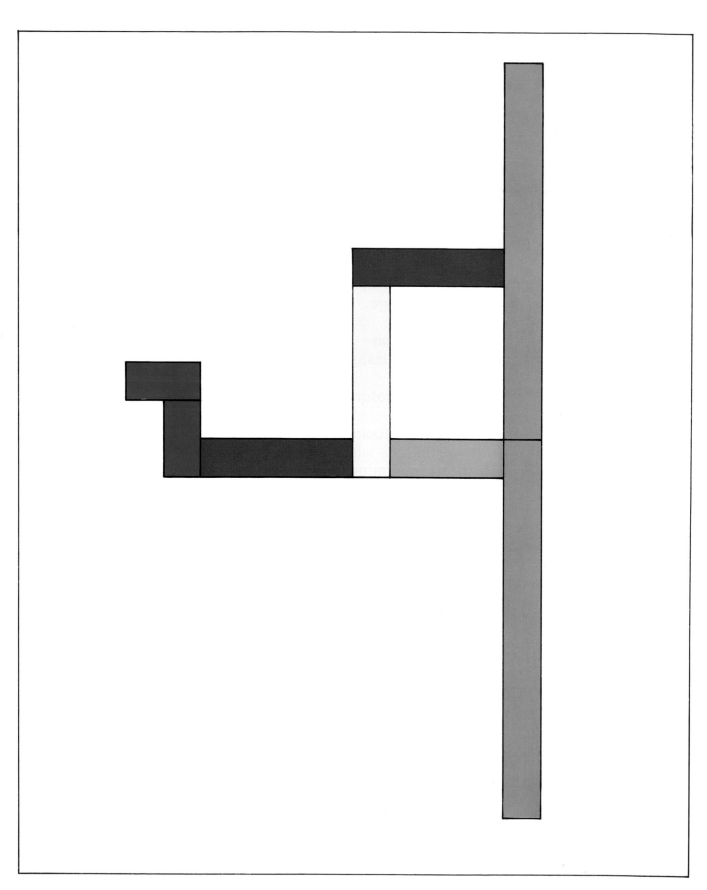

A Design to be Matched

Matching Designs Across the Table

Materials:
Cuisenaire rods for each child

Settings:
Two children working together
A small group, children working in pairs
A whole class, children working in pairs

Learning Experience:

The pair of children should sit across the table from each other.
A train of two orange rods should be placed to define a line of symmetry between the children.

Ask one child to build a design with six rods on his side of the line. At least one of the six rods should touch the line.

The other child matches the first child's design so that the two orange rods define a line of symmetry.

Check to see that the children's completed design is symmetrical.

Then the children switch roles. The second child places six rods on his side of the line of symmetry. The first child completes the symmetrical design.

The children now should exchange seats and repeat the activity. They may wish to increase the number of rods in their design.

Underlying Mathematics :

Symmetry
Congruence of shapes

Building Symmetrical Designs with a Partner

Matching Designs Side-by-Side

Materials:

Cuisenaire rods for each child

Settings:

Two children working together
A small group, children working in pairs
A whole class, children working in pairs

Learning Experience :

The pair of children should sit side-by-side at a table. A train
of two orange rods should be placed between them to define
a line of symmetry.

Ask one child to build a design with six rods on her side of the line.
At least one of the six rods should touch the line.

The other child matches the first child's design so that the two
orange rods define a line of symmetry.

Check to see that the children's completed design is symmetrical.

Then the children switch roles. The second child places six rods
on her side of the line of symmetry. The first child completes
the symmetrical designs. Then the children should exchange seats
and repeat the activity.

Underlying Mathematics :

Symmetry
Congruence of shapes

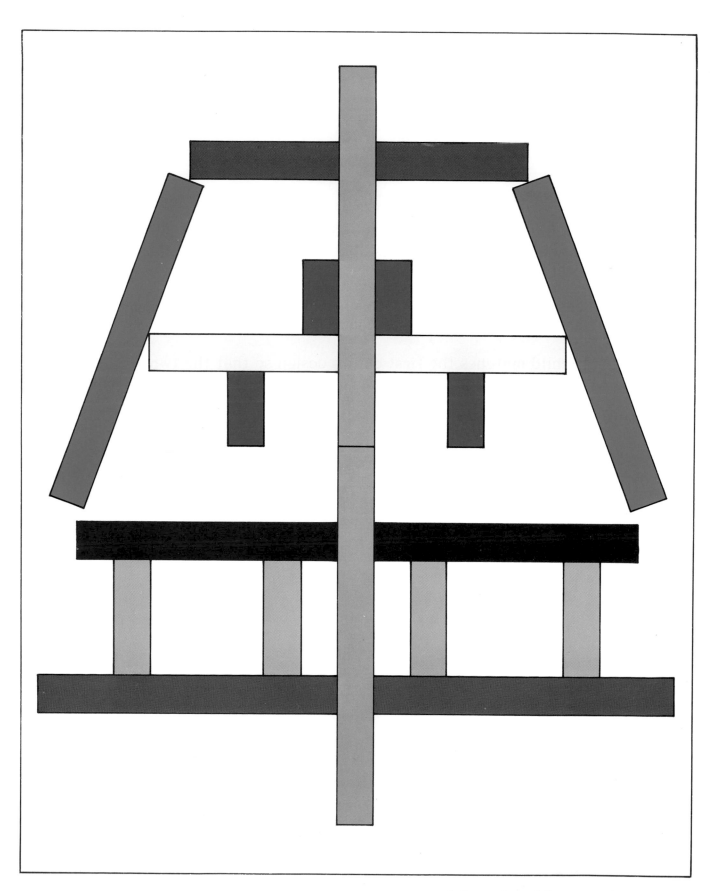

A Completed Symmetrical Design

Matching the Leader Game

Materials:

Cuisenaire rods for each child

Settings:

Two children working together
A small group, children working in pairs
A whole class, children working in pairs

Learning Experience:

The partners may sit side-by-side or across the table. A train of two orange rods should be placed to define a line of symmetry between them.

One child starts to build a design on one side of the line by placing one rod in position. The rod does not need to touch the orange rods, nor does it need to be placed horizontally or vertically.

The second child must place a rod of the same color on the other side of the line of symmetry so that it is symmetrical with the first child's rod.

The first child places another rod on either side of the line. The second child matches it. Play continues until the design is completed.

If the second player misplaces a piece at any time, the first player scores one point.

The players switch roles, so that the second player becomes the leader. If the first player misplaces a piece at any time, the second player scores one point.

The first player to score five points is the winner. After each round, the players should change the seating arrangement.

Underlying Mathematics :

Symmetry
Congruence of shapes